SONGS IN THE KEY OF MP3

Liam Inscoe-Jones is a music and fiction writer who has written for *The Quietus*, *Line of Best Fit* and *Spectrum Culture*. He has interviewed members of 5 Seconds of Summer, Dirty Projectors and Tame Impala, alongside Lianne La Havas, Bartees Strange, Enter Shikari, Xenia Rubinos and Amber Mark, among others. His debut short story 'You Have Been Notified' was published in *The Social* in 2021. He has released playlists of the best new songs from each month, every month, since 2018.

SONGS IN THE KEY OF MP3

THE NEW ICONS OF THE DIGITAL AGE

LIAM INSCOE-JONES

WHITE RABBIT

First published in Great Britain in 2025 by White Rabbit,
an imprint of The Orion Publishing Group Ltd
Carmelite House, 50 Victoria Embankment
London EC4Y 0DZ

An Hachette UK Company

The authorised representative in the EEA is Hachette Ireland,
8 Castlecourt Centre, Dublin 15, D15 XTP3, Ireland (email: info@hbgi.ie)

1 3 5 7 9 10 8 6 4 2

A CIP catalogue record for this book is
available from the British Library.

ISBN (Trade Paperback) 978 1 3996 0963 0
ISBN (Ebook) 978 1 3996 0966 1
ISBN (Audio) 978 1 3996 0967 8

Typeset by Born Group
Printed and bound in Great Britain by Clays Ltd, Elcograf S.p.A.

MIX
Paper | Supporting responsible forestry
FSC® C104740

www.whiterabbitbooks.co.uk
www.orionbooks.co.uk

Contents

'WHOLE NEW WORLD' (INTRO) 1

1. DEVONTÉ HYNES / BLOOD ORANGE 15
2. TAHLIAH BARNETT / FKA TWIGS 90
3. DANIEL LOPATIN / ONEOHTRIX POINT NEVER 161
4. THEBE KGOSITSILE / EARL SWEATSHIRT 200
5. SOPHIE (OUTRO) 279
6. (CODA) 336

Essential Listening 341

Acknowledgements 347

Sources for Quotations 349

Credits 351

Index of Artists 353

For Mom, Dad, Beth & Karen Carpenter

'WHOLE NEW WORLD' (INTRO)

One morning, at the height of summer 1948, in an anonymous conference room deep in the sprawling corridors of the Waldorf Astoria – a great grey symbol of post-war, boom-time opulence whose rooms, at that very moment, Frank Sinatra and Grace Kelly called home – an extremely neat, bespectacled scientist from Budapest stood between two stacks of shiny black discs, preparing to change the music business forever.

Peter Goldmark had always been an inventor. He studied physics at the University of Vienna but knew, even as a child, that he preferred making things to studying them. In the 1920s he built a kit television to receive the first signals sent across the continent by a newly minted BBC. In 1937 he took his talents to the United States and joined Columbia Broadcasting System's own burgeoning TV department. He was a creative, passionate and lonely man – a stubborn workaholic who unlocked the laboratory door at 5 a.m. – but his work paid off for the rest of us. It was Goldmark who helped to invent the first colour television and, in the 1960s, developed the first video recorder too. Startlingly though, neither would prove to be his most enduring creation.

Goldmark loved music. More specifically, as a Hungarian born in 1906, he loved German, classical music. It was something he liked to listen to sitting in the armchair of his study before six hours of sleep. In the early decades of the twentieth century though, listening to music at home was also a pretty considerable pain in the ass. To enjoy a new recording of Johannes Brahms' Piano Concerto No. 2 (to use his favourite as an example), you had to buy an actual album of ten-inch discs called 78s and flip them, one after the other, five minutes at a time. Every one of the concerto's four movements, from the tense melodrama of the second to the thrilling, florid climax of the last, were spliced into halves. Add to that the cost of those 78s, and the fact they were made of a shellac resin so brittle it could survive no more than a dink, and you come to realise that you'd have to *really* like Brahms to bother at all. Goldmark decided to do something about it.

To perform the minor technological marvel which would be required to make listening to symphonies at home even remotely enjoyable, Peter and his team had to make a series of radical adjustments. Firstly, they decided to replace the fragile and expensive shellac with a new polymer called polyvinyl chloride, made from salt and oil rather than the secretions of a female bug. Then they swapped the thick steel styluses of gramophones for ones made of sapphire. These innovations enabled one crucial evolution: the shrinking of the grooves which contained the music itself. They had invented the 'microgroove' and it quadrupled the amount of music each side of a record could hold from five minutes, to a colossal twenty-one.

When Columbia Records asked Peter Goldmark to launch his new product before the waiting press, in the depths of the Waldorf Astoria, it was stacks of these two types of records – the 78s and the new, polyvinyl discs – which stood either side of him. The difference was comical. The pile of 78s stretched eight feet off the ground, stretched towards the ceiling. Goldmark's polyvinyl records, on the other hand, was hardly a tower at all; only sixteen inches high. Both contained the exact same amount of music. Columbia christened their new product the 'long-player', or 'LP' for short. It was an invention which completely transformed the art of songwriting, the joy of listening and the shape of popular culture to follow. The age of flipping was over.*

Technological leaps like the micro-groove have had an unfathomable impact not only on the way we can listen to music, but on what we even consider music to *be*. Thirty years ago, inside a mossy cave on the banks of Slovenia's Idrijca river, a group of archaeologists found the hollowed out thighbone of a young bear, with two perfect holes cut into either side. It was a flute from 60,000 years ago; the oldest musical instrument modern man has ever found, so old that it wasn't even made by humans, but a Neanderthal. For almost the entire history of playing notes and chords in sequence, which followed the sound produced by that piece of bone, 'music' has meant to each new generation almost exactly what it would have done to that primordial flautist: something which happened once, and never happened the same way again.

The very idea that music could exist beyond the moment it was first produced is, by comparison, still less than two

* Peter Goldmark died at seventy-one years old in a car wreck on the Hutchinson River Parkway. His car clipped the bumper of another while he was changing lanes and it spun out with such violence that his body was flung across the highway. It was 1977, only three decades after he invented the micro-groove, and Linda Ronstadt – who made a kind of music inconceivable in 1949 – was at the top of the Billboard Chart, selling three million copies in America alone. The year's bestselling album, Meat Loaf's *Bat Out of Hell*, sold 43 million. All forty-six minutes and twenty-one seconds of *Bat Out of Hell* fit onto a single black disc with ease. I don't know whether Goldmark ever heard 'Two Out of Three Ain't Bad', but I hope it was Brahms playing as he went.

centuries old. It was basically inconceivable until 1857 when, in a workshop in central Paris, Édouard-Léon Scott de Martinville created a machine which could scribble lines onto paper in correspondence with the sonic vibrations detected in the air. It was two decades more until those recordings could actually be played, when Thomas Edison designed a tool to follow the instructions of those waveforms and reproduce the vibrations in audible form. When his little brass cylinder played the first sounds ever recorded – Edison himself saying 'Good morning, how do you do?' – it was a form of time travel: sounds made in the past, being heard in the present. Only when the gramophone was made available for sale at the end of the nineteenth century could anyone really begin to think of music in anything like the way we recognise it today: something which happened in exactly the same way every time we chose to hear it.

It was perhaps for this reason that, in 1948, Columbia Records knew that their pitch to affluent Americans – listening to twenty-one minutes of music in your own living room, uninterrupted – would be an irresistible one. The LP turned recorded music into a genuine, viable prospect and artists quickly seized upon all the opportunities it gave them. Jazz musicians no longer needed to truncate their improvisations; they could lay down full, fifteen-minute tracks knowing they could be heard without interruption. Labels began compiling multiple singles onto a single disc, and artists started to think about the way those songs transformed into something greater when listened to together. The age of musician as auteur was born.

The effect of the likes of The Beach Boys' *Little Deuce Coupe* and Bob Dylan's *Highway 61 Revisited* – the first proper, fully fledged *records* – must have been dazzling, but even they didn't change everything about the way music was understood overnight. For example, listening remained a communal experience at heart. Portability was confined to the living room and so records were heard most on dance-floors, or on the radio. The first Sony Walkman – 1979's TPS-L2 – was fitted with two headphone jacks because its designer, Norio Ohga, couldn't comprehend that people would be interested in listening on their own.

The advent of computers and digital compression software eventually rendered polyvinyl, cassette tapes and CDs, if not obsolete, then utterly inessential. The invention of WAV and MP3 files in the early '90s did something remarkable by removing the need for physical album formats entirely, turning recorded music – itself impossible less than 150 years ago – into something as abstract and immediate as air. At the precipice of a new millennium, Steve Jobs debuted a new device called the iPod with a size-based gimmick of his own: a thousand songs in his jean pocket.* Within eight years, iPods had become the most popular MP3 player in the world. By 2012 the iTunes Store replaced physical media as the way the majority of people purchased their music, but the giants of Silicon Valley were only just getting started.

In June 2015, Aubrey Graham (a teen actor and one-time hockey prodigy who now goes by Drake) pulled a stunt which was to the iPod what that stack of LPs had been to that tower of 78s. From the giant, lilac-lit stage of a Californian

---

* Goldmark and Jobs' stunts were just two in a long line of product demonstrations which sought to make great leaps in technological advancement explicit to the naked eye. In 1981, Kieran Prendiville – the presenter of BBC One's *Tomorrow's World* – demonstrated the durability of the CD by furiously scratching at its surface with a rock, something which would have rubbed Goldmark's micro-grooves clean off. Tragically, the album printed onto the CD was the Bee Gees' sixteenth studio album *Living Eyes,* making that demonstration one of the first instances outside of a Roman stoning where people were rooting for the rock to win.

convention centre named after an assassinated mayor, the soon-to-be biggest rapper on the planet stood before the teleprompters and announced the launch of not a store, but a library of songs: a streaming service named Apple Music. The competitor they sought to dethrone, Spotify, had already been active for nine years, but its subscriber base stood at only 77 million; chump change compared to the half a billion it boasts today. TIDAL (who launched six months earlier with an *Avengers*-style line-up including JAY-Z, Madonna and Nicki Minaj) gambled big on people caring about hi-fidelity music, found out most didn't, and flopped.

Shortly after the keynote, Drake announced that his fourth studio album, *Views from the 6*, would be released on Apple Music exclusively. It was the year of 'Hotline Bling' and an explosive, one-sided beef with Philly MC Meek Mill. People were waiting on his magnum opus. The endorsement all but guaranteed that streaming was here to stay. It was, in effect, the dawn of the streaming era. Six short years after Apple Music was launched, streaming didn't just become people's favourite way to buy music, it became the most popular way to *listen* to it in general, usurping a form of listening which has survived everything from the micro-groove to the MP3: the radio. But what was most remarkable was the extent to which technology had dwarfed Peter Goldmark's stack of polyvinyl LPs. Only sixty-seven years earlier, listening to twenty-one uninterrupted minutes of music had been a revelation; that number had now exploded to near-infinity.

Even in the early days of the twenty-first century, there was already a fair bit of anxiety about what the newfound access granted by the Internet was doing to creativity. Past technological advances, from the wah-wah pedal to the Akai MPC60, once fuelled the creation of original styles of music at a blistering pace; from rock to disco to acid house, all being forged, one after another, at an unprecedented speed. Figures like cultural theorist Mark Fisher posited that, on the other hand, the new technological breakthroughs like Napster, Limewire and MP3 stores were not about musical creation, but simply musical perseveration, and he found great swathes of new artists beginning to simply remix or rehash the great leaps of decades past.* If the past was granted equal status to the present, then culture was in stark danger of becoming frozen in history. 'How long can a culture persist without the new?' he asked in 2009. 'What happens if the young are no longer capable of producing surprises?'

Forecasts like these were premature to say the least. The 2010s did not, in fact, transpire to be a decade of stagnation at all, but instead became a period of startling *transformation*, one where the entire landscape of music was remade in a way unseen since the 1960s. A new generation of musicians responded to the MP3 era with furious creation; forging new aesthetics at an incredible rate. Styles of music which simply didn't exist in 2009 – from hyper-pop to Brooklyn drill – now predominate. In 2016, hip hop, a style of songwriting invented by children of Caribbean migrants in New York City, overtook rock and pop music as the most-listened-to genre in the world, shattering a paradigm which had lasted half a century.

* It was these file-sharing platforms, often made by teenage coders in their bedrooms, which actually facilitated the culture of infinite access, rather than the streaming services of today, but their efforts were also just signposts pointing towards an enormous shift to come. Your average Britney-loving Joe was not downloading early Aphex Twin rips online in 2002. When Napster was launched, half of households in the UK didn't even own a computer. In fact, downloading music using dial-up Internet was almost as effortful as flipping a 78 nine times over. Instead, their most important contribution was forcing the music industry to do something about them.

Streaming services also fuelled an unprecedented appetite for international music in the culturally conservative West, and the modern era has seen the unimaginable happen: acts from Korea, Nigeria, Japan and Spain becoming enormous stars in America. In 2023 the biggest musician on the planet, in terms of sheer numbers, was Bad Bunny, a Puerto Rican rapper and singer who performs almost exclusively in Spanish.

Digital audio workstations (DAWs) became the most ubiquitous instruments of all, and music can now be made just about anywhere, or on several continents at once. Many artists seized upon the utterly boundless capabilities of the Internet age. In 2023, Canadian chief-of-chill Mac DeMarco released *One Wayne G,* a 199-song collection of demos, each simply named after the date they were recorded. This kind of self-archiving was nearly impossible in the time of physical-only recording, but no longer. It was as if Arthur Russell had simply released every song he ever recorded in one go, back in 1991.

Even more fascinating than the material changes of the music industry are the stylistic alchemy which manifested within the music itself. Poptimism has been popularised, and the once-gaping oceans which existed between the mainstream and the underground have been transformed into tributaries. This is a world where an indie darling like Grimes and the world's wealthiest man are just the space of a tweet apart, and everything has been urgently squeezed together. DIY music imitates pop stardom, and the actual stars are sounding stranger than ever.

As such, the 2010s were far looser about the dividing lines of taste. In decades past, self-elected connoisseurs – from the classical purists of the '30s to the Internet bloggers of the mid-2000s – preferred to make their cultural savvy known by separating art into scales of High and Low. With all music blurred into one though, with extremely fringe figures subsumed into the centre of pop, those same tastemakers began advertising their supreme *lack* of pretension, embracing a love for pop and obscure electronica alike. In many ways, this attitude better reflects the truth of the creation behind the music. Some of the world's biggest artists, from Billie Eilish to Lil Uzi Vert, make their music in much the same way a niche, cult artist like Daniel Johnston once did: sat in a bedroom, surrounded by kit.

If the 2010s will be remembered for anything though, it will be as the decade genre became redundant once and for all. Genre-blending musicians have always existed. It's how some of the most thrilling music of the twentieth century was made. Even as the new millennium began, the music industry and the listening public stood by the old dividing lines between rock and soul, between rap and electronica, which had been conjured up by industry executives in the 1950s. No more. Even the most casual music listener now seems to be comfortable with – nay, expects – a certain amount of genre-hopping within even the most commercially successful records.

In 2018 *A Brief Inquiry into Online Relationships* became a UK number one record for Manchester band The 1975. It opens (as all their albums do) with a song also called 'The 1975', here rendered as a haunting piece of a cappella auto-tune, performed through the iZotope VocalSynth plug-in first popularised in Florida rap. The second track – 'Give Yourself a Try' – is a taut indie-rocker fitting of the scene they emerged from in the late 2000s, but *that* song is followed by the buoyant, gentrified tropical house of 'TOOTIMETOOTIMETOOTIME'; a pop-song whose sound nestles nicely among the Biebers and Clean Bandits. By the time we arrive at 'How To Draw / Petrichor', this group of Mancunian twenty-somethings sound like Laurie Anderson being remixed by DJ Luck & MC Neat. The point is not that this is incredibly innovative (or even necessarily good): the point is that it was streamed by millions of fifteen-year-olds. It's *normal.*

Across music of the modern day, genres are thrust together not just across albums but within the space of a single song. Take a track like JPEGMAFIA's 'Jesus Forgive Me, I Am a Thot', one of the wildest songs of a pretty wild decade. It opens with shots of glitchy crowd noise and stuttering drums, like something Fugazi would have laid down in 1995, but they're soon replaced with solemn, down-tempo piano, which plays through his first verse. In the chorus, Peggy shouts from the back of his throat and the beat picks up intensity, but the piano echoes on; Mobb Deep meets Nils Frahm. The song is piano ballad and industrial rap all at once, and the effect is eerie; the sound of a man raging through tears.

Audacious genre-blends like these can be supremely entertaining too. Take a song like 'Concrete', the opener to one-time YouTube sensation Poppy's 2020 album *I Disagree.* It somehow washes seamlessly through nu-metal, dream pop and dubstep, before finally breaking into a chorus of torch-waving arena-rock; the kind of moment which would have made her a star in 1987 if not for lyrics like 'bury me six feet deep / bury me in concrete / turn me into a street'.

More contentious is the way in which digital technologies have begun to bring the very concept of musical authorship into question. In 2010, a beautiful, thirty-five-minute song called 'U Smile' was uploaded to SoundCloud. It's a shiny, oscillating piece of music which begins with a few tentative flutters and expands, incrementally, into something vast and elegiac. Snatches of choral vocals float in and out of focus and lashings of dense, rumbling noise rise and fall like waves on the shore. It sounds like Godspeed You! Black Emperor at their most hopeful or Sigur Rós in the midst of a moment of great, celestial wonder. 'U Smile' is also a Justin Bieber song, from his 2010 album *My World 2.0*, slowed down 800 times. Florida producer Nick Pittsinger had processed the track through a piece of software called PaulStretch and uploaded it to SoundCloud as a joke. Within weeks it was an Internet phenomenon. It's also (and I mean this sincerely), a gorgeous piece of music. Does it matter that this beauty was entirely incidental to the creative intentions of the teenager who made the original in 2009? These questions, once ridiculous, are becoming increasingly relevant. Through apps like TikTok, everybody with a smartphone now also owns tools which can write music, create sounds and remix songs at a moment's notice. From Neil Young to Tinie Tempah; no song is sacred or – as was always the case when Edison spoke into his gramophone – permanent either.

This diminishing of artists is, therefore, the *other,* more tragic story of our time. Even in the early years of the music industry, where artists were far more dependent on labels to get their stuff heard, it would have been utterly inconceivable that a musician would be required to sell a song 3,000 times to earn a single pound; yet that's exactly the rate which Spotify – the streaming service with 80 per cent of market control – offers its artists. From 2024 onwards, if an artist's song was heard fewer than one thousand times, they received no money at all.

The rampant theft initiated by the likes of LimeWire and PirateBay was not solved by the music industry, then; record labels and streaming giants simply took up the mantle themselves. It's now commonplace for all but the artists with the biggest marketing budgets to rely on live performance to pay the bills. With economies stagnating and government support for the arts vanishing worldwide, many of the music venues which hosted small or independent acts began to shutter too. In 2023 alone, 125 of Britain's grassroots venues closed, making it the worst year for live music on record. As livelihoods diminish, the powerful stranglehold which centres of capital have always maintained over art and artists have tightened further, and these companies will likely determine the shape of music's future. Soon after all of recorded music became available to us in an instant, a future is already coming into view where it could vanish from our lives completely.

This quest for ease which drives these predatory practices is everywhere in a hyper-consumerist world, from the food we eat to the way we communicate. The beauty of art though – what distinguishes it from ready meals and iPads – is that the role of humans cannot be completely erased from it. For all the ways in which tech companies and record labels have shaped the artistic shifts of the era of recorded sound, they still can't do what Lana Del Rey does in the final seconds of *Norman Fucking Rockwell!*, when the piano falls silent and she whispers 'I have it, I have it', like she's drawing her final breath. They can't do what Kendrick Lamar does on 'For Free?', when his words drop effortlessly between kinetic drums and squealing sax in a way which feels like gymnastics. They can't sing like D'Angelo, or write like Lauryn Hill. Columbia Records and Apple Inc. may have had an oversized hand in tilting the direction of culture, but they didn't create it. Musicians did.*

* The twenty-first century has also seen an increase in the scientific understanding of just *how* essential music is for living. We now know, for example, that music activates more regions of the brain than almost anything we can expose it to: more than food, more than smell, more even than sex. (Those who listen to Billy Ocean have understood this for years.) Music messes with the brain in ways only drugs otherwise can: it can change our perception of time and strengthen our immune systems; it can make people who cannot otherwise move dance; it can make people who cannot otherwise remember begin to do so. Even more incredibly, researchers

One of the more insidious consequences of listening to songs in the Internet age however is that the work which goes into a single song – the pure miracle that ordinary, breathing people are able to make astounding art – is sometimes hidden by the effortlessness with which it all arrives at our ears. Albums which were anticipated for months now seem to arrive one Friday and vanish the next. New Radiohead album? Next. New Ariana Grande? Thank you, next. The result is that new and monumental music – my generation's equivalents to *Pastel Blues* or *Illmatic* and *Songs in the Key of Life* – tends not to garner the same folklore as those LPs, or even the same stature in our lives. This is a not a testament to the quality of the music. Sons of Kemet's *Your Queen Is a Reptile*. Xenia Rubinos' *Black Terry Cat*. Danny Brown's *Atrocity Exhibition*. Arooj Aftab's *Vulture Prince*. Isaiah Rashad's *Cilvia Demo*. Chat Pile's *God's Country*. Fiona Apple's *Fetch the Bolt Cutters*. Frank Ocean's *Blonde* . . . It's obvious to me that these records deserve close examination every bit as much as *Led Zeppelin III*.

As such, the book in your hands intends to act as a corrective of sorts. Beginning roughly in 2013 – the year that the aesthetics which shaped the modern era coalesced – it seeks to ensure that the music made during this great, productive Internet age doesn't vanish into a pixelated ether. It tells the story of all of the great stylistic and cultural shifts of the 2010s and beyond through the stories of five artists – Devonté Hynes, FKA twigs, Oneohtrix Point Never, Earl Sweatshirt and SOPHIE – whose art best encapsulates what was special about this thrilling and transformative era.

---

now tell us that neuro-ensembles (the unique firing of our brain's neurons in response to music) means that our brains themselves are instruments contributing to our perception of a song. The obsessiveness of nerds like me is, in short, completely justified.

It likely goes without saying that these artists are not household names. Ask your gran who they are, and you're liable to elicit a reaction somewhere between confusion and disgust. Instead, their careers have operated in the vast and fertile ground between the avant-garde and the mainstream; entering culture on the periphery before, over the course of a decade, becoming utterly central to it. Each of them is a member of the first generation of musicians raised in the time of MP3s, the specific, unprecedented moment at the beginning of the twenty-first century when recorded music suddenly became as abundant and pliable as the air we breathe.

Because of this, their work begs an obvious question: if Peter Goldmark's LPs had such a seismic impact on the nature of music – the way we perceive it, and the things it's capable of being – then what has been the effect of this digital age, heralding as it did shifts which dwarfed his creation so completely? The artists and the music contained within this book, and throughout this great, thrilling new time for music, are and will always remain the very first answers to that question.

1. DEVONTÉ HYNES / BLOOD ORANGE

On the 27th of October 2013, after a long night listening to Roberta Flack, Frank Ocean and Ornette Coleman, Lou Reed died at his home in Long Island, Laurie Anderson by his side, looking out at the Atlantic Ocean. Lou Reed was a Buddhist and, in accordance with his faith, a life is celebrated for forty-nine days until, on the fiftieth, the soul is finally set free. Lou Reed's spirit, if the Tibetans are to be believed, was released on the 18th of December 2013, fifty days after his death, during a memorial concert in Harlem's Apollo Theater.

The Apollo Theater is just a small distance from where the junkie narrator of 'I'm Waiting for the Man' hopped off the Lexington Avenue subway to score. The Harlem of 2013 though was another universe from the rat-ridden outpost for Black American art Reed visited as a teenager on trips from Long Island, his heart stolen by doo-wop and Ornette Coleman's careening, improvisational jazz. Harlem is now the scene of a different kind of plague, one drawn along the lines of luxury condominiums and the haute cuisine of Restaurant Row.

The stars were out for Lou Reed's final night. Paul Simon and Patti Smith sat among the crowd. Debbie Harry delivered a version of 'White Light / White Heat', and saxophonist John Zorn represented Reed's fondness for the avant-garde, letting rip a screeching solo of the kind he'd played alongside Reed and his wife Laurie Anderson through their uninhibited twilight years. Lou's most punishing songs, tales of prostitution and assassination, were bookended by a Kaddish prayer, played by Philip Glass, sat alone at the piano. As a night of music, it was bewildering; as a farewell to an artist whose music traversed jazz and metal and whose interests remained intemperate to the last, it was the only thing which made sense.

Devonté Hynes had been an acolyte of Reed's for years. He used to take a book of his lyrics to Washington Square Park, sit opposite the great marble arch and listen to 'Street Hassle' on a loop. Reed's music was one of the reasons why Hynes, a boy from Essex, posted up in New York City to begin with. Hynes was at the Apollo Theater on the 18th of December too, watching Debbie Harry play from the cheap seats.

The night Lou Reed's soul dissipated into energy was also the night Devonté lost everything he held dear. Just as he and his girlfriend emerged onto the sidewalk at the end of the show, Hynes' phone began lighting up. It was his friend Keith, who lived on the same block as Hynes in Greenwich Village. Dev, it's your apartment, Keith said. Be quick.

Hynes hopped on the subway and raced from Harlem to Greenwich Village, but it was too late. His entire fourth-floor apartment was gone, swallowed by a raging fire. Poor electric wiring had sparked and set the flat ablaze. In the fire Hynes lost everything his owned. Unfinished work; his piano; his computer, and his puppy Cupid. The next day, his friend Adam had to buy him new boxers and socks. Hynes had been suffering from panic attacks for weeks. The blaze pushed him over. Two days afterwards he collapsed and was hospitalised with a diagnosis of extreme exhaustion. He woke the next morning propped up in a bed with IVs running from his arms, unable to remember a thing.

This crushing low, and perhaps a good amount of the exhaustion too, came at the end of two years of perpetual highs. That year Hynes had released his second album as Blood Orange, a name he had taken from a comic book he'd scrawled in the back of a maths textbook as a kid. *Cupid Deluxe* was easily the most acclaimed record of his career and afforded him a new level of exposure. He'd produced his first soundtrack, for Gia Coppola's *Palo Alto*, and sat down with one of his heroes, Jimmy Jam. A year earlier his songs with Solange and Sky Ferreira, 'Losing You' and 'Everything Is Embarrassing', were received as instant classics. The right places were beginning to talk about him as The Next Big Thing. Then, in a single night, two days before his twenty-fourth birthday, everything was gone.

Devonté's first response upon waking in the hospital bed was to do the one thing he knew best: he booked a gig. By 2013, a good portion of his fans knew him only as Blood Orange but, on that night, he planned to play again as Lightspeed Champion, the moniker which earned him a cult following among the indie kids of the late 2000s, and one he hadn't used since 2010. He played the show with his girlfriend at the Cameo Gallery in Brooklyn just hours after being discharged from the ward. In the New Year, he'd have to start again, but Hynes was more used to that than most. Once that show was over, he retired Lightspeed Champion for good.

Devonté Hynes is a renaissance man and dresses like one. He tucks fishnet vests into Levi's jeans. He pairs Hawaiian shirts with hiking shoes, and beige, rugby-tour trousers with durags. Sometimes he looks like a creative writing teacher caught between class and a track day, other days like a tennis star with a passion for the Cocteau Twins. His clothes lean towards the feminine but, when posing for cover shoots, sat topless with his legs spread wide, a guitar strap running through bristles of chest hair, he's all man.

Across two decades, the eclecticism of Devonté's style has been matched only by the *wild* eclecticism of his music. In his late teens he was a member of a British punk band, only to go it alone and make an Americana album for his debut offering instead. He's helped craft songs with pop stars like Kylie Minogue, Blondie, Lorde, Mariah Carey and Carly Rae Jepsen, but he's just as likely to pop up on a hardcore record, a Vampire Weekend album, or on rap songs with Mac Miller, A$AP Rocky or Skepta. Devonté has been both a peripheral figure and central player in some of the most obvious cultural shifts of recent times, from the mainstreaming of poptimism to the re-evaluation of music which, around lines of class, race and sexuality, was once treated as far less important than music made by dudes with amps and arpeggiators.

Devonté is one of the few artists working today who acts on the idea that the sounds of rap, commercial pop, jazz and classical music do not exist on a hierarchy of merit. Despite being most famous for synth-pop songs, his first project was a punk band and his first instrument was the cello. As an adult he returned to concerts and symphonies: playing piano at the Kennedy Center, the Barbican and Carnegie Hall. He has composed his own percussive suites and symphonies, alongside a glut of film scores, including Paul Schrader's *Master Gardener* and a TV show by Oscar-winner Luca Guadagnino, where the teenage protagonist is – you guessed it – a Blood Orange fan.

Despite a handful of monikers and a seemingly limitless array of extra-curricular activities, it is only under this name – Blood Orange – that Hynes melts all of his disparate interests into a single, rich stew, often within the space of a song. Records like 2016's *Freetown Sound* and 2018's *Negro Swan* feel distinct to the time they were made in: amalgams of funk, minimalist classical and rap, which exude a sensitive masculinity borne by the likes of Prince and Lou Reed, and a multitudinous depiction of Blackness. From the photographs which cover them to the street sounds they sample, Blood Orange albums are so distinctly American that, like *Exile on Main St.* and *Tumbleweed Connection* before them, they could only have been made by a Brit.

Devonté *was* born in the States, but he didn't grow up American. His mother and father met in their twenties; two immigrants who came to London just as Thatcherism gripped the capital. His dad was Sierra Leonean, his mum – Wendella – Guyanese. His dad's work took them to America and Devonté was born David Joseph Michael Hynes in Houston, Texas on the 23rd of December 1985. He is the youngest of three siblings. His family returned to the UK nine years later; first to Edinburgh and then to the tarmacked suburbs of Illford, east London. His mother worked as a nurse, conducting home visits for the elderly, and his dad took up the most English of all occupations: working in Marks & Spencer. They were neither poor nor rich, holding the kind of jobs familiar to anyone who grew up in working-class homes after 'working class' became synonymous with tills rather than tools.

The Hynes home was close; open, and talkative. Like most prefab houses, the walls were thin, and so the first soundtrack to his life was the music of his siblings, leaking through their walls into his bedroom. His sister was into '80s pop and '90s rock: Madonna and Prince cut with Nirvana and Blur. She was also a fan of musicals, and so some of the first songs Devonté ever tried to play were from *Hair*. His brother wasn't so into *Hair*, and instead was embroiled in the first golden age of rap: A Tribe Called Quest, DMX, Tupac, and a particular love for Bone Thugs-n-Harmony. Every time their dad drove them in the car, Classic FM would play the whole ride through.

Wendella also loved the classical stations, but was a devotee of British soul too. These dissonant tastes led to an eventual harmony. 'I think it explains me now,' Devonté one day told A Tribe Called Quest's Ali Shaheed Muhammad. 'Hearing all those things, I just see them as all the same . . . and the idea of them being in conversation is so natural to me.'

When he was small, Devonté's sister began taking piano lessons and filled the house with Bach and Beethoven as she practised. When she left Devonté would cry out of jealousy and so, in an attempt to keep him quiet, his mum let him go with her too and Devonté, a little earlier than planned, began learning too. When his primary school began a music programme and asked which instrument he wanted to learn, Dev watched as the other boys in his class said 'guitar' and 'drums' and (already suspecting a difference between himself and them) requested 'cello' instead.* As his teacher showed him Yo-Yo Ma and Bach and Pablo Casals, a now-teenage Hynes began a lifelong hobby of studying the words of people he admires, from Julius Eastman to Thelonious Monk. When he read that Casals practised every day into old age, he set about planning to do the same thing.

As a Black kid with an endpin between his legs, reading about great composers yielded fast lessons in the relationship between European classical music and Blackness. Devonté would later remember opening a book on the modernist composer Charles Ives and immediately finding a picture of him in blackface. Indeed, the more you hear about the men behind the art, from Richard Wagner to Heinrich Schenker (the Austrian theorist who praised Hitler) the more the clas-

* Hynes' family couldn't afford a cello and so they rented one from the council. It was the start of his lifelong status as a transient music-maker; writing music in his head and recording it in hotels and friends' apartments. He didn't buy a cello himself until 2014, or a guitar until 2016, over a decade into his career.

sical canon begins to feel like a carnival of horrors. The idea of dismissing the beautiful art written by these reprehensible men was immortalised in the 2022 Todd Field film *Tár*, where Cate Blanchett's titular conductor mocks a young student's refusal to play Bach given all of his moral failings. Her stance is one Hynes doesn't fall far from: 'If he's a piece of shit,' he told Lauren Martin in 2016, 'then I'm going to take some of his atonality lessons and use it for myself.'

Almost all of the albums a teenage Hynes brought into his life were found in the Virgin Megastore on Tottenham Court Road. He did his hunting in the bargain bins: primordial versions of today's YouTube playlists, filled with *X Factor* cast-offs and random, discarded songs of the past. He bought Neil Young and Philip Glass CDs based on their covers alone, and listened to them with no knowledge of the men who made them. His favourite TV channel was MTV2 and, if you watched that for long enough, they would play through the gamut of popular music in all its various permutations. Destiny's Child into LL Cool J. The Pet Shop Boys into Alice in Chains. He didn't discriminate. Devonté treated his hobbies with an academic rigour and, as all nerdy kids come to realise eventually, that is, to certain teenagers, a mortal sin.

Hynes loathed almost every second of school. He was bullied horribly. He was called 'faggot' and spat at, mostly by other Black boys. He got into Slipknot and Korn and began to dress like it. He painted his nails and started hanging out with the gay kids. He tried to hide the bullying from his mum but he couldn't disguise the evidence of his body, so she sent him to karate lessons for self-defence, which he hated just as much. 'I was living in hell,' he told *Out* in 2014. 'I was so depressed and distraught about my existence.'

The worst of these beatings was so brutal that it sent him to hospital. He immortalised the attack on 'Dagenham Dream' from his album *Negro Swan*, a ghostly song where Hynes delivers every line like he's peeking his head around the corner to check the coast is clear. He sings of the decision he made after he was discharged: to play down the parts of himself which had turned him into a target. The next morning, still stinging from his bruises, he stood in front of the mirror and chopped his hair, took out his piercings and buzzed a line through his eyebrow. When he arrived at school the next day one of the younger teachers saw him and started to cry.

Devonté had a dozen potential careers in mind for himself before he even started secondary school. In the late '90s Hynes was one of the millions of English teenagers with a biblical infatuation with Sir Alex Ferguson's Manchester United (even though he was, officially, a Tottenham fan). The posters on his childhood bedroom were split equally between pictures of Damon Albarn, The Smashing Pumpkins and posters of David Beckham, platinum hair draped across his forehead. He could have been a comic book illustrator, or scriptwriter. For a time, Hynes imagined himself as a biographer, writing the kind of tomes he'd studied about Casals and Bach. Ironically the talent which turned him into an icon was one of the few he intended to keep as a hobby.

As Blood Orange, Devonté's music is so evocative of a particular era: that specific breed of rhythmically dynamic, funk-flavoured 'indie' which gathered steam at the beginning of the 2010s. What is often forgotten though is that Hynes had *already* been part of a distinct cultural moment even before that one, on the other side of the pond.

A decade before *Cupid Deluxe*, when Hynes was seventeen, 'indie music' began to take over the charts. Bands forged in the fires of The Libertines and Franz Ferdinand began popping up in suburbs across the country. In 2002, songs like 'Dreaming of You' and 'Don't Look Back into the Sun' were so ubiquitous that they seized hold of the next decade of British chart music, the latest (and probably last) enactment of a tradition which lasted half a century, thrusting each new generation of British four-piece bands straight to the top of the charts. Acts like Mystery Jets, The Coral and The Zutons were more eclectic than history gives them credit for – dabbling in New York dance-punk and Liverpudlian psychedelia – but eventually those bands became so ubiquitous and derivative that, in 2008, writer Andrew Harrison began to call them 'landfill indie'. It was as part of this ecosystem that Hynes got his start.

By the time he was twenty, Devonté had played in at least a dozen bands, beginning in the practice rooms of his east London comprehensive. Social scenes formed around them and, when they left sixth form, many of the kids kept playing, underage, around the indie club circuit of central London. It was at club nights like Kill 'Em All and AfterSkool that Devonté met Rory Attwell and Sam Mehran, with whom he would form the first of his several acts to make it. Unfortunately, they decided to name themselves Test Icicles.

To be fair to Test Icicles, they didn't technically choose their name at all. Attwell and Mehran were already part of another group called (of course) Balls. In August 2004, when they were all eighteen, Balls' lead singer Ferry Gouw received a call asking if the band were free to support Canadian outfit The Unicorns at The Old Angel pub in Nottingham. Gouw was out the country but, not wanting to cost his mates the spot, he told them Balls couldn't make it but his good friends Test Icicles (a group he invented on the spot) could. After hearing the good news, Attwell and Mehran asked Devonté whether he wanted to take Gouw's spot and, twelve hours after forming, Test Icicles played their debut gig.

There were a glut of bands starting like this every day in the summer of 2004, but Test Icicles didn't reside in obscurity. Within a year, they were opening for Death from Above 1979, who were becoming a pretty big deal. They signed to Domino Records in 2005, and were sent on tour alongside their label-mates, Arctic Monkeys.* Test Icicles were proof that 'landfill indie' was not a monolith. Like Franz Ferdinand and – later – Hot Chip, they were as interested in electronic dance music as Julian Casablancas. Many of the venues they frequented were descendants of Trash, a pioneering club night which ran from 1997 to 2007 in New Oxford Street. Those nights were true sonic melting pots, where New York rock music was pressed against French house. It was at Trash that LCD Soundsystem played their first UK show in 2002, and it was that kinetic combination of squelching electronic music and noise-rock which defined Test Icicles' only album: 2005's *For Screening Purposes Only*.

There are plenty of fans of Blood Orange who wouldn't even know that Devonté was in bands like this at all, so it's crazy to think that he wasn't simply in bands, but that those groups were rubbing shoulders with the biggest names of the era.

---

* It feels strange now, but Arctic Monkeys were among the first successes of the Internet age. They took advantage of being among the first bunch of teenagers who could burn live recordings of their songs onto CDs at home, and the fans who bought their CDs for a few quid started to upload those songs on early, primitive forms of social media – the type only school kids knew how to access. It wasn't a major label single which first found a wide audience, it was a bootleg compilation, *Beneath the Boardwalk*, which could be downloaded for free online. Just as rappers sharing cassettes of their mixtapes had learned in New York and LA, giving away free music was very good for business. Now, it's essentially the only model there is.

NME were absolutely rapturous about the band's debut, calling them 'the ticket inspectors to the wormhole of the future', and said that 'Test Icicles will inspire a generation who are striving for the next noise, the next trip.' The *Guardian* even ran a column speculating on who would be the first to break big: Test Icicles or Arctic Monkeys?

Listening to their debut now, there's very little of the Hynes who would eventually emerge as Blood Orange on *For Screening Purposes Only.* To call that record rough around the edges would be generous, as the band's members were eager to make clear. 'We're not very good,' Devonté told *The Guardian* in 2005. 'We can be absolutely horrible live. And we've got a bad name.' In fact, Test Icicles did not enjoy much about their first taste of fame. They embarked on a long European tour in 2005 which left them sick, tired and miserable, and split in February 2006, cancelling a US tour before it began.

It would have been reasonable to assume that, like the members of so many bands of that era, we wouldn't be hearing from any member of Test Icicles again. Even when he was playing MTV stages though, Devonté never really stopped making music. He started a MySpace page to upload demos of folk-rock songs he was recording in his bedroom away from the band. For his profile, he tried out the names of the comic books characters he'd drawn as a kid (including Blood Orange, which was taken) and landed on 'Lightspeed Champion'; a character he'd sketched in the back of his maths notebooks, whose super-power was saving the world by solving equations.

After breaking up Test Icicles, Devonté killed time in 2006 by performing solo shows at venues like The Barfly in Camden, covering 'Xanadu' and the *Grease* soundtrack and testing out those demos in front of crowds. Perhaps looking to recoup their losses, the founder of Domino Records – Laurence Bell – attended one of those shows and asked Hynes whether he'd been working on any new songs. In response, Devonté handed him not one but three CDs, with twenty songs apiece. Without Hynes knowing it, Bell began passing those tapes out to various producers, and the demos caught the ear of Mike Mogis. Mogis was the in-house producer for Saddle Creek, the Nebraskan label who helped craft the baroque, country-tinged sound of Bright Eyes and Jenny Lewis. Before long Domino was flying Devonté to Omaha to meet with him. He was still only nineteen.

When it became apparent that he and Mogis were a good fit, Hynes quit everything and moved to Nebraska. For the first time in a decade, he was living in America again. He stayed in a guest house decorated by Justin Oberst, the co-founder of Saddle Creek and brother of Conor. Months after trudging around the dive bars of Europe, he was thrust into small-town living, with little to do aside from dedicating his days to the studio and his nights to Wikipedia, editing pages on the Eminem/Benzino beef.

The sessions eventually took the form of the debut Lightspeed Champion album: 2008's *Falling Off the Lavender Bridge*. It was a total about-face from the brittle edges of Test Icicles, its shrieking guitars replaced with pedal steel, fiddle, jaunty piano and soaring, harmonised choruses. Several songs began as rap songs from Hynes' private mixtapes, leading to bizarre moments where he sings 'sketchy motherfucker' over a violin solo and a song named 'Everyone I Know Is Listening to Krunk'. There are wonderful highlights, like the soaring chorus of lead single 'Galaxy of the Lost' and the epic centrepiece 'Midnight Surprise'. There are also moments where you can practically hear Hynes straining at the walls of the new box an image-obsessed industry had squeezed him into. Now he was no longer the 'new Bloc Party', but 'the English Bright Eyes'.

In truth, no one album could capture the breadth of the music Devonté was working on from his bedroom in Nebraska. He once compared the way he made music to a football fan, kicking a ball against a wall to pass the time: he did it as easily as breathing. Musicians have noodled on a Sunday afternoon since the invention of song, but only with the advent of websites like MySpace could an artist without a recording contract release entire albums the day they were made. Hynes was one of the first artists who embraced doing, in real time, what streaming services would one day allow all artists to do. Fifteen takes of 'A Case of You'? Have them all! On the mixtapes Devonté uploaded to his MySpace page like *I Wrote and Recorded This in Less Than Five Hours* and *House-Sitting Songs,* the illusion that he was 'a folk-rock musician' was undermined because he was releasing raps and covers of Slipknot too. 'I found it really funny,' he later said. 'Everyone thought that was all I did. To me, [that's] just one of seven albums I made in that time.'*

When *Lavender Bridge* was released in 2008, Devonté toured furiously again, although only occasionally played songs from the

---

* In the 2010s the attitude Devonté held in 2007 had become commonplace. More artists stopped thinking about music in that traditional, album format and began releasing exactly what they wanted to. In 2010, San Franciscan rapper Lil B released 1,500 songs through MySpace, Soundcloud and Twitter. Many were recognisably Bay Area rap songs like cult hits 'Wonton Soup', but others were New Age tracks and spoken-word snippets. Many rappers began to run their entire catalogues in this way. In 2021, Rochester rapper RXK Nephew released over 400 songs, and why not? 'I don't think we've ever seen the Internet that advanced,' Earl Sweatshirt said of him. 'He lived an entire rap career in a year.' As if to acknowledge the audaciousness, *Pitchfork* ran an article entitled: 'The 100 Best RXK Nephew Songs . . . of 2021'.

record. At his own album's launch party, he didn't play a single Lightspeed Champion song, instead announcing 'Who wants to hear some indie?' and ripping into covers of The Strokes, Interpol and The Walkmen instead. He also formed Team Perfect with Florence Welch of Florence & The Machine, who he'd befriended when they were teenagers, hanging out in the pubs of Elephant and Castle. They played house parties together, Hynes laying into the guitar while Welch belted out Iggy Pop covers to a room of twenty-somethings trying to enjoy their Aperol spritzes. In 2007 they uploaded a mixtape to Devonté's MySpace which was simply Green Day's *Nimrod,* covered front to back.

Hynes shared his talents generously. He appeared on a Chemical Brothers song and sang at a tribute to American composer Moondog at the Barbican. He was even drafted to join the in-house banks of songwriters behind British taste-making institution *The X Factor*, which accidentally landed him his first ever production credit after he played guitar and drums on a song for 2008's runner-up, Diana Vickers. 'I was slightly horrified,' he said about the day he received an email offering him the fee, 'because I didn't bother to tune anything.' By late 2008 Devonté was spending so much time touring that, for a time, he didn't actually have a home at all. With his visa still valid from the abandoned Test Icicles tour, he decided he might as well be a nomad in America, and decamped to New York City.

The first release Devonté wrote in the Big Apple was the second Lightspeed Champion album. It is, ironically, the most British-sounding record he's ever made. Recorded mostly in Abbey Road and produced by Ben Allen (who has been behind the boards for Gnarls Barkley and Animal Collective), *Life is Sweet! Nice to Meet You* is also his safest. Allen mostly follows Mogis' lead, but with even more bells and whistles which give it a Kinks-esque affect. There are gorgeous songs, like 'There's Nothing Underwater', and a piano étude in the album's final leg but, mostly, the songs are pretty and unobtrusive in a familiar way.

Hynes wrote its songs in late 2008 but he wouldn't record them for almost a year, and the album wasn't released until February 2010. After relentless touring Hynes was diagnosed with growths on his vocal cords called nodules, a painful condition which blights countless vocalists but tends to occur, as with Elton John, far later in their careers. By the time Hynes was twenty-three though, he had already been performing for a decade in punk and metal groups which demanded power and strain. Devonté had emergency surgery which left him unable to talk for two months. He needed speech therapy to get his voice back at all.

Because there was such a gap between writing the songs and recording them, Devonté's focus was drifting away from Lightspeed's second album before it was even finished. While unable to sing, he began composing a classical piece he called the *D-List Symphony*, a tribute to his favourite composers which he published the sheet music for in increments on his blog, and invited followers to submit their own recitations. In 2009 he covered around thirty albums in their entirety from his living room, and promptly filed them away on his laptop, never to be heard by anybody. He recorded two albums of cello compositions, which didn't see the light of day either. He also began experimenting with a project he'd been teasing for some time.

For years, Devonté had been joking to crowds at Lightspeed Champion shows that he wanted to start a funk and soul group. When asked about it by *The Quietus*, he laughed and said that might be the direction of the third Lightspeed album, something like Marvin Gaye's first disco record, *I Want You*. 'I want to do something like that,' he told them, 'percussion heavy.' In 2009, when he began getting his voice back, Devonté finally decided to channel his inner Marvin.

The clean break between Lightspeed Champion and Blood Orange does not exist. Devonté was, for a few months at least, performing as both. But, by my estimation, the very first Blood Orange song released was a cover of a doo-wop tune from the 1950s, and it was released under the name Lightspeed Champion.

The Fleetwoods were a pop group from Olympia, Washington, comprised of two girlfriends and a dude named Gary. They're best known for 'Come Softly to Me', a near a cappella song built around only their three voices, guitar, and percussion played by a rattling set of car keys. It became a US number one in 1959. Often comprising little more than brushed drum skins and gently cooed vocal lines, The Fleetwoods made music of a sweetness which is almost incomprehensible today, a distinctly Christian utopia where passion exists only in glances and supple kisses. In 1961, two years after 'Come Softly to Me' made them a household name, The Fleetwoods released '(He's) The Great Imposter', a song where a woman's friends watch helplessly on as she's seduced by a malevolent man. With that positively sinister subject matter and drums which are actually drummed, for The Fleetwoods it might as well have been death metal.

At one point in 2009, '(He's) The Great Imposter' was the only song on Devonté Hynes' iPod. He listened to it incessantly, and eventually released a cover too. His version – 'He's The Great Imposter' – abandons the ambiguity of the parentheses and emphasises the song's strangest parts. That Pacific-coast guitar riff is dragged to the fore and tuned tight and sharp, each chord striking like a flicked blade. When he uploaded the cover to his blog, he explained that he was about to begin a new project and that The Fleetwoods' sound – a blend of oriental melodies paired with soft, lovelorn vocals – was what he wanted it to sound like.

Hynes posted the first official Blood Orange song on the 3rd of August 2009, six months before *Life Is Sweet!* was released. 'S'Cooled' is a short, strutting tune with snapping, 'sha!' percussion straight out of the DFA Records playbook. It's sexy. The bassline is fatter and groovier than any which had appeared on a Lightspeed Champion song, but the biggest change was to Devonté's voice. The shift wasn't simply a stylistic one. After recovering from surgery, Hynes decided to sing in a way which wouldn't do the same damage that the first decade had. To do so, he abandoned the angsty projection he'd learned from the likes of Billy Corgan and began to develop a softer, sultry tone inspired by LL Cool J and French synth-pop singer F.R. David instead.

'S'Cooled' would eventually land on Blood Orange's debut album *Coastal Grooves*, released in August 2011 on Domino Records. Back then, the pivot from the country-pop of Lightspeed Champion to this new material felt like a complete about-face but, in retrospect, Blood Orange's first record still evokes aspects of Hynes' indie era, its songs deploying the stalking basslines of Franz Ferdinand and The Rapture in a way he never would again. It was an album born more directly from his bedroom experiments, playing around with the sounds which obsessed him: the melodies of Joe Hisaishi and the electronic whims of Yellow Magic Orchestra, all cut through with Chris Isaak's brittle guitar lines and surf-punk bands like Agent Orange and The B-52s.

Working from a cramped apartment, he didn't have much space to practise, and so he took the new songs for walks. He played them all over New York City, tweaking them live in front of half-empty bars with just a microphone, his guitar and a laptop. By the end of 2009, before *Life Is Sweet! Nice to Meet You* was even out, Hynes had already recorded twenty Blood Orange demos. Then, in December, he debuted Blood Orange publicly with the song 'Forget It', played live on MTV's *It's On with Alexa Chung*.

With everyone under the assumption that this stuff was just a side project, Devonté was able to work without the weight of expectation or pressure of time. He signed up to a basketball league in the West Village (a storied tournament set up by the Beastie Boys) and began to make more acquaintances in the American side of the industry. One of those friends was Theophilus London, a rapper and singer from Trinidad and Tobago, by way of Flatbush, Brooklyn. After Hynes heard his self-released project, *This Charming Mixtape*, he and London began hanging out, starting work on a new, pop-leaning EP. Theophilus would never really become a household name himself, but those sessions would give birth to somebody who would.

In the early 2010s, certain age-old dividing lines between so-called alternative music and pop began to break down for good. The collaborative spirit of rap music began to be reflected in all around it, and it became the norm to not only ask another MC from the city to hop on a beat, but for artists from entirely different worlds to coalesce on a single track. Justin Vernon of Bon Iver, the grizzled über-hipster, was a key collaborator on *My Beautiful Dark Twisted Fantasy* and *Yeezus*, his soft drawl interacting with snarled verses by Rick Ross and JAY-Z. Kanye West was already tapped into indie music (as a noted Fiona Apple fan, he recruited her producer Jon Brion to work on his first epic, *Late Registration*), but Bon Iver had a different audience entirely.

Also emerging were a new crop of underground and alternative artists who didn't feel so compelled to ride for the Pixies or die by the Backstreet Boys. Grimes, for example, began in a distinctly indie mode (she was signed to the 4AD of Cocteau Twins and Deerhunter) but her songs, like 2012's iconic 'Oblivion', were not startling because of how strongly she reacted against the zeitgeist but because she didn't. Grimes made electro-pop songs, just like Lady Gaga; she simply reimagined them on softer, shyer terms: blockbusters, as sketched in a kid's notebook.

One of the artists who defined this particular critical moment was Sky Ferreira. Ferreira grew up around fame. Her grandmother was Michael Jackson's stylist, and she spent her birthdays in Neverland. She was ready-made for stardom. By the time she was fifteen she was already a model with an EMI contract. They hired the directors of Britney Spears' 'Toxic' video for her first single. But that single – boilerplate EDM at the height of boilerplate EDM – flopped. The budget for her second single was slashed and when that song, 'One', did almost as badly, rather than drop her, EMI gave her the opportunity to pursue a sound closer to her idea of herself, abandoning their plans for a chart takeover and allowing her the chance to see what she could recoup of their losses instead. She was paired with young producers like Ariel Rechtshaid (himself a landfill-indie alum who had produced Plain White T's 'Hey There Delilah'), and Devonté Hynes. The three of them emerged with 'Everything Is Embarrassing'.

Released in 2012 (and again in 2013), 'Everything is Embarrassing' became the archetype for a new breed of pop song. It makes its pleasures known early, as most great pop songs do, with a massive clattering kick drum right out of the gate. But really, it's all tease. Those drums press on, decorated by jagged guitar lines and a heavy, downtempo piano. Listening to it brings joy but it's not about joy: it's about the bottom falling out of somebody's world. It wouldn't work without Ferreira's voice. She delivers a palpable yearning and her vocals are stalked, even in the song's pretty bridge, by a pitched-down version of herself, pitching the mood of the song somewhere between devotion and utter humiliation. It's all the things a great pop single should be – infectious, danceable, propulsive

– and yet, as with Grimes, it's more complicated and reticent than pop songs usually are. It was an enormous critical success – *New York* magazine called it the best song of the year – and yet an utter commercial failure, charting in only one single country: Belgium. The only difference was that, this time, landing a hit no longer seemed to be the point.

One EMI signee who did step away from her contract was Solange Knowles. She was better positioned for stardom than even Ferreira, by virtue of happening to be Beyoncé's younger sister. She started as a backup dancer for Destiny's Child when she was barely a teenager. Like Ferreira, she too was primed for stardom by inference and, when she turned sixteen in 2002, EMI signed her up. Her debut album, *Solo Star*, boasted production from Timbaland and Pharrell. With a feature from Lil' Romeo to top it all off, what could go wrong? Well, everything did. The album didn't even make the Billboard Top 100 and is now unavailable for sale. Her second album, a Motown-influenced departure which somehow featured both Q-Tip and Boards of Canada, did better but Solange still didn't feel like she'd captured the sound she was vying for. She'd fallen in love with European downtempo and some of hip hop's most involute producers, and she wanted to pursue her bliss without compromise. In 2008 she left EMI and signed with a label co-run by Chris Taylor of Grizzly Bear instead.

Solange's first EP with Terrible Records – 2012's *True* – saw her finally arriving at the sound she was after. A dance album at heart, its seven songs were both pop and the antithesis of it; a taut sound driven by pulsing, squiggly grooves and snatches of piano and bass, but almost entirely chorus-less, her vocals delivered with the nonchalance of a woman leant against a wall, delivering dispatches with one eye on the door. Its first single, 'Losing You', boasts one of the finest openings to a pop song ever: a stomping sample of the drums from

Euro Funk's 'Dynomite' paired with the sound of – well, I've never quite worked out what that sound is – but it sounds like a cat trying to flirt. Like 'Everything Is Embarrassing', it's everything a heartbreak song shouldn't sound like: the palette hit songs use to denote supreme confidence deployed to soundtrack extreme doubt.

The *Village Voice* called the track 'a stunner' and declared a '"Losing You" Week' the day of its release. Even with the association of her sister however, the song also didn't chart in the US.* What 'Losing You' *did* do was prove to Solange herself that she could succeed making music far more eccentric than what EMI had expected of her. When she finally released her third album, eight years after her second, it was *A Seat at the Table*, a genre-crossing classic which exists in the cracks between rap, soul and funk, and delivered Solange a style of her own. It was an evolution which began on *True*, which was produced by Devonté Hynes.

When Theophilus London first made the call to Solange, she was at the beach with her son. London and Devonté were working on his single 'Flying Overseas' together, building around a demo Hynes had written when he was recovering from throat surgery in his apartment. Theophilus was blown away. He was so excited by what he was hearing that he insisted that Solange needed to come straight to the studio. Don't even wait around to find a sitter. Knowles took his enthusiasm seriously, and drove straight to the studio in central LA, baby in tow.

Solange loved 'Flying Overseas' and eventually lent her vocals to it, but what really captivated her was its producer. Within a single track, Devonté had melded the still-new sound of melodic, Kid Cudi-influenced rap with the electro-funk of

* It did make it to number four in Belgium though!

Afrika Bambaataa and West Street Mob, and a dash of new wave drums. When Devonté played her the unreleased demos for 'Champagne Coast', Solange, still seeking a new direction, was ecstatic. She and Hynes hit it off in a big way. For a time they became, by their own accounts, like brother and sister, bonding over a love for Willow Smith and The S.O.S. Band. The next time they met he showed her a playlist of muses, filled with the likes of Chaka Khan and French MC Jimmy Jay. She had one which was almost identical. That day Knowles told her boyfriend: 'I've found the person I want to make my next album with.'

Solange invited Devonté to Santa Barbara to join the sessions for her first Terrible Records release. At first Hynes was just one of a roster of producers but Knowles became excited only by what he was doing, and asked him to produce the entire thing instead. As the sessions began in earnest, with just the two of them in a room, Hynes quickly became a presence on every song. They made expansive, electro-funk suites spanning twelve minutes in length, which they would riff on and whittle down into pop songs. Two of the tracks – 'Losing You' and 'Bad Girls' – were developed from the Blood Orange demos Hynes used to pass around, but the rest were created by Solange, with assistance from Devonté, entirely from scratch.

Drawing from their shared playlists, Solange and Hynes pulled heavily from an iconic production duo: Jimmy Jam and Terry Lewis. Producers of Janet Jackson, Mary J. Blige, Boyz II Men and The S.O.S. Band, their signature sound – the walloping kick drum of the Roland TR-808 – bore them forty-one US top ten hits and became central to the sound of *True* and Blood Orange too. When Devonté met Jimmy Jam for a 2013 magazine feature he told him that he had once ordered vintage keyboard magazines from the '80s online, just because he knew that he and Lewis had been interviewed in them. After scouring the pages, Devonté downloaded software plug-ins which imitated all of the gear they'd referenced on the page so that, if he ever got his hands on the real things, he could get to work straight away.

True was a love letter to passions shared by Solange and Hynes, yet it's easy to forget just how unique it sounded in 2012. Among critical circles, the likes of Jam and Lewis were not fashionable reference points. In 2012, music fans were well used to '80s revivalism thanks to the 'Quiet Storm'-infatuated 'chill-wave' scene, with the likes of Toro y Moi, Washed Out and How to Dress Well producing luscious, sultry music so laid back that it was often entirely flat. They may have shared some of the same musical lineage, but 'Everything Is Embarrassing' and 'Losing You' were lightning bolts in comparison: angular, potent and emotionally bare.

On the day of *True*'s release, Devonté and Solange took a trip to Michael Jackson's star on the Hollywood Walk of Fame and took a picture holding a poster for *Bad* to celebrate. Weeks later, Hynes – drunk on too many glasses of champagne – sang 'What Have You Done for Me Lately' to JAY-Z at Beyoncé's birthday party, and was hired as a consultant to his Rocawear fashion label on the spot. Nonetheless, Solange and Devonté's partnership was short-lived. Hynes claims to have never read a review of his albums but Knowles did read reviews, and what she found there pissed her off. Journalists covering *True* often wrote about the EP as if it was a Devonté Hynes project, with Solange Knowles on vocals.

'Y'all got it all the way wrong,' she tweeted. 'I've been writing and producing my own voice since 02 . . . I find it very disappointing when I am presented as the "face" of my music, or a "vocal muse" when I write or co-write every fucking song . . . Sexism in the industry ain't nothing new.' Sky Ferreira expressed irritation too, in her case at Devonté directly. When performing 'Everything Is Embarrassing' live, Hynes introduced it as a song he wrote for her, which Ferreira bristled at. Like Solange, she claims to have dramatically altered Hynes' demos to make them what they became. These feuds were written about excitedly by publications who didn't even comment on the singles themselves, and it caused such panic for Hynes that he traded in his iPhone for one which was less Internet-ready.*

Ferreira and Solange's anger was a response to a framing of their work which will be familiar to many a pop artist, especially the female ones. Collaboration is a cornerstone of all music, but that truism has often been emphasised unequally depending on the type of artist and type of music being made. Some classic albums are treated as if they're the work of a single genius, as if the engineers and session players who worked on them were effectively interchangeable. For other types of artists – the likes of pop and R&B – the inverse often occurs. Over the years, pop artists have often been treated as if they're puppets on their own songs, fronting music which – even when great – must surely be due to the other people who worked on it.†

The alternative-pop scene which emerged around the likes of Grimes and Sky Ferreira (which *Pitchfork* christened 'small pop') proves the opposite point. Here were artists – some who

* Hynes did get small production credits on Solange's next two albums and they've since performed 'Losing You' together again, so the pair have somewhat reconciled. It's not clear whether Ferriera and Hynes ever hashed it out.

† It's an attitude which still, maddeningly, persists. When Jann Wenner (the co-founder of *Rolling Stone*) was asked in 2023 why he didn't speak to any female artists in his book of interviews with great musicians, he responded that no female musician was 'articulate enough on this intellectual level'.

rejected major label deals, others who were making music in their bedrooms – who made increasingly brilliant pop music the more they had control over it. Figures like Hynes and Rechtshaid, artists who were not in-house songwriters, instead used their talents to facilitate the creation of the kind of music Sky and Solange wanted to create. Songs like 'Losing You' and 'Oblivion' are songs which encourage *more credit* for their stars, not less.

It's also music with an ongoing legacy. DIY artists like Rina Sawayama and Clarence Clarity soon began making huge, eccentric pop songs of their own, and major-label signees like Carly Rae Jepsen and Charli xcx soon stepped away from zeitgeist-chasing hits to bring weirder, more fascinating ideas into their songs. Songs like 'Everything Is Embarrassing' and 'Losing You' are proof of the magic artists like Charli are capable of when they're given the space to do whatever they hell they please.

After releasing *Coastal Grooves*, Devonté didn't plan to make another Blood Orange album. He didn't plan *not* to either; he just kept making music every day, as he always had. He followed that album quickly with a Tumblr mixtape named *Blood Orange Home Recordings*, which features vocals from Erika Forster and Solange. When he started Blood Orange it was his first solo project; insular and experimental and made mostly in his bedroom. But now, just like the Saddle Creek sessions in Omaha, his friends were becoming woven into his process, and that excited him. Producing and writing with others had been liberating. The stakes of a song were lower when he knew he might not have to be the one to see it through. 'I just write songs and think: this will be a cool song for someone to sing and then either it gets rejected, or everyone forgets about it,' he told the *New York Times* in 2013, laughing. 'I get my own leftovers.'

By 2012, Hynes had gone through several break-ups, romantic and creative. He had recorded dance, country and punk albums. The likes of 'Losing You' had even made him (to a certain, blog-reading crowd at least) a celebrity. But his discography was messy too, split between Blood Orange, the singles he helped craft with other artists, and Lightspeed Champion, which many were still expecting to hear more from. It began to seem like no single project could fit all of his disparate loves in one single space, and messy is how it would remain. That is, until it didn't.

Even though, by the age of twenty-five, Devonté had already amassed an enviable CV, *Cupid Deluxe* was still a startling leap forward. Recorded over two years and released on the 18th of November 2013, it so completely eviscerates the rougher edges of his earlier records that it's startling to realise it was released only two years after the one before it. Despite the evocative mood of *Coastal Grooves*, that album sounds like unfinished business, with songs which begin with great ideas before stalling into stasis. *Cupid Deluxe* is, on the other hand, radiant. It's spotlit by synths which are bright and warm, shimmering beds of sound set ablaze by heavy, clattering 808s. It's strange that this record was released (unlike all of the Blood Orange albums to follow) outside of summer, because it's made to be paired with muggy, hot days; its details are sticky and sun-kissed, and it's perpetually wrapped in the state of lethargy and agitation the summer heat cooks out of us. In terms of discographies, it's an album in the vein of New Order's *Power, Corruption & Lies* or Outkast's *ATLiens*: a second album (technically Hynes' fifth) where a promising, occasionally brilliant, artist suddenly delivers something masterful and complete, front to back.

Like his work with Solange and Ferreira, *Cupid Deluxe*'s songs are often confounding. The tempos are upbeat, its grooves borrowed from disco, and yet it often feels too melancholic to dance to. It had a legacy as a decidedly American album but *Cupid Deluxe* is still a deceptively British record, if you look beyond the references to Bowery Ballroom. Hynes modelled the structure of the record after Bristol's own Massive Attack, with a smattering of Gorillaz along the way. There is a cover of 'I Can Only Disappoint U' by Mansun, an alt-rock band from Chester which only people of Dev's specific age, interests and proximity could possibly remember. The *Cupid Deluxe* version, retitled 'Always Let U Down', is one of the most transformative covers I've ever heard, remaking a slightly stiff psych-rock tune as a slick, yearning ballad – dropping the tempo drastically and adorning it with a sample of reggae-funk from Grace Jones' 'Nipple to the Bottle', and beatbox hiccups.

The LP's singles – 'Chamakay' and 'You're Not Good Enough' – arrived just days before the album did, and signalled something great to come. The latter became the finest song in Hynes' catalogue the second it was released. It's almost full-blown disco. A tight little guitar riff wrapped around shuffling drums, with a New Age organ breakdown in the second half. It's a classic kiss-off, written about a past relationship and sung as a duet with a new girl. It takes the most horrible words you can conceive of hearing from an ex – 'I never was in love / you were never good enough' and delivers them softly, like a piece of sage advice. Hynes' music had so often been sung from the perspective of the defeated lover, but here he and Samantha Urbani sound victorious: equal parts nasty and sexy.

The other, opener 'Chamakay', conjures a mood of pensiveness which seeps out across the rest of the record: hollow wood bouncing off thick, cavernous columns of bass. The voice of Caroline Polachek, another emerging underground-pop stalwart, joins Hynes almost as soon as the song begins. 'I'll never leave you if you're thinking that it's all the same,' she pants over a groove which moves like lapping waves; 'I'll never trust you if you're thinking that it's just a game.' It sounds like someone got Elizabeth Fraser of the Cocteau Twins to sing over '80s Marvin Gaye.*

I spoke to Caroline about the making of 'Chamakay' back in 2011. She and Devonté had first met at an illegal basement gig in Brooklyn in 2008. 'Even there, there was already a mystique around him then, people going "that's Dev Hynes, that's Dev Hynes". Back then, that was the real fun of going out; you did hear about people first IRL before hearing about them online, which is almost unfathomable now.' Soon after meeting her, Devonté asked Caroline to come by the studio to record. '"Chamakay" was wild!' she told me. 'I was going through a very fraught period in my life, and I showed up at a very chic studio in a high-rise where Dev was working. It had these huge glass windows which opened onto the city. When I got there, he played me a recording of an African choir where this woman was singing at full pelt and told me "I want you to try something like this". It didn't sound like my voice, but I was excited to try something different.

'The whole process was quite spooky because we were barely speaking to each other. We started tracking takes, one after the other, and I almost fainted! I blacked out for lack of oxygen because I was going so hard. He added reverb and we listened back and it had this urgency and fantastic sense of atmosphere. At that point Dev showed me some lyrics. They were cast off, like he'd found them in his pocket after they'd been through the wash a couple of times. I didn't even bother writing them out,

* The word 'chamakay' is Guyanese slang which means something close to 'young, mischievous girl'. It was a word Hynes learned when he visited his mother's home country for the first time during the making of *Cupid Deluxe*, and you can see footage from that trip in the music video for the song, where Devonté dances along the shoreline and meets his 95-year-old grandmother for the first time.

I just started singing along to his patchwork beat along with the choir. It was one of the quickest sessions I've ever done. I was there for like an hour max. But there was an urgency and severity in the room; it's so really rare to not have a warm-up chat or banter or anything. That was a very special day.'

In the 2020s, we are used to artists like Travis Scott ceding the stage of their own song to the likes of James Blake or Beyoncé, but in 2012 it felt strange to just have a singer from another group come and open your record. Hynes was hanging out with Polachek in his home studio, just having fun, and asked her to sing the words he'd recorded for himself as a jape. When he heard her voice on it though, Hynes considered the song complete for the first time.

This idea, that only an album's named artist should be the one to sing every note of every song, was another rule which Devonté quickly discarded. He claimed that one of the main aspirations for Blood Orange was that it never sounded like a solo project, even though he wrote many of the songs alone. What's remarkable about *Cupid Deluxe* is that the menagerie of voices Hynes brings to the table don't just sound like he's put an imaginary band together: they sound like a community of voice contributing to one single, idiosyncratic style. Despite the many guests, despite the fact he doesn't even sing on one of the songs, it sounds like a Devonté Hynes album through and through. Visiting players like Polachek, Urbani, Tawiah, Dave Longstreth and Skepta somehow help to complete the Blood Orange 'sound', even though most hadn't worked with Devonté before and wouldn't again.*

---

* One reason for this is that Hynes' post-surgery vocal style – which Solange showed him new ways to deploy when they worked on *True* – is so distinct that even though he doesn't sing on 'No Right Thing', Dave Longstreth's diction is so notably his that it feels like he's there anyway.

Despite his love for The Fleetwoods and Philip Glass and Boyz II Men, the greatest sonic influence on that sound (and perhaps Blood Orange's aesthetic in general) was Malcom McLaren. Alongside a great many other things, McLaren was curator above all else. As the man behind the Sex Pistols, one of the architects of the look of British punk, he understood the power of image intuitively and, although the Pistols are synonymous with venomous rebellion, McLaren crafted the band to suit the image in his mind, much as Simon Cowell would later do with kids from the North in skinny jeans. The look was the thing, and he pulled together myriad cultures to make it happen.

Just as McLaren pieced together bands (he'd done the same with New York Dolls and Adam and the Ants), so too did he act as a curator on his own LPs. His first, 1983's *Duck Rock*, is a total Frankenstein album, taking various South American, Caribbean and South African iterations of rock music and melding them with post-disco hip hop. McLaren was the original DJ Khaled, recruiting a roster of players and slapping his name on the cover. Despite the continued acclaim for *Duck Rock*, I prefer his second record, 1984's *Fans*, which took the same idea and applied a different equation: rap, electro-funk and opera. Yes, opera.

The first track from that record, 'Madam Butterfly (Un Bel Dí Vedremo)', had long been one of Devonté's favourite songs, and the track is killer. Thumping gated drums rattle beneath a majestic soprano and it finishes off with an energetic, rapped verse from Debbie Cole. Each element works in isolation: the rhythm is crisp and heavy, Cole's bars are joyously goofy and then there's the opera: an element which has the potential to feel like a joke but somehow achieves the opposite. The voice of soprano Betty Ann White remains gorgeous, granting McLaren a shimmering performance whose beauty isn't diminished by the nature of her collaborators.

'Madam Butterfly' suggested to Devonté – a fan of electro-funk, hip hop and classical – that it was possible to put all of those disparate components in one place and watch the sparks fly. Accordingly, the palette of *Cupid Deluxe* is an unbridled blend of all these different worlds. At first glance, it might feel like '80s revivalism – a homage to electro-funk, new jack swing and disco – but the album is an open book, and the presence of other genres takes those sounds in myriad directions: there are flashes of jazz, diversion into hip hop on the Despot-featuring 'Clipped On', and – as on 'Madam Butterfly' – of classical. When the Dirty Projectors' Dave Longstreth appears on 'No Right Thing' his vocals are statelier and more angular than you're used to hearing paired with a supple, R&B instrumental: an alternative history where Jimmy Jam recruited Mark Hollis for a guest verse on *Rhythm Nation 1814*.

Hynes was working on several projects during the making of the record – one of them being the score for Gia Coppola's film *Palo Alto* – and he carries that cinematic instinct into these Blood Orange songs. Most of them – from 'It Is What It Is' to 'Chosen' – start with serene, scene-setting introductions which are loudly shattered by booming kick drums. The remarkable third song, 'Uncle ACE', boasts a vamping, Blaxploitation guitar riff dancing around a motorik beat. It's funky, but what seems like a disco song is another trick. In the song's second half, a saxophone enters the fray and, as the wind rushes in, the whole thing collapses. The song breaks into Philip Glass-style ascending woodwinds which circle upwards frantically, a vibe become vortex.

McLaren and Devonté don't simply play with a sandbox of sounds and styles from across popular music, but with their cultural connotations too. 'Madam Butterfly' isn't simply exciting despite its blending of the supposedly high and low but perhaps *because* of it. It feels a little wrong, a little punk, like these two worlds – the unabashed funk of electro-funk, the soaring pomposity of opera – shouldn't exist in the same space. Like McLaren, Hynes looks at the music of Lil Wayne or Philip Glass or Lou Reed and sees them as equals. This equal footing unlocks the potential of sounds which were once trapped in archetypes. A hungry rap verse can become melancholic; booming drums can become dreamy and sad.

That's what happens on the LP's last and best song, 'Time Will Tell'. It opens with that massive sequenced beat, but this track has none of the bounce of classic electro-funk hits like The S.O.S. Band's 'The Finest' or Janet Jackson's 'When I Think of You'. Instead the drums are left unadorned, creating vast caverns between them which Hynes slips his voice into. Stripped and alone like this, that drum loop feels cold and cruel, a Roland R-70 sounding like the machine that it is. Licks of wah-wah-drenched guitar playing limply, like spurious snippets of a lifetime of Billboard hits. There isn't a huge chorus; a gorgeous, Puccini-esque piano part enters instead. The song's title comes from track 5, 'It Is What It Is', and the aching motif 'come to my bedroom' is a revival of the hook of *Coastal Groove*'s 'Champagne Coast'. As a writing practice, Hynes often uses lines from older songs to fill unfinished lyrics in this way, but here he just leaves them there. 'Time Will Tell' sounds how memory feels and, by scooping the beating heart out of classic hits and presenting their skeletons nakedly, reminds us that those memories are often soundtracked by pop songs.

One of the most beautiful things about the way music evolved in the 2010s, in a post-Internet, post-poptimist age, is that so many albums now approach music in exactly the same way. Caroline Polachek, who sang on 'Chamakay', became a major indie-pop star in her own right, and her solo albums – like 2023's *Desire, I Want to Turn Into You* – runs roughshod over the sounds you can and cannot use on a pop record. There's Spanish guitar, dembow, children's choirs, trip-hop, folk and bagpipes, and all of that eclecticism hardly seems worth commenting on anymore, aside from how fun it all was. Enormous commercial albums, like Drake's record of the same year – *For the Dogs* – move between beats ridden by New York classists Griselda, the punk-ish rage of Playboi Carti and ratchet dance music. On their brilliant 2022 album *I Love You Jennifer B*, Warp Records signees Jockstrap run the gamut of dubstep, folk and hybrids of the two. I saw them play live in Finland two years later and there was no dissonance. Sometimes their songs make you want to jump into the air, sometimes stand in poignant reflection. A paintbox has been opened up. It's all music. If you like sound, then embrace what they're giving you.

One of the things which made even the less radical *Coastal Grooves* feel so distinct from the identity of Lightspeed Champion was the way Devonté began to present his records. In the 2000s his albums featured himself prominently, in all his cardigan-wearing, bespectacled glory. Hynes' image had changed drastically since then but, from *Coastal Grooves* onwards, he vanished from his sleeves entirely, and chose evocative images of Ballroom queens, shot at the height of '80s drag culture instead. *Cupid Deluxe*'s music serves as an accompaniment to the stunning photograph of an androgynous queen in Manhattan which appears on its cover; stood only in bikini and bright yellow heels, hands on hips, bathed in pink light. Like the songs, it's both glamorous and tawdry, a queen treating a battered-looking side-room like a catwalk.

As all great album covers do, those photographs create a world for the music to live in, and the people who litter Blood Orange album covers join the swathes of voices deployed as avatars for Devonté within the songs of the albums, from Dave Longstreth to Caroline Polachek who, on 'Chosen', adopts a French accent to deliver a short monologue luxuriating over the body of another man; words spoken by her but written by Hynes.

Devonté isn't queer himself but, because he hung out with the gay kids at school, he was often bullied as if he was. Even for adults, homophobia remains part of the public laceration many artists raised in the age of social media have to endure. When Test Icicles opened up about struggling under the stress of touring, Kasabian's lead singer Tom Meighan dismissed the band and others like them as 'King's Cross rent-boys' in *NME*. In 2013, when Hynes' popularity was rising, the most popular search term pertaining to him wasn't about the music, it was: 'is Dev Hynes gay?'

Shortly after he moved to New York, there was a series of much-reported suicides of young gay men in the city. Devonté was shaken by the stories, and wrote 'Uncle ACE' in their honour. In New York City, a radically disproportionate number of the young and homeless are LGBTQ, and 'Uncle ACE' is the nickname some had given to the A.C.E.: the network of subway lines which runs from Manhattan and which many queer homeless youths use for shelter at night.

In 2009, before much of *Coastal Grooves* was written, Hynes came across Jennie Livingston's cult 1991 documentary *Paris is Burning*, an incredibly influential and starkly unpretentious portrait of queer Ballroom culture. The Ballroom scene has long roots which wind back to Harlem's Black artistic renaissance in the 1930s, through the African and Latino-American gay men partying in the traditional ballrooms of the 1960s and the house clubs of the 1980s. Livingston's film is remarkable in its candour, capturing both the confidence and nonconformity of queens like Dorian Corey and Angie Xtravaganza, alongside the way in which the exuberance of the Ballroom nights intersected with music,

HIV, hate crime and sex work.

By the time of *Paris Is Burning*, much of the Ballroom scene was centred around house music. By 1991, house had evolved from a niche, Chicago subculture to a New York phenomenon. The term 'house' comes from the Chicago club The Warehouse where the genre's progenitor, Frankie Knuckles, once held a regular slot, but the word also aligns appropriately with the 'houses' competitors are grouped into in Ballroom clubs; so called because they provide homes for people who were once rejected from theirs. As a hobbyist dancer (in a 2015 interview he told Julian Casablancas that dance was his favourite form of expression, above even music), Devonté fell in love with the voguing culture depicted in Livingston's film: a combative style of dance which merges elegance with sharp angularity, the body trying to emulate geometric shapes struck by models in fashion magazines. Like 2005's *Rize*, which captured clowning and krumping, or Pablo Larraín's 2019 drama *Ema* – which focussed on reggaeton – *Paris Is Burning* captures voguing as a passionate, rageful outlet for the American underclass. It's utterly upfront, shameless stuff, developed and often performed by people who have at some point being told explicitly that they should stay ashamed.

Many expressions of queerness are not explicitly associated with working-class culture but – like boxing, or rap – voguing is essentially working-class, Black expression. It aligns with those cultures as an outlet for the poorest and most disenfranchised among us, a type of dance which didn't necessarily require equipment, or expensive professional training: just a community and a ballroom. The protagonists in *Paris Is Burning* are often tragic figures. They often shoplift and do sex work just to survive. Voguing has fluidity at its core but melds that complexity with a frantic aggression, an exhalation of passion and pain.* As Hynes was working on the first Blood Orange songs, he played *Paris Is Burning* on a loop in the background.

One evening Devonté was looking for photos of Sally's Hideaway; the club in New York where many of the scenes in *Paris Is Burning* are set. In his search, he came across an archive of club photography from that era: drag queens in various states of undress, relaxing with a cigarette at the end of the night. At the bottom of the pictures he noticed a credit: 'Brian Lantelme'. Lantelme had been a photographer for the *New York Times*, the *Village Voice* and *New York* magazine through the '80s and '90s, and Hynes found his email to send him the demo of 'Sutphin Boulevard', alongside a video he'd made for the song out of clips from *Paris Is Burning*. Lantelme emailed him back to say that the video had made him cry; the photographer was actually *in* the footage Hynes had chosen, and it was the first time he'd seen anything from the film in more than a decade. He gave Devonté full access to his archives, from which he selected the image for the cover of *Coastal Grooves*: a nameless drag queen taken at the entrance of Sally's Hideaway.

* If it feels like the radicalness of subcultures like voguing is being overstated, especially as they drift towards mainstream culture through artists like Rihanna and FKA twigs, then it's worth remembering the extent to which many people still absolutely loathe public displays of pride and flamboyance from queer people, because they loathe queer people. As I was writing this chapter O'Shae Sibley, a gay Black man from Brooklyn, was dancing to Beyoncé's *RENAISSANCE* at a petrol station in New Jersey with a group of friends when a group of teenagers began hurling homophobic abuse at them. An argument broke out, and one of the teenagers stabbed Sibley, killing him instantly. To a limited, bigoted mind, free expression – even joy itself – is still very threatening indeed.

*

On the 17th of July 2014, Eric Garner, a Black gardener for the NYC Parks and Recreation department, was selling loose cigarettes on the pavement in front of a beauty store in Staten Island. Garner had just broken up a fight which had erupted in front of his spot, and that fight caught the attention of Daniel Pantaleo, a 29-year-old plain-clothes police officer. Pantaleo didn't follow the men who'd actually been scuffling but approached Garner instead, his attention piqued by the bundle of cigarettes he was holding in his hand. Selling loose cigarettes is a crime in New York City and Garner, who had been arrested for several similar offences a bunch of times already, knew what was coming.

'Every time you see me, you want to mess with me. I'm tired of it. It stops today,' Garner protested. 'Everyone standing here will tell you I didn't do nothing.' Pantaleo wasn't listening. He walked behind Garner and began squeezing his hands together, readying his wrists for the cuffs. Garner pulled his arms away and Pantaleo snapped. He yanked Garner backwards and tried to force him to the ground. Garner was a big man – forty-three years old, heavy and tall – so it was a struggle to get him down. Pantaleo bounced him off the glass of the beauty store and Garner dropped to his hands and knees. Five more police officers rushed out of nowhere and surrounded them in a circle. Pantaleo latched his hands onto the back of Garner's head and pushed his face into the concrete, pinning him in position as the others wrestled to get his hands into cuffs. 'I can't breathe,' Garner said, and said it eleven times more as Pantaleo shifted more weight onto his neck. Garner struggled, but struggled less forcefully by the second. He remained silent, even once Pantaleo lifted his weight off him. Garner lay there unmoving, face to the ground, for seven long minutes until an ambulance arrived. As they drove him to the hospital, he had a heart attack and died just hours later. It's illegal to sell loose cigarettes in New York State, and Eric Garner was killed for it.

When Devonté and then-girlfriend Samantha Urbani performed their Lollapalooza set at Chicago's Grant Park two weeks later, Hynes wrote Eric Garner's name on his shirt in marker pen. Alongside it, he scrawled the names of Oscar Grant (the 22-year-old whose death at point-blank range was immortalised by 2013's *Fruitvale Station*), Jordan Davis and Trayvon Martin, the seventeen-year-old who was shot in the back by neighbourhood-watch coordinator George Zimmerman while he was visiting family. Urbani wore a shirt which read only 'STOP POLICE BRUTALITY'. During his set, Hynes spoke about his shock at the death of Eric Garner and begged the crowd to take care of one another, and to film any more arrests which seemed to be heading in that direction.

When Urbani and Devonté walked off the stage at the end of the set, one of the security guards grabbed her by the arm. When Hynes asked what the guard was doing, three more suddenly leapt on him and knocked him to the floor. The assault tore the patella in his knee, and left him in a leg brace for sixth months. The exact reason for the attack remains unclear, even to Hynes, but it's not unreasonable to assume that Hynes and Urbani's onstage protest was the trigger.

The day after he killed Eric Garner, Daniel Pantaleo was stripped of his gun but stayed on the job, consigned to desk duty. He had been on trial before when two Black men had filed lawsuits against him the previous year, claiming that he made them strip naked to be searched in the street. In that instance, the charges made against those men had been quietly dropped, but this was different. Eric Garner was dead. The New York Medical Examiner's office ruled Garner's death a homicide, and said that his death was caused primarily by the compression Pantaleo had exerted on his neck. These findings and the video footage of the incident which had gone viral on social media, recorded by Garner's close friend Ramsey Orta, seemed damning but, on the 3rd of December 2014, a jury cleared Pantaleo of all charges.

Devonté joined a crowd of thousands in one of the protests which erupted across American cities in the wake of the verdict, from Baltimore to Minneapolis to Atlanta. Protestors staged theatrical 'die-ins' and began to use Garner's last words, 'I can't breathe', as a rallying cry. 'I feel like, in our culture, you associate time with learning and progression,' Hynes told *Complex* in an interview he gave at the time, still in crutches. 'You assume, in any field, in regards to anything, that over a period of time, there's a progression, and you learn. I think in our culture it's just a real shock when you actually realise that that doesn't add up to everything.'

Hynes' music had dealt explicitly with race and exclusion before. He sang about bullying at the hands of other Black kids on the first Lightspeed Champion album in 2008, but, perhaps because that record was considered an indie-folk record, it was an aspect of the album which wasn't picked up on by many. When he was a teenager, Hynes would often go to the public library to read about Black history, which in school had been reduced simply to the story of slavery. One of the reasons Hynes settled in New York was because he received far less racial abuse there, but he was still reminded of his skin colour perpetually. In 2017, when he played at New York's iconic Boiler Room (with a set which ended with an impromptu cover of Nina Simone's arrangement of 'Nobody's Fault but Mine'), Hynes wrote on Facebook that, before the show, the local police had looked through every page of his notebook with a flashlight, while his white friends passed through without interference.

'You may see me write on this page or playing music and see me as Blood Orange or Dev Hynes, but I turn the corner and I am just another black man,' he wrote on Facebook in 2015, 'a black man that can't get a cab, a black man that has to be careful how I walk if I want to overtake a young white woman so that she doesn't feel scared, a black man that has to sit down and be silent when a police car circles the basketball court I play at, a black man that could be shot down at any time in my life, and as I'm dying know full well that, even if they were to catch who killed me, he will get off free. It is an incredible sadness & heaviness.'

During the making of *Cupid Deluxe*, Hynes was working on multiple full-length projects, one of which was an entirely separate Blood Orange album which he decided not to release, passing it around as a mixtape to friends instead. Another he planned to call *Black Out*, an album of racially charged songs which he made in a single week after he attended another rally at Union Square, the day after Trayvon Martin was murdered. His plan was to create a fake email account and send it to various publications, but he changed his mind at the last moment, afraid that the aesthetic of his music would get in the way of his intent.

In 2015, though, he did release two singles which directly addressed his despair at the list of violent injustices committed against Black Americans which seemed to be growing daily. One of these songs was 'Sandra's Smile', a skeletal cut which he wrote in tribute to the mothers of the many victims he'd read about in the headlines. It was named after Sandra Bland, a Black woman who died in a Texas jail cell after being arrested for a minor traffic violation.* The other, released

* The sheer volume of Black deaths at the hands of police in America led to some of the 2010s' most powerful protest songs. In their 2017 song 'Cleveland', the lead singer of Atlanta rock

on the 1st of July 2015, was 'Do You See My Skin Through the Flames', a sombre, eleven-minute piano piece which he recorded quickly in his bedroom and uploaded to SoundCloud the same day. He played every instrument – from the piano to the Wurlitzer – improvising a verse and chorus before breaking into a long, spoken-word passage where he expresses dismay at his white audience's inability to comprehend the experience of being Black in places where most people are not. On the song he recalls researching his surname and realising that 'Hynes' came from the Irish name 'O'Heyens', which means 'servant'.

'Not only is my last name a name originated from the slave trade, but it literally means a servant,' he says on the song. 'It's a weird thing to have to carry around. I'm proud of my name, I'm proud of my dad, I'm proud of my family: but it's very strange to have to carry that every day. We all carry that, every black person carries that.' In 2016 he spoke to a *Pitchfork* journalist in New York's Washington Square Park and commented on how he was conscious that the space had originally been given to freed slaves to help ease relationships with other Americans. 'That's just one part of our day,' he told them, 'because I want to sit in a park.'

In the wake of the apartment fire of December 2013, Hynes continued to collaborate, writing, producing and playing on albums by Theophilus London, FKA twigs, Jessie Ware, Tinashe and Heems. He produced the huge, sparkling 'Crystallize' for

---

and rap group Algiers lists the names of Black people killed by the police or who died under suspicious circumstances in custody. In 2020, they released an updated version of the song which added all of the additional victims who had been killed since the original, named 'Cleveland 20/20'. A four-minute song stretched to thirty-four minutes.

Kylie Minogue – one of her best singles in years – and made his presence known on the third record of an artist who came to embody porous boundaries between cult fame and superstardom in this new decade: Carly Rae Jepsen.

Three years before she reached out to him, Jepsen was being heavily promoted as the first signee and prodigy of Justin Bieber (despite him being only eighteen – a full nine years younger than her – at the time). Her first album, the now (and then, to be honest) forgotten *Tug of War* was another in a long lineage of Canadians going country, but her songwriting had been twisted and polished to fit the Scooter Braun-industrial complex. In 2012, the first single of her rebrand was a little song named 'Call Me Maybe'. That massive, maximalist, bubblegum hit exceeded just about everybody's expectations. The Bieber-boost helped. He was near the peak of his baby-faced, and 'Baby'-born, fame at the time, but I doubt even he expected her song to immediately became one of the best-selling singles of all time.

'Call Me Maybe' was everywhere, but Jepsen was an uneasy fit for mega-stardom. She was sweet, and a little shy. Like Solange, she wasn't keen on the direction producers like LMFAO's Redfoo had led her sound into either. Around the time that *Kiss* came out, the *True* EP was released. Jepsen was smitten. She delved into the production credits to find who was behind it and asked her team to reach out. When Hynes heard that she wanted to work with him, he became suspicious; he was wary of a huge pop star seeking indie credibility. When he met her though, he discovered the artist Jepsen would emerge as in the decade to come: a sharp songwriter, with a speciality in bashful self-depreciation and an utterly maddening knack for a chorus. The song Hynes eventually wrote and produced with Jepsen and Ariel Rechtshaid was called 'All That', and it's a classic, a Prince-flavoured ballad which sees two sexually bashful writers taking their sultry side for a spin. Despite his luscious sound, there isn't a lot of sex in the world of Blood Orange (uniquely, almost none of his songs are even love songs) but 'All That' is pure heat: acoustic drums crashing against honey-thick slap-bass, building to an orgasmic peak.

Around this time Devonté also began working on new songs of his own. For the first time he began noting down scraps of ideas in notebooks. It was a useful tool because he wrote as he moved around the city: headphones on, passing the roller skaters and the homeless and the hipsters. Inspired by the chaos, he began trying to transfuse some city life into the songs themselves, sometimes literally.

One day Devonté was walking with a friend in Central Park when they passed under a bridge, with a female opera singer singing gorgeously on one side, and a saxophonist busking on the other. Hynes loved the way their different pieces mingled in the air, and so he recorded them on his iPhone from his pocket as he walked. He built the song which would become 'With Him' around it; writing piano melodies in place of the singer's voice and additional sax parts to add to the busker's. If you listen closely, you can still hear his friend talking to him on the song. Those sounds and recordings would coalesce, over the course of almost three years, into *Freetown Sound*, the third Blood Orange album. It was released on the 28th of June 2016. Hynes wrote that the LP was for anybody 'not black enough, too black, too queer, not queer the right way'. It was his attempt to provide a home for the culturally homeless, and to give himself something to listen to as he cycled around town.

Freetown Sound was first conceived two years before its release, with the track 'E.V.P.' That song, which features both his close friend BEA1991 and Debbie Harry of Blondie, is a complete amalgam in itself.* Hynes started work on its components for an Eckhaus Latta catwalk in 2014, and then revisited it occasionally across two years. 'E.V.P.' ended up sounding somewhere between '70s funk band Zapp and a Leonard Cohen song, with some drawling, Arthur Russell-style strings as a final flourish. In the 2020s, a lot of post-genre acts like to forecast their genre shifts with a bang, but Devonté works differently: pouring them into a stew and letting them simmer without comment. Hynes had always made music in this loose way, but more of that instinctual music making made it onto this record than ever before. 'But You' was constructed from melodies which had sat unused on his hard drive for years. One day Hynes spontaneously committed to the song, recorded all of the instruments and the vocal line in a single take, and then stopped, because he'd planned to play table tennis. He didn't make another adjustment.

More so than ever before, *Freetown Sound* is rife with Devonté's impulse to share. In the album's liner notes, some credits are noted by percentages and, for the song 'Augustine', Aaron Maine of synth-pop band Porches is credited with 'third chords and hook suggestion', after simply being present during a session one day to add an F-sharp to the B-minor.† Integrating

---

* Devonté had sparked a friendship with Harry a couple of years earlier, and returned the favour of 'E.V.P.' by co-writing and producing 'Long Time', the propulsive stand-out from Blondie's 2017 album *Pollinator*.

† The lack of distinction Hynes draws between the work of others and his own is why there's a whole swathe of his finest work which would go unremarked upon in the traditional style of reviewing an artist's work, because some of his finest songs appear on the records of others. There's his loose, cold-blooded turn on The Avalanches' The Roches-flipping masterpiece 'We Will Always Love You', and some bright, snapping guitar work on John Cale's 'I Know You're

other voices on work which is so personal has alchemical results. He said that on the clipped, jungle-hybrid 'Better Than Me' Carly Rae Jepsen is singing about the uncomfortable feeling of not being Black enough for his Black listeners, even though she might not have known that as she sang them. 'I use women singers because there's a lot of emotions that I want that I can't get to,' he told *Pitchfork*. 'The woman's voice, and not necessarily just her singing voice, is powerful and needs to be heard. It's the most important voice in general, and that can't be denied. And on a musical level, I just prefer it. It sounds better. And the male voices I've loved in my life have all been somewhat androgynous, like Michael, Prince, Marvin, or Curtis Mayfield.'

Freetown Sound was acclaimed upon its release. 'Prince's radical pop spirit lives on in many artists,' wrote *Rolling Stone*, three months after the Purple One's passing, 'but none are channelling it more fully, or artfully.' Despite the praise, some of the writing about the album seemed misplaced. The album was released in the wake of a pair of enormous and beloved records which were explicitly concerned with Blackness in America: Kendrick Lamar's *To Pimp a Butterfly* and D'Angelo's *Black Messiah*. Those projects were so instantaneous in their brilliance that listeners and critics became hungry for more like them, and the experience of everyday Blackness *does* run through the Blood Orange album too. On 'Love Ya', Baltimore author Ta-Nehisi Coates is sampled listing off all of the small things he had to consider as a schoolboy to appear unthreatening; 'Every morning, how I, ya know, when I was gonna wear my backpack, was I gonna strap it over one shoulder or two shoulders? How was I gonna cock my baseball hat? Wear it straight, cock it to the left, to the right?'

Happy'. My favourite though are his two appearances on Brooklyn hardcore band Turnstile's 2021 album *GLOW ON*, where his vocals drift between thrashing guitars like gaps in the clouds.

But, in actuality, *Freetown Sound* isn't much like those Kendrick or D'Angelo records at all. It doesn't make large, political proclamations in the way songs like 'The Charade' or 'The Blacker the Berry' do. It's political only in the sense that it's hard for a Black man's life in America not to be. What it is instead is a sonic scrapbook; an interrogation of personal history made by a musician who happens to be Black; a fifty-nine minute investigation into the legacies of family, history and faith which form, in ways which are difficult to parse apart, a person's sense of self in the present.

When he was a boy, skateboarding to school in Ilford, one of Devonté's favourite records was the Beastie Boys' *Paul's Boutique*. Hynes wasn't listening to the bars. What he loved were the instrumentals; a tapestry of samples and sonic references so dense that songs felt like leafing through the pages of a book. (Produced by the Dust Brothers, the story goes that it contains so many samples, they're still getting sued for them.) A devotee of '90s rap and the great beat-makers like J Dilla, Devonté understood the explosive power of taking fragments of old music and twisting them together to create something new. An avid record collector, Hynes lost many hours to the record shops of Bed-Stuy, and it was there that he came across forgotten relics of primordial sampling: mega-mixes made by DJs like The Latin Rascals in the early '80s. These artists didn't write new songs at all, but they still made perfect dance records by physically cutting and splicing tape reel together.

Aside from pieces of speech, Devonté hardly samples other music at all. Instead, he was inspired by the *aesthetic* of these mélanges, and realised how the effect of blending styles of music could be as thrilling as hearing them anew. As a result, *Freetown Sound* is utter magpie-music. It glides between disparate sources effortlessly, from Charles Mingus to Carly

Rae Jepsen, from Missy Elliot to Tupac and Boogie Down Productions. Nelly Furtado and Blondie make appearances, as does Ballroom-performer Venus Xtravanganza. There are wisps of Puccini, snippets of Eric Dolphy-style sax and dispatches from New York, Sierra Leone and Essex. The album is a tapestry which becomes more startling when the sum of its parts are taken as one: an artist presenting many facets of himself and then stepping away, shirking definitive resolution. As an artist, Devonté had always been a collector and curator, but it's on this record that he applies that instinct purposefully, loading the album not simply with the genre fusions of *Cupid Deluxe* but ones rich with meaning.

It's there in full effect on the first song, 'By Ourselves'. As with any decent piece of musical theatre, the first instrument we hear on the record is the piano. One hand taps a melody, the other presses out the rhythm. This refrain is actually from the first few seconds of a Charles Mingus improvisation called 'Myself When I Am Real'. Out of the hundred or so albums Mingus made, that LP – *Mingus Plays Piano* – is his only solo performance, and the only one on which he set aside the upright bass and sat at the piano instead. When Devonté heard that part for the first time, he rushed to the studio and clipped the MP3, knowing that it was special. He later removed Mingus' hands and played the part himself, rewriting the notes towards an apex which wasn't there in the original, and wrapping a vocal melody around them – turning one melodic moment from a jazz improvisation into a pop song.

The most important voice on 'By Ourselves' is the slam poet Ashlee Haze. In the poem which she recites in the second half of the track, Haze remembers being a child, sat on the carpet seeing the music video for the remix of Lil' Kim's 'Not Tonight' appearing on MTV. That song came with a music video where Kim dances cheek to cheek with the likes of Missy Elliot, Da

Brat, Angie Martinez and Lisa 'Left Eye' Lopes. It was also, says Haze, the first time she'd seen anybody on TV who looked anything like her.

Even though it's no longer a novelty to see the likes of Ice Spice, Megan Thee Stallion and Cardi B thriving commercially, Missy Elliott holds a unique place in the history of '90s rap. Upon the release of her 1997 classic *Supa Dupa Fly,* her persona was distinct among female MCs of the era. Before her, they tended to slip into one of two acceptable types: hyper-sexualised divas or hardened street veterans, keeping pace with the men. Elliott was neither. Spitting dextrously over clattering G-funk beats, she veered between sung and spat vocals which were braggadocious, but proudly feminine too. Her style feels decidedly modern now, but being tough and feminine, in the '90s . . .? It was like showing up to a party uninvited and becoming the main attraction.

Charles Mingus was another uninvited person. Among the hyper-masculinity of gangster rap, Elliott's voice was a lonely one, but she at least had the opportunity to trail-blaze in her chosen craft. Mingus, on the other hand, was born in Jim Crow-era America. He was a respected virtuoso of the upright bass, a bandleader on the Blue Note label, and endures as a true icon; but he was among several jazz performers whose first love, like Devonté himself, was classical music. Mingus was a devotee of harmonically inventive composers like Strauss, Debussy and Stravinsky but, like Bud Powell before and Nina Simone after him, his classical aspirations eluded him, despite his obvious talent. In the twentieth century – and to this day – labels like 'soul', 'jazz', 'blues' and 'R&B' were used to repurpose music which, when played by white people, was called something else.

In the liner notes for his 1971 album *Let My Children Hear Music* Mingus wrote that 'I'd like to write a symphony myself

. . . I'd like to write a suite of three or four hours and have a solo in spots.' Mingus died at fifty-six of Lou Gehrig's disease but, after his death, a piece named 'Epitaph' was discovered, a work for a thirty-piece orchestra which would have taken two hours to play. In his lifetime, nobody performed it. 'Let my children have music,' Mingus wrote in 1971. 'If we so-called jazz musicians who are the composers, started including these instruments in our music, it would open everything up, it would get rid of prejudice because the musicianship would be so high in caliber that the symphony couldn't refuse us.'

On *Freetown Sound*, Devonté's music began conversing with the past in this way. Ashlee Haze speaks for herself in her poem but, when Hynes saw the clip of her performing it at a poetry festival online, it captured a feeling which had sat with him a while; feelings inspired by Charles Mingus, Missy Elliott, and maybe ever Haze herself. Sometimes the great talents of artists were limited, under-appreciated or unseen entirely, in no small part because they were Black. 'I'm aware, as a Black musician, that I will never be seen on par with white people that do what I do,' Hynes told *Pitchfork* in 2016. 'That's just what it is. A white guy showing soul is so much more interesting to people than a black person showing soul.'

Arranged by Hynes' close friend Adam Bainbridge, the propulsive, squealing saxophone which scores Haze's words is of the kind Bernard Herrmann ensured will be forever associated with movies set in New York City after dark. As a song, 'By Ourselves' is full of this noir tension: between Mingus' right hand and his left, between Hynes' cello and Jason Arce's sax and between the three distinct voices which muscle for space in the motif. All of it though is in service of a frisson at the heart of the song, of voices which have often gone under-appreciated playing in chorus, loudly and emphatically. Decades of history woven together in a song.

Plenty of other music contains allusions like these – every song is written by people with their own tastes and histories – but Hynes uses the collage style of DJ mixes and beat tapes, not only the lyrics themselves, as a way to tease at his personal history. The song 'Love Ya' is an interpolation of an Eddy Grant song; a Guyanese artist who Hynes grew up listening to. His mum loved to play him round the house, so much so that Hynes said that Grant was his 'black man with a guitar', rather than Jimi Hendrix. Devonté merges that legend of his mother's culture with the language of his father's. Sitting beneath the instrumentation is a woman speaking in Krio, the first language of Sierra Leone, talking about the civil war, remembering when rebels arrived to destroy her village. Hynes merges their histories as his parents merged their lives.

The album's second single, 'Augustine', delves even further: directly tackling his parents' arrival in the UK, both having landed in England at the same age he later emigrated to New York. His mother was devoutly Christian, and the song is named after Augustine of Hippo, the saint who denounced Roman Christianity and moved to West Africa in 393, bringing to Guyana the form of Christianity which endures in Georgetown, the city of her birth. The song contains fragments of Augustine's writings; the line 'late have I loved and chose to see' comes from there. Hynes bakes Christianity into the music too, the chorus melody an ode to Puccini, whose work was steeped in church traditions. (It goes without saying that Puccini isn't often paired with Roland R-70 drum pads.) In the music video for the song Devonté dances with a leather jacket draped across his topless shoulders before the tri-colours of the Sierra Leonean flag. The camera flits between books on Black, queer history; a cover of the *TIME* magazine issue which memorialised Trayvon Martin; and Hynes himself, sat in a café, sharing a coffee with Julian Casablancas.

Out in the world, these things take centuries to coalesce, but in music, they can come together in just a few chords.

By this point in his career, Devonté was on a rip. Almost two years after releasing his most accomplished album to date, he topped it with another. Released on the 24th of August 2018, *Negro Swan* is at once a companion to, and inversion of, *Freetown Sound*, right down to the dark hues of its cover. Retreating from the dense arrangements of his third album, on his fourth Devonté remade the Blood Orange palette through sonic scarcity, each song spotlighting a different facet of his sound, from the fidgety guitar of 'Charcoal Baby' to the rich, harmonised vocals of 'Saint'.

In the wake of the expansive and cosmopolitan records which came before it, *Negro Swan* is shyer and moodier, despite an abundance of blissful moments. On 'Orlando' and 'Charcoal Baby', he sings about his traumatic teenage years for the first time on record, and 'Chewing Gum' is an extended metaphor for tiredness, a sigh at the state of things which runs throughout the record. Those songs are intersected by a firm sense of resilience – provided by author and trans activist Janet Mock – whose voice is heard throughout the album. Where *Cupid Deluxe* created electric moments before drowning them in melancholy, *Negro Swan* exists mostly in those liminal spaces.

Hynes was taking an increasingly relaxed approach to the recording of his songs. He was still obsessive (he said that he rerecorded the vocals of 'Take Your Time' over a hundred times), but he was also getting in the habit of using the world as his toolbox, recording songs wherever he found himself, like Monet's 'en plein air', painting outdoors. He began making the record on the move, in hotel rooms and friends' apartments across Asia, Europe and the US. He also got into the habit of writing only with the instruments at hand. There was very little guitar on *Freetown Sound* because Devonté simply didn't own one, and it appears so prominently on 'Charcoal Baby' only because Fender sent one his way. He would sometimes rent a studio and bring nothing besides a mic and a hard drive. 'Smoke' sounds the way it does because he arrived in a room and the only thing there was an acoustic guitar.

Devonté had the album's name scrawled in a notebook for years before a note of the record was even played, turning it slowly into a journal of drawings, lyrics and images which eventually set the tone of the record. He carried around the songs in much the same way. He played instrumentals to almost everyone he encountered and, if they expressed interest, he invited them to record. 'Saint' features vocals from a menagerie of Hynes' close collaborators – Aaron Maine, BEA1991, Adam Bainbridge, Ava Raiin – but their voices were recorded months apart, whenever Hynes encountered them.

'Saint' opens with another sax solo snatched from a busker Hynes encountered in his borough. There are still fragments of street noise on the recording because, when it came to laying down the vocals in his apartment, the sound was leaking in from outside. 'I got to see you live for more / you said it before / you wish I'd seen / the saint you were before.' The opening words are wide and warm; regret, empathy and hope folded into just a few bars. When the drum machine kicks in, thick and pounding, it's as startling as any dubstep drop, but the vocals continue, sweet among the thunder. It's a love song to the self, not to someone, so says Devonté, but that doesn't matter; it's an impossibly romantic song, pitched right in the blush of love.

My single favourite moment from Devonté Hynes' entire discography appears on *Negro Swan*: the transition from track nine to track ten, from 'Chewing Gum' to 'Holy Will'.

The former begins as one of the album's looser moments: a downtempo, misty rap song upon which both Hynes and A$AP Rocky deliver loose, languid flows. But when Rocky's verse ends, the bottom suddenly falls out of the beat and Project Pat appears. The Memphis rap legend (older brother to Juicy J) arrives on the beat like a man possessed, pitched down and lumbering, sounding devilish as hell. He shouts out the classic Tommy Wright III mixtape *Feel Me Before They Kill Me* as the synth pads shimmer, the equivalent of Moneybagg Yo rhyming over an Enya instrumental. That's when things start suddenly spiralling, the mix filled with a pulsing wash of arpeggios which build into a cacophony until they're halted completely by the clear and gorgeous voice of Ian Isiah, singing a sustained note. 'Holy Will' is a cover of a 2007 song by The Clark Sisters, a Detroit gospel group. It's a simple, gorgeous song, and Isiah's version is enchanting, with long, sustained notes followed by steep, blissful come-downs. It's a song about being shrouded in the Lord's grace.

One of the four voices who sings alongside Ian Isiah's startling performance was Caroline Polachek. 'It was LA in 2016,' she told me. 'Once again Dev text me to say, "I'm working on an album, come by the studio," which is fun because it means whatever song he's working on is the one you'll sing on, which is pretty amazing when you think about it, spinning the roulette wheel like that. When I arrived, Dev was workshopping the vocal arrangement with Ian . . . I just sat back and watched, like a fly on the wall. I think it was a dance studio; it had rickety wooden floor and house plants and hanging mandalas, and Dev had his drum machines strewn all around. It was a beautiful environment. Then Dev indicated to jump in and lay down a harmony. There's four of us singing on that song. Normally you'd do that in a separate booth with headphones on, but the amazing thing was that Dev had all four us of us stand around one mic, like a 1940s radio show. The backing track was playing out loud in the room and bleeding back into the mic. No headphones. No metronome. My jaw was on the floor. I've never done anything like that in my life, and my hairs were standing on end. Hearing someone else singing next to you was an experience I hadn't had since I used to sing in choirs, and it made everything so much more high stakes. Being surrounded by amazing singers, so it makes you *really* wanted to hit the note,' she laughed.

Atheist or believer, placing a Project Pat verse next to a beauteous piece of gospel music can't help but feel a little sacrilegious. The Memphis scene which Pat was born out of was once one of the grimiest, most crime-addled pockets of rap, but Hynes' ode to that era, and the hymn which follows, feel equally sincere. The transition between the two feels like Saturday evening and Sunday morning, two of the defining sounds of African American culture whose proximity implies that they have more in common than either of their advocates would care to admit. As Monet knew: placing two contrasting colours side by side changes our perception of them both.

As soon as the technology made it possible, musicians began exploring the explosive power of remaking and reworking past music. In the 1940s French composer Pierre Schaeffer made 'sound art' from taping, looping, pitch-shifting and sequencing sounds in a sequence. On *Paul's Boutique* the Dust Brothers were just two of a wave of rap producers making use of new, portable samplers like the Roland F-10 and Akai S900, which made that process easier than Schaeffer could have ever imagined. Around the turn of the millennium though, this phenomenon went into overdrive. In 2000, Australian act The Avalanches made the beautiful and nostalgic dance record *Since I Left You* out of 1,000 different samples, while Danger Mouse made *The*

Grey Album by melding The Beatles' *White Album* with JAY-Z's *The Black Album*. In the '10s, Neil Cicierega's *Mouth* mixtape series mashed myriad pop classics like 'Imagine' and 'Billie Jean' with the one real musical anthem of my generation: Smash Mouth's 'All Star'. (Play a hipster in 2004 his mash-up of that song with Modest Mouse's 'Float On' and watch them bristle at just how easily they slide together.)

As the twenty-first century began to bed in, critics like Simon Reynolds took critical praise for acts like Girl Talk – pop songs made from collages of older pop songs cut at hyper-speed – to be evidence of a worrisome cultural stagnation. He said 'what was "new" about Girl Talk was the sheer number of thefts per minute'. In 2010, Reynolds received a PR email which sold British producer Ikonika's LP *Contact, Love, Want, Have* as being both reminiscent of a raft of past electronic genres from dubstep to UK funky, but somehow, assuredly, completely modern too. In response Reynolds wrote a famous blog post questioning the legitimacy of that claim, praising the intelligence of the music but saying that 'the artist . . . avoids having one influence by having lots of influences . . . Too often though, it just means that the artist in question is diversely derivative.' He coined a new term to define this manic but supposedly backwards-facing state: 'hyperstasis'.

It is true of course that the genius art of the past can act as a crutch in the present. Remarkably, for example, November 2023 saw both the release of a new Rolling Stones album *and* a new Beatles song. The culture of reissuing classic records hasn't slowed, in fact the vinyl resurgence which manifested after Reynolds coined 'hyperstasis' has incentivised it further. There have been so many retrospective David Bowie box sets since his death that he was more prolific in 2018 than most working artists. There are plenty of younger acts who weave the crutch of the warm feeling of nostalgia into the songs they write too.

Harry Styles, for example, might as well be a Frankenstein himself, a walking tribute act to David Bowie, Mick Jagger and – somehow – A-ha. The same criticism can be levelled at artists I don't like (Dua Lipa) and plenty I do (Jessie Ware).

Despite its fair share of accurate observations, the concept of hyperstasis is nihilistic to a fault. Firstly, determining the value of music by the extent to which it's innovative is a strange and depressing way to think about art. The vast majority of songs which have ever been written do almost nothing to contribute to new genres or sounds or styles. My favourite song of all time is Sam Cooke's 'That's Where It's At', an exquisite, joyful piece of music which brought absolutely nothing new to the table, if you were judging it by that metric.

In the decade after Reynolds wrote those words, each and every week there have been great swathes of records filled with striking new ideas, they just weren't necessarily ones based around the pioneering of a new type of song. I had never, for example, heard a track like Xenia Rubinos' 'Mexican Chef' before: a tight, bouncing funk tune which explores the army of working-class Latino cooks behind half of America's restaurants. How about Little Simz' thundering, cavernous 'Offence' or Nick Cave's utterly haunting 'Hollywood'. These songs are stunningly creative and original in almost every *other* sense of the word, so why discount them?

Underpinning the concern for the future of music espoused by the likes of Reynolds was a mourning for the loss of the political radicalism supposedly baked into stylistically revolutionary art. Unfortunately, conflating bold new stylistic ideas with a social or spiritual advancement vastly overstates how revolutionary much of the music which would succeed on the basis of Reynolds' metric truly was. In *Retromania*, he claims that the twenty-first century's fetishisation of the aesthetic of bands like the Sex Pistols dilutes those acts' radical potential.

'As we've seen,' he argued, 'the deluge of retro coincides with the decay of all sorts of old dialects to do with opposition, identity, rebellion, change that were essential to expressing what pop might stand for.' I learned that the political potential of the Sex Pistols was bullshit right about the moment when the band themselves produced an 'Anarchy in the U.K.' Virgin Money credit card. Overstating the claim is part of excitable music writing's DNA. Here is storied music critic Lester Bangs talking about Iggy Pop and the Stooges in 1973: 'the Stooges, or any band that challenges its audience, are the answer. Power doesn't go to the people, it comes from them, and when the people have gotten this passive, nothing short of electro-shock and personal exorcism will jolt them and rock them into some kind of fiercely healthy interaction.'

Well (and excuse me because I do love the Stooges), but this transpired to be just a little off the mark. In 1982, James Williamson, the guitarist responsible for the band's nasty, jagged energy, left the band to study engineering and moved to Silicon Valley to start developing computer chips. That particular technological revolution would result in the steepest upward financial movement *away* from the people in the history of mankind. Iggy Pop went on to make some vastly underrated albums, but I first saw his face when he was starring in a 2009 advert for Swiftcover car insurance. The only radical restructuring of society which followed *Raw Power* was a capitalistic one, as Ronald Reagan's White House enacted Milton Friedman's vision of total capitalism on a global scale.

I'm being flippant. You could say that the late-life choices of these once-revolutionary artists simply flew in the face of what their art once stood for. But stylistic advancements have always helped to adorn tepid politics with sonic thrills.
The visceral immediacy of punk, for example, blew through the social mores of the middle classes above all else; saying the

unacceptable and making a lot of noise doing it, but dredging up little of substance. Much of the substantively revolutionary music of the counterculture era, from Archie Shepp's *Attica Blues* to Eddie Gale's *Ghetto Music*, didn't make much of a cultural dent at all. In the final chapter of *Retromania*, one of Reynolds' concluding thoughts is a plea to leave the culture of nostalgia behind us. 'Maybe forgetting,' he claims, 'is as essential in culture as it is existentially and emotionally necessary for individuals.' What this overlooks is that the shape of culture, the history of art itself, is defined by stubborn, active remembering.

This is why the archiving capabilities of Peter Goldmark's LPs were so significant in the creation of a zeitgeist of popular music, with the most readily available art being the ones which societies remember most. After all, the very first attempts to preserve music in a solid state were what shaped our understanding of the fundamentals of music. Many of us might assume that the names of composers like Ludwig van Beethoven and Wolfgang Amadeus Mozart tower so high in the history of music because of their brilliance, and they *were* brilliant, but beauty alone does not guarantee survival. In their day, Beethoven and Mozart were not in fact among the most popular or beloved European composers. What they were was lucky. They were German in the late eighteenth century, and it was only at that particular historical moment that the universities of the German Confederation had the idea to begin keeping repertoires of music: libraries of written sheet music which told people who hadn't even been born yet exactly how a Beethoven symphony should sound. Ludwig and Wolfgang's music was among the first to enter those repositories and so, because their compositions were stored, their names became iconic. If the first universities to have that bright idea had been Egyptian, who knows how the Proms would sound today.

Being able to determine what cultures remember and forget has, in a way, even become a geopolitical resource. In between the North Pole and Norway sits Svalbard, a remote and barren territory covered almost entirely in ice. There, in 2017, a new library was begun. Inspired by the nearby Svalbard Global Seed Vault, this underground, reinforced concrete library stores not biological matter, but artwork from mankind's vast repository. Named the Arctic World Archive, it has a motto etched into its steel doors: 'protecting world memory'. Stored in the archive is a digitised version of Edvard Munch's *The Scream* and the works of Olga Tokarczuk. In 2023, the Global Music Vault followed in its footsteps, serving the same purpose for the world's recorded songs. Stored on sheets of silica glass, the vault is designed to preserve the music for at least a thousand years.

It's still unclear exactly what the Global Music Vault will contain or how large it will grow – (so far only recordings of traditional music from New Zealand, Kenya and Lebanon have been checked in) – but the very existence of the Vault makes literal the kind of decisions cultures make across decades: to exclude or include, to dismiss or embrace. The people who write about music – today's historians of sound – do so explicitly. The choice to forget certain artists and certain styles becomes complicated when those decisions are made in bad faith; when music is forgotten or written out of history due to their creator's gender, race, sexuality or politics. The aspiration to move perpetually forward is to risk ensuring those artists remain as historical footnotes for evermore.*

* There is also the matter of public reception. Hip hop, for example, still a predominantly Black art form, continues to be vilified by right-wing media outlets like Fox News and The Daily Wire. Such perpetual, systemic dismissal of certain styles and sounds works its way into decisions which eventually become The Vault.

Sometimes, 'forgetting' can manifest in ways which are quite insidious, like the extent to which some forms of music have been praised above others by music writers who, for the majority of the twentieth century at least, predominantly looked the same way: white, middle class and male. It's easy to forget the extent to which things have changed even within the last decade. Much of Devonté Hynes' work already feels less radical because the way we think about music in the 2020s is closer and closer to the way he always did. In the mainstream music press at least, the influences he and Solange used to create the *True* EP were once jokes. The S.O.S. Band, Sade, Janet Jackson and even Prince were not treated on an equal footing to the guitar-rock bands of the same era. Even when *Cupid Deluxe* was released, the notion that much of '80s Black dance music was somehow inherently inferior to the various permutations of rock persisted. There have been changes. When *Pitchfork* listed their best albums of the 1980s in 2002, the highest Prince came was twelfth, but when the list was redone in 2018 he had been promoted to first, signalling a shift which occurred across the decade, doubtlessly helped by the degree to which taste-making indie writers took an album like *Freetown Sound* seriously.

Several of Devonté Hynes' own idols were neglected by the industry in this way. Nina Simone's mental decline quickened when she became a Black Power activist at the end of the 1960s, and she was promptly exiled from the music industry at large, ending a run of magnificent records prematurely. As a lover of dance, Devonté idolised figures like the Nicholas brothers, two Black dancers whose routine for 1943's *Stormy Weather* Fred Astaire called 'the finest dance sequence ever put to film'. The Nicholases didn't act in the films they appeared in though, they only danced, so that when their films were shown in the South, their scenes could be cut with ease.

These acts of forceful forgetting have often cost cultures some remarkable leaders. Paul Robeson, for example, was remarkably talented: a Black bass-baritone who was also an actor *and* a professional footballer. His name is almost forgotten today because, when his Communist beliefs came under question by the House Un-American Activities committee, his name was literally removed from the many record books it appeared in. Culture exile is enforced through financial means too. There were swathes of female composers and musicians before the twentieth century, but they were normally paid so much less than their male counterparts that maintaining full-time careers in the arts was almost impossible for women who weren't born wealthy; their ideas and talents went unheard.

Entire volumes have been written about these kinds of cultural excisions, but the most egregious examples are presumably ones we aren't even aware of for the very fact they were so successful. These cultural un-remembrances have a great impact both on the music we remember and the music which succeeds today. As the moral philosopher Alasdair MacIntyre wrote in *After Virtue*: 'the possession of an historical identity and the possession of a social identity coincide'. Reynolds, notion of the total rejection of the past as a form of revolution assumes that the history of popular music unfurled in a way which isn't worth re-interrogating or, at least, isn't as worthwhile as creating brand-new styles of sound. But what is beautiful about art is that, even while these figures from history are long gone, their music can still be played with, their contributions remembered in current, living songs.

In 1912, Picasso took the idea of the collage – once seen as a hobby for Victorian housewives – into the world of high art by merging Parisian daily newspapers and incorporating them into his oil paintings. The idea was directness: instead of references and allusions, the painter actively cut up his subject matter and pasted it into the work itself. In 1919, Hannah Höch's *Cut with the Dada Kitchen Knife through the Last Weimar Beer-Belly Cultural Epoch in Germany* used the same method for more political ends, taking cuttings from newspapers to critique the failings of the Weimar government. As the past was made permanent in print, these collagists realised they were able to deploy the past to say new things about the present.

Inspired by the early collagists of music – DJs and hip hop beat-makers – on records like *Freetown Sound* and *Negro Swan* Devoné Hynes does the same with his music, piecing together his classical training, his love for rap and pop, the music he heard around the streets of New York City, and pieces them together. Charles Mingus and Missy Elliot. Gospel and Memphis rap. Puccini and New Order. Reynolds thought that this kind of influence-heavy music could only be cumbersome and unoriginal ('glutted musicians make clotted music', he wrote in *The Wire*) but Hynes' music integrates each reference effortlessly. His music is not nostalgic either. Mark Fisher talked about cultural stagnation creating 'lost futures' but, by contrast, Devonté creates *alternative presents* in his songs. What if Black, '80s pop had been treated with the same reverence as '90s rock? What if Charles Mingus got to conduct a symphony while he was alive?

To be fair to those critics, those claims were largely written before 2011, when aspects of culture did indeed feel less vibrant than they have since. The world has changed quite radically too. As police brutality shone a harsh light on the persisting ghosts of America's racial divisions, historical injustices were thrown under unprecedented scrutiny, and the Black Lives Matter protests in the wake of George Floyd's death were among the largest the West has ever seen. In that context the idea of revisiting the past stops feeling like nostalgia, and becomes vital interrogation instead. Films like 2016's *Hidden Figures* began attempting to correct historical narratives, writing the contributions of NASA's Black female scientists back into a history they'd been written out of. Around the point a statue of slave trader Edward Colston hit the bottom of a Bristol canal, it became clear that young people were questioning the landscape of the past in unforeseen ways, and plenty of music in the 2010s followed suit.

If Reynolds posed 'forgetting' as an act of rebellion, then these records treat remembering in the same way. On her remarkable 2022 album *¡Ay!,* Lucrecia Dalt takes the perception of Latin American folk music as staid and eviscerates it. To make the record, she imagined another alternative present: picturing an alien, arriving on Earth, and the first music they heard wasn't Drake or The Beatles, but the bolero and son music of her youth. Songs like 'El Galatzó' twist traditional forms into fascinating, electronically warped shapes, giving them new life. In fact, South America was home to much of this kind of exploration, a bevy of small labels like Ecuador's También and Mexico's Antimateria Sonora releasing ambient records which take folk styles like cumbia and apply them to dazzling modern contexts.

On their phenomenal 2018 album *Your Queen Is a Reptile,* London jazz band Sons of Kemet reject the nation's monarch, and name the personal heroes they'd prefer to memorialise instead. Beginning each song's title with 'My Queen Is . . .', they name a different woman in Elizabeth's place. 'My Queen Is Ada Eastman'. 'My Queen Is Yaa Asantewaa'. 'My Queen Is Doreen Lawrence'. Away from that ingenious device, the tracks themselves are rich with the diverse musical infatuations of the men who made them: recreating fat garage basslines and lumbering dub reggae with the instruments of a jazz quartet.

Reynolds coined the concept of 'hyperstasis' because he struggled to find the radical in contemporary music, but he was so fixated on locating new genres and styles that he was looking in the wrong places. This *is* radical music, not because it memorialises the past but because it re-examines it, bringing forgotten parts of history to life in the present. As Charles Mingus said, 'I admire anyone who can come up with something original, but not originality alone, because there can be originality in stupidity, with no musical description of any emotion or any beauty the man has seen, or any kind of life he has lived.' With his radically non-discriminatory music, Hynes was exploring what essayist Perry Anderson termed 'the history of possibility', but he was about to go further: dedicating the next part of his career to a man whose brilliant talents had been, for a long time, confined unjustly to the past.

In the autumn of 1998, the composer and lecturer Mary Jane Leach was asked to teach a course in composition at the California Institute of the Arts. She had been given the challenge of focusing specifically on traditional, so-called 'real' instrumentation rather than the electronic infatuations which had been sweeping the campus in the final decade of the century. To fit the remit, Leach had the idea of choosing a composition which was heavy on multiple voices, and one particular piece – a performance which had been lodged in her memory for decades – immediately came to mind.

In the early 1980s Leach had been a regular at the various storied experimental art institutions scattered throughout Manhattan. It was at one of these venues – The Kitchen – that she happened upon the debut performance of 'The Holy Presence of Joan d'Arc'. It was a vibrant, undulating piece written for ten cellos, composed by a young polymath named Julius Eastman. Leach remembered the electricity of the piece and knew it was exactly what she was looking to bring before her students, but she ran into a problem almost immediately. 'The Holy Presence of Joan d'Arc' was nowhere to be found.

It's now almost inconceivable to imagine – in the time of YouTube and ZIP files – that it was once possible (quite recently in fact) to simply not be able to hear something. Despite being something of a legend among the classical scene of downtown New York, Eastman's piece had never been officially released in any official form. To find it, Leach had to make dozens of phone calls to old friends. By the time she did get her hands on a copy (a dub made from a tape passed to a composer friend by Eastman himself) Leach realised something bigger: it wasn't just 'Joan' which was hard to find, but nearly every piece Eastman had ever composed.

The story of Julius Eastman was already served poorly by history. For a long time he was remembered simply as a vocalist, known for his performance on the Grammy-nominated 1973 recording of Peter Maxwell Davies' 'Eight Songs for a Mad King'. But singing was just a fraction of who Eastman was. Julius had studied composition at Philadelphia's prestigious Curtis Institute, under revered pianist Mieczysław Horszowski. He was one of only two Black students enrolled in the entire school. He was penniless, and so lived at the local YMCA while he studied. When he graduated in 1963, he played only his own works at his recital. By the end of the 1960s he joined the Creative Associates programme at the State University of New York at Buffalo, which had become a centre of avant-garde activity, and there Eastman immersed himself in the radical new wave of classical composition led by John Cage and Morton Feldman, who also studied there. For a man like that to be remembered simply as an obscure and half-forgotten singer . . . something had gone sorely wrong.

After realising that so much of Eastman's work was missing – even in sheet music form – Leach embarked on a seven-year mission to recover his missing work. She launched a primitive website where she tracked the status of lost compositions and put out a call for information, like a missing person campaign. She began weaving an endless web of phone calls and referrals. One lead referred Leach to another, and sometimes back to herself, often without unearthing a single fragment. Over the course of years, pieces did eventually begin to resurface. Some were scores, some were recordings dug up from dust-ridden archives. In June 2004 she hit upon her most substantial find yet: recordings of three of Eastman's major pieces for multiple pianos from a performance he'd given at Northwestern University in 1980. They had existed, to that point, only as rumour.

In 2005 Leach released what she had so far recovered of Eastman's work as a box set entitled *Unjust Malaise*: three hours of music pieced together from a resolute absence of it. What appeared on those CDs wasn't simply an archive of an obscure artist's work; according to one appraisal in *The Guardian*, it 'completely rewrote the history of post-war American new music'. *Unjust Malaise* forcefully and undeniably inserted Eastman into the lineage of American minimalists like John Cage, Terry Riley, Steve Reich and Philip Glass, expanded the oeuvre, and complicated the timeline.

Even though Eastman drew from the controversial (often reviled) minimalism emerging from the State University, his approach had been completely different. He developed what he later termed 'organic music'. Instead of evolving from a single repetitive pattern, organic music instead presents all of its component parts at once at the outset of a piece, and stretches forever onwards. Instead of moving section by section, his music spirals hypnotically in on itself, a method which seems to engender intense, devotional focus in the musicians who play it. His sheet music was often simple and disobliging: the manuscript for 'Femenine' for example (a seventy-minute long piece) is only five pages in length, and most of the action happens in the first few minutes; it then just continues to happen, for sixty minutes more. It was an idea which musicologists thought hadn't developed until at least a decade later.

Just as Mary Jane Leach helped to recover the first resurrected pieces of Eastman's oeuvre, so too did her research help to explain why so much of it had disappeared. Julius Eastman was a true original. Many of his friends and colleagues attest to it. He was an openly Black, gay man who studied classical composition five years before the Civil Rights Act: an impossibly rare thing. He was a tall, lithe man, but he also had a five-octave range. Like Devonté Hynes, he had no concern for the dividing lines which often kept various strains of music in isolated silos. As well as playing and composing for piano, Eastman sung in barber shop quartets and contributed to early recordings by legendary performance artist Meredith Monk. He collaborated with Lou Reed's future stage director Robert Wilson, made disco music with Arthur Russell (it's his voice you hear on the outrageously funky '#5 (Go Bang!)') and played in jazz groups with his brother Gerry.

Julius also showed absolutely no regard for the high-society mores which compositionally radical provocateurs like John Cage stayed true to. Eastman's friend Ned Sublette said 'Julius was anti-pompous. He would talk with absolutely anybody. Julius did not have a nickel of snobbery in his body.' Indeed, in a 1979 essay 'The Composer as Weakling,' Eastman wrote that composers had become isolated figures, cut off from the life-force of music making. He suggested that his ilk should 'reassert him/herself as an active part of the musical community . . . to be only a composer is not enough'. Eastman delivered on this promise with flamboyance and wit. On the night of the 1974 premiere of 'Femenine', Eastman – dressed in either an apron or dress, depending on the story – cooked soup and served it to the audience while the concert played.

The ideas of genre and gender-fluidity which are so familiar today all existed in Eastman's work half a century prior. 'What I am trying to achieve is to be what I am to the fullest,' he explained in a rare 1976 interview. 'Black to the fullest, a musician to the fullest, a homosexual to the fullest.' Unsurprisingly, this choice was not without its detractors. On the 4th of June 1975, during a recital of John Cage's 'Song Books', Eastman invited a young man onstage, and promptly undressed him. Cage (himself, privately, a gay man) was incensed. As the years wore on, Eastman's own work became more political and more confrontational. The three major pieces which Leach recovered in 2004 were named 'Crazy N****r', 'Evil N****r' and 'Gay Guerrilla'.

When he performed them, Eastman explained his rationale for their names carefully, but his brazenness won him plenty of enemies even among Black students, and tenured institutions began to turn their backs. Eastman's life, once erratic in a creatively fruitful direction, took a more devastating turn. In 1980 he was refused a teaching job at Cornell University and, increasingly struggling for work, turned to drugs and alcohol instead. Before long he could no longer pay his rent and became homeless too. A state enforcer broke into his flat and threw almost everything out including, presumably, great masses of his now-lost work. His mental health spiralled and he spent most of the '80s homeless, moving between shelters and Tompkins Square Park, just half an hour from The Kitchen. In May 1990 Eastman died alone in a Buffalo hospital aged forty-nine. It took the *Village Voice* eight months to run his first obituary.

In the wake of *Unjust Malaise*, Eastman's work began to spread in increments. Some of his pieces began to be worked into the repertoires of concert halls across America. In 2015, a decade on from Mary Jane Leah's first compilation, a recording of 'Femenine' was finally found and released by Frozen Reeds Records. The same year the London Contemporary Music Festival put on the first major festival of Eastman's music, followed closely by a 2017 exhibition and concert series in Philadelphia, pieced together following three years of research.

After the release of *Negro Swan*, Devonté found himself becoming increasingly involved in classical composition again, to an extent he hadn't since he was a teenager. He'd long called his score for *Palo Alto* the work he was proudest of. It was, after all, the first project which allowed him to explore a taste for classical minimalism he'd acquired in the bargain bins of Virgin Megastores. In 2018, Philip Glass invited him to perform his *20 Etudes* with four other pianists live at the Kennedy Center. Hynes frantically began retuning his skills as a pianist. He practised incessantly, on any surface he could find, including restaurant tables and his thighs, sat on park benches.

Devonté, drawing from his adolescent enchantment with Stravinsky and Nico Muhly, began devoting himself to orchestral composition in earnest. He resumed an old habit of pursuing two careers at once. In the exact same period he was opening as Blood Orange for Harry Styles' residency in Madison Square Garden, he was composing concertos for the Tokyo Chamber Orchestra. In 2020 he wrote *Fields*, a buoyant instrumental work which evolved out of a piece he'd written for the Chicago company Hubbard Street Dance, which was later nominated for two Grammys.

As he was writing original compositions and exploring other composers more incessantly than ever before, Devonté discovered Julius Eastman too. 'When I was younger, I remember going to the library in search – consciously or not – of my reflection in music books. I would only find this reflection there much later,' Devonté wrote in the foreword to the French edition of *Gay Guerrilla*, a collection of essays about the composer. 'To finally discover the illustrious universe of Julius Eastman was like discovering a lost secret that I wish was revealed to me many years ago . . . He is for me the most inspiring artist.'

In the summer of the first pandemic year Hynes joined the Eastman revival properly, playing a portion of 'Evil N****r' for the Black Power Live Broadcast, a virtual fundraiser held in the wake of George Floyd's murder. After establishing himself as a fan of Eastman's work, Hynes was invited to contribute to the most ambitious project of the revival to date. In 2021 Wild Up – an LA-based chamber collective led by Christopher Rountree – announced that they would spend the next six years arranging, recording and releasing an exhaustive seven-volume anthology of every one of Eastman's found pieces. They invited Devonté and the prize-winning pianist Adam Tendler to help bring a new arrangement of 'Evil N****r' to life, eventually realised on their 2023 collection *Julius Eastman Vol. 3: If You're So Smart, Why Aren't You Rich?*

Released as the second part of his most blistering triptych, 'Evil N****r' is Eastman's idea of organic music taken to a confrontational extreme. It begins pensively with a jagged, undulating piano part, played on the Wild Up recording by Devonté's right hand. Strings vamp in the distance, pensive and taut, but nothing really prepares for the sudden jolt which occurs one minute and twenty-three seconds in. A voice suddenly counts off '1, 2, 3, 4!' and those violins and cellos hit like a tsunami. It's a startling exercise in counterpoint – as vast as the height of a cliff – and those bombardments keep coming, each time the piano chords becoming less assertive until, after fifteen minutes or so, they're just brittle fragments of melody twinkling away in a mass of strings. It's one of the most jolting, astounding pieces of music I've ever heard and so it's unnerving to think that, until 2004, it stopped existing at all. Even in the age of streaming, all music is somewhat fragile in this way.

Make no mistake: Julius Eastman didn't make it easy to preserve his work. His score sheets were impressionistic at best and he didn't place a great deal of stock in the staying power of his own work (an ex-boyfriend once recounted that he used the sheet music of 'Joan' to line his cat's litter tray). There were institutions who could have given him a steadier career and instead he bristled against them. He was, by all accounts, a mediocre student and even patchier as a teacher. But this is true of a great many of history's great artists, and it's hard to imagine the music of David Bowie being allowed to simply vanish. Julius Eastman is, in short, the living embodiment of The Vault: that great, hypothetical repository where all of our culture and the hierarchies we enforce upon it reside. In the 2010s, through a process of resolute remembering, Julius Eastman's scattered, mostly vanished catalogue was slowly pieced together in reverse. For two decades his music existed only in a haze of obituaries and anecdotes but, over the next twenty years, through the labour of dozens of composers and musicologists and players like Devonté Hynes, it was dragged kicking and screaming back into vivid recognition.

As the 2020s came into view, it seemed that it was classical composition, out of the half-a-dozen musical outlets Devonté Hynes had forged for himself, which was rising to the top of the pile. I was sat in the audience at London's Barbican Hall in March 2023 when Devonté made his British debut as a composer, true and proper. The London Symphony Orchestra took to the stage (as strong a statement of credibility as it gets) and performed 'Naked Blue', Hynes' thirty-minute symphony and a sweeping piece of music which contains something entirely absent from the taut, nimble songs of Blood Orange: grandiosity, on a vast scale. The orchestra scattered and Devonté took to the stage himself, his Steinway positioned dramatically opposite Adam Tendler's as they launched into 'Morning Piece' and 'The Long Ride II'; two pieces for two pianos. Hunched over his stool dressed down in a grey sweater and black baseball cap, it was starling to see a man who had already helped to transform the sound of my generation's pop music looking so completely himself among the wood-panelled walls of one of the capital's premier stages. This was not a novelty event – a crowd of a few thousand Blood Orange fans gathered to humour their idol – but a bona fide performance and yet another artistic identity, only this time with his own name.

Devonté didn't play any of Eastman's music at his own recital but he did include two of his pieces ('Stay on It' and 'Gay Guerrilla') in his score for 2020's *We Are Who We Are*, the first TV series by Luca Guadagnino, the director of *Challengers* and *Call Me by Your Name.* Hynes became involved in the project after Guadagnino saw him play a Blood Orange show in Bologna in 2016. The director was so impressed that, when he came to write the script, he worked the concert into the story and made its lead character a Blood Orange fan. Guadagnino asked Hynes to recreate the Bologna concert for the show's final episode and, as they got to know each other, eventually asked him to write the show's score too.

In the sixth episode, two of the characters, Caitlin and Fraser, recreate the music video of 'Time Will Tell' in its entirety. It was the kind of homage Hynes used to pay to his favourite acts as a teenager himself. Devonté, who grew up with Slipknot and Weezer posters on his wall, was now the artist on theirs. '*We Are Who We Are* is the first time I've had to confront myself as someone who makes something,' he told *The Independent* in 2020. 'The show takes place in 2016, and Fraser is into a song I wrote that came out in 2013. A seventeen-year-old was nine when I wrote that song. All of this got things turning into my head. It was very touching and emotional. I'm turning thirty-five next month so, you know, I'm thinking about these things a lot.'

In the time since Devonté was a teenager himself the landscape of popular music has changed dramatically. In the year 2000, in order for most people to play two random songs from two different places one after the other, they would have to be downloaded and burned, or recorded off the radio. Two decades earlier, you'd have had to splice them together from tape, by hand. Now streaming services allow songs from different continents and decades to slide into one another endlessly – they'll even find them for you – and it's the least remarkable thing in the world.

Devonté was one of the first artists of the twenty-first century who made music the way the streaming age eventually convinced most of us to consume it. An adolescent disregard for whichever music was considered worthwhile persisted as he began to write songs of his own. It's no wonder that the discovery of Julius Eastman was a revelation: he was someone who showed as little concern for the dividing lines of high art or low art as himself. Devonté is interested in the ways different types of music can fit together, and how the music of our lives, often without us knowing it, helps to create our ideas of who we are. He just doesn't much care whether that's jazz or a pop song. In recent years he's played with John Cale, Lou Reed's greatest muse, adversary and closest collaborator. He produced a remix for Paul McCartney. He got a shoutout on a hit Doja Cat album. Of all the great musical minds he's worked with, he says that Mariah Carey is the greatest.

A musician like Devonté makes us question the responses we have to the many types of music we encounter and the preconceptions we hold about them. Alongside making his own art, Devonté helped to give the forgotten greats of the past new life. It's now normal to see the likes of Julius Eastman, Alice Coltrane and Arthur Russell given their fair dues, or for house music to receive the same thoughtful consideration which was reserved exclusively for rock, but it didn't happen quickly, and it didn't happen by accident. Artists like Devonté *made* it so. The alchemical creations of Blood Orange are as radical as any new genre. His music is unapologetically committed to the idea that all art has the potential to be beautiful, and his approach clears the way for an alternative future, one where true genius is appreciated while it's still being made, and not simply once it's over.

APPLE MUSIC

SPOTIFY

2. TAHLIAH BARNETT / FKA TWIGS

As long as art has existed, artists have been altering and changing the shape of reality. Goya's open-mouthed cannibals. Raphael's glowing Christ in the sky. In the final years of the nineteenth century though, painters began to depict objective reality, for the first time, through the lens of the mind's eye. 1893's *The Scream*, painted by the paranoid and death-obsessed Edvard Munch, depicts a man in a state of existential panic. The sky is scarred blood-red; his skull is melted into a deep, impossible gasp. Munch was depicting a real-life panic attack he once experienced on that very bridge, but his genius was to not depict himself directly, and shape the world around himself to appear as that frightening moment felt to him. The reality of the Self.

Munch's idea – expressionism – started a movement. In the age of psychoanalysis, German and Austrian painters like Egon Schiele and Franz Marc developed new styles which strove to depict life as experienced by the mind. Their colourful, freaky paintings were often portraits, but the way they portrayed their subjects no longer upheld the rules of physics. What is physics, after all, compared to feeling? Their works dredged up people's emotional, inner lives, and spilled *those* onto the canvas.

If you try to find examples of expressionism in music, you will come across academic literature about composers like

Arnold Schoenberg and his *Five Pieces for Orchestra*, music which is 'expressionist' because it claims to be written directly from the subconscious. When it comes to popular music though, expressionism hardly seems to have made a dent. Perhaps this is because *all* music is expressionism, of a sort. It is comprised of the intangible: the vibration of airways, articulating ideas conceived only inside the musician's brain.

In the 2010s, just as in the decades after Nietzsche declared the death of God, a new crisis of the Self was in full swing. Or rather, the crisis of the self-ie. The work of expressionist painters did amazing things with the mind's eye but there was no mistaking their reality-warping imagery for real life. It was art, plain and simple. No more. In the Internet age, in a time when social media and digital information rule the world, our faith in our own eyes is no longer quite so concrete. As social media companies began encouraging us to turn our very selves into brands, objective truths and constructed realities became far harder to tell apart.

Through these digital technologies, it's now possible for something to claim to be real, to *look* real, while it isn't. Body dysmorphia rose. Conspiracy theorists did too. Some surgeons even began offering surgeries to make people's real faces look more like Snapchat filters. Somewhere in the middle of the 2010s, this Instagram-expressionism began leaking into political arenas and warped our perceptions of the world. On the Internet, with news relayed by digital images, there is no objective reality, and we can interact with whichever version of the truth we choose.

As deepfakes and AI art begin to infiltrate the hundreds of fleeting images we encounter every day online, questions are raised about a conceivable future which would make the distortions of social media editing look like an age of innocence. Music isn't safe from this fate. On the 4th of April 2023, an artist called ghostwriter977 released a song named 'Heart on My Sleeve' which sounded like a new single from The Weeknd and Drake. In reality, those former labelmates haven't collaborated in years but, through the help of AI, here they were: reunited on a track. 'Heart on My Sleeve' was listened to by 600,000 people on Spotify before it was removed and a legal firestorm ensued, but a terrifying question had already been raised. In a material sense, what makes 'Heart on My Sleeve' any less of a Drake song than a *Drake* song? 'I got my heart on my sleeve, with a knife in my back' sounds exactly like something which would come out of his mouth, and the AI vocals are plausible enough that they sound like they had. It raps, therefore, he is.

Throughout the history of popular music, artists have made personas for themselves and presented them as real. Prince became Camille. Johnny Cash was The Man in Black, and Beyoncé Sasha Fierce. The artists in this book, however, are the first generation who work in this time of digital self-creation, where the abstraction of the expressionists became the abstraction of our lives. This chapter looks at an artist and two close collaborators who embraced this new reality to create expressionist music at last. They used new, digital technologies to create impossible new sounds and indulge in fantastical versions of the self.

Tahliah Barnett always loved playing dress-up. When she was eight years old, she marched up to her parents wearing home-made tights and a thong, claiming to be Jane Fonda. Tahliah was a pretty solitary child. When she was born in 1988, her mum – Bonita – moved them from the sleet-grey streets of Birmingham to rural Gloucestershire, intent on raising her daughter surrounded by clean air and green fields. Barnett would later claim that the most exciting thing which ever happened there was being stuck behind a tractor on the way to school. In their house Bonita painted stars on the ceiling of Tahliah's bedroom.

Throughout Tahliah's early years, it was her imagination which kept her company. As a child she was obsessed with the cartoon *FernGully*, and spent hours imagining that she lived there amid the forest. At school, while her classmates played, she took herself to the furthest end of the field and sat there alone with her daydreams. 'I would imagine pulling myself up a solitary spider thread,' she would one day tell *DAZED*. 'In my head . . . it was the most real thing.'

Barnett's musical upbringing was different to most of the other kids in Gloucestershire. Bonita was a Latin-dance specialist and a seamstress, and when she taught classes at salsa clubs, she dragged Tahliah along too, hiding her beneath the table under the DJ's decks with copies of *Vogue* as the music played. Bonita Barnett is half Spanish, and she didn't play much music from the kind of bands whose names appear on T-shirts in HMV. For Tahliah, household names were the likes of Brazilian singer Tania Maria and other greats of Latin jazz. When Bonita met Tahliah's stepfather – a jazz lover of English, Spanish, Jamaican and Egyptian descent – he brought a whole raft of new sounds with him. Living in rural England, he was one of the few other Black faces Tahliah ever saw. When he drove her and her friends around she was embarrassed as he blared rotations of bee-bop, acid jazz, Nina Simone and Fela Kuti through the car stereo.

Even though she was surrounded by music, even though she loved to sing, nobody – *nobody* – thought that she was going to end up making it herself. She was too busy dancing for that. Tahliah took her first ballet class at only six years old. Her instructors quickly decided that her feet weren't designed for pointe shoes so she switched gears, developing a love for tap and modern dance. Her friends nicknamed her 'Twigs' because of the way her joints cracked as she moved. By the time she was a teenager, Tahliah's name was being etched into the trophies of dance competitions across the country. It was a deathly serious business. When she was seven, her stepfather told her that, if she wanted to stand out from all the white girls in her class, she'd have to be at least twice as good as them. 'If I wanted to win a competition,' an adult Tahliah explained to the *New York Times,* 'I couldn't afford to be good. I had to be excellent. It had to be so obvious that I was going to win, that it would be ridiculous [if] I didn't.' Barnett's family couldn't afford private lessons and so Tahliah practised alone in her bedroom after school and on weekends, studying YouTube clips, demanding excellence from herself in private.*

As a child, Tahliah was fascinated by Matthew Bourne's *Swan Lake.* She was enthralled by the greats of American jazz too: legends like Ella Fitzgerald, Dinah Washington and Billie Holiday. She even volunteered to go to church to sing 'Wade in the Water' with choirs made up of only local grannies and herself. Tahliah was so excited by any chance to perform that her parents often had to catch up with her, rather than push, but that didn't mean Bonita wasn't clear about her wishes for her daughter. Years later Tahliah told the story of how, as a teenager, in the middle of a TV dinner, her mother once turned to her and told her, unprompted: 'Tahliah, you don't want a normal life.'

---

* This was an ethos Tahliah would never deviate from. As an adult, Barnett retains total control over every aspect of her work. 'Imagine you're an artist that didn't know how to do your own makeup, didn't know how to do your own hair, didn't know how to put an outfit together, didn't write your own music, didn't direct your own videos, didn't produce your own music . . .' she told *Allure* magazine in 2016, in a tone of sympathy rather than disdain. 'They're not artists. They're vehicles.'

But by the end of the 1990s, even a normal life was becoming something the Barnett family had to fight for, tooth and nail. In the wake of various job disasters, the family's finances entered a steep decline. They were never wealthy to begin with but suddenly government cheques were paying for buses and school lunches. Sometimes her mother asked to borrow her daughter's pocket money just to pay for the shopping. Despite everything – and unbeknownst to Tahliah – her parents decided that the one thing they couldn't cut back on was her classes. They knew that ending them would be devastating for her. A single trip to Blackpool became the sole holiday of her childhood. But their faith in their daughter's talents paid off, and Tahliah won an academic scholarship to St Edward's, a private Catholic school in Cheltenham.

Throughout her teenage years, Tahliah didn't make a great deal of effort to fit in. She knew that, no matter what she did, she would likely remain a curiosity to her classmates regardless. 'I was never the pretty girl at school. I'm tiny and mixed-race,' she told *Pitchfork* in 2013. 'I grew up in a white area. I was always the loner. I was always kind of off . . . a little weird.' To compound things, she suddenly found herself in classrooms with kids who owned ponies, and had pools in their back gardens. What was the point in trying to compete with that? Instead, Tahliah did what she knew best and dived headfirst into performance. When she was eleven, she shocked the judges of a choreography competition by debuting a dance routine she'd written about the life of a slave, set to Marvin Gaye's 'Calypso Blues'. Bonita helped to make the costumes.

In 1996, when she was eight years old, Tahliah had bought her first ever album: a CD of Prince's *Emancipation.* She chose it because, with his sharp cheeks, caramel skin and soft, effeminate lips, she thought that he looked like her. He wasn't the only icon of the 1980s she fell in love with.

Fifteen years too late, Tahliah was a new romantic at heart. As a teenager, she became besotted with Siouxsie and the Banshees, Kate Bush, Shakespeares Sister and X-Ray Spex – all-female acts fronted by singers with eccentric, singular voices. As a shy girl with an eye for big stages, the likes of Poly Styrene appealed to her strongly, and Barnett later said that her song, 'I Am a Poseur', defined her teenage years. In secondary school Tahliah followed her lead and became a singer in a punk band herself. It was short lived. Her voice didn't suit the shouting.

Barnett lived and breathed the artists she listened to, and few influenced her style quite as much as Annabella Lwin. Lwin was the lead singer of new wave band Bow Wow Wow in the early '80s, another of Malcolm McLaren's curatorial creations. The band had started without him as Adam and the Ants but, when lead singer Stuart Goddard (the Adam) approached McLaren to manage the band, McLaren stole the band from him instead. He changed the band's name to Bow Wow Wow and took six months to audition new lead singers for the band. One was Lwin, and the other was George Alan O'Dowd, who quickly left again to become Boy George. Lwin was just thirteen when she joined the group, recruited after McLaren's talent scout overheard her singing in a West Hampstead dry cleaners, and persuaded him to give her a chance.

A Londoner of Burmese descent, Lwin was very much a child when Bow Wow Wow released their debut song 'C·30 C·60 C·90 Go' (which happened to be the world's first ever cassette single). To see her then, at the beginning of the '80s, she looked remarkably like Tahliah Barnett, and Tahliah loved that fact. 'I used to dress up like Annabella Lwin every single day,' she told *Red Bull Academy*. 'I thought I was her. I remember going to some cheesy West End club dressed as

Annabella Lwin and everybody else was dressed up in designer clothes, and I just looked mental."*

Like Lwin, Tahliah was also thirteen when she was paid to dance for the first time. Her talents were striking enough that the gig soon turned into regular work, and Tahliah spent the next three years on the train between London and Cheltenham, dancing and modelling. But as it became an even greater part of her life, a crucial realisation began to dawn on her. It wasn't dancing she loved after all. It was dancing to *music*.

Tahliah first tried her hand at singing in Gloucester youth club. The boys in the club would make beats and rap and, as one of the few girls in the room, they'd sometimes call on her to sing the chorus on their songs. Eventually, they encouraged her to write some songs of her own. Secretly at first, she began putting together songs in her bedroom, making samba beats on a cheap little Yamaha keyboard and sharing them with nobody.

When Barnett finished her GCSEs, she did what seemed only natural for a girl who had been dancing since she was six, and applied to join the BRIT School. As a college which counts Amy Winehouse, Adele and King Krule among its alumni, places were prestigious and hard to come by but Tahliah felt disillusioned before she even arrived. Her first glimpse inside the entertainment industry alienated her and, unlike a lot of the sparkling young hopefuls in class, she had no ambitions to join the Mickey Mouse Club. Part of her just wanted to open a carpet shop and live a normal life. She dropped out after only six weeks and enrolled in Croydon College to study her A levels instead, just like an ordinary teenager would.

At eighteen Tahliah took a job working in south London youth centres, deploying the many talents she had studied in

* Tahliah had plenty of love for Stuart Goddard too. When she was eighteen and living in London, she saw him walking down Old Compton Street, ran up to him, and gave him a hug.

her childhood to teach teenagers to dance, write poetry and sing. Tahliah was getting to know and love the local teens but, after three years, the government withdrew funding; the clubs shuttered, and her job went with it. She was heartbroken. Soon, she was working three or four jobs at a time, just to make her rent. 'It was like hell,' she told *Rolling Stone* in 2014. 'I didn't really have any friends. If I wanted to go to a rave, I'd go by myself . . . But I'm an only child. If you want to get something done, you've just got to do it.'

One of the jobs Tahliah took was as a hostess in a strip club, where clients could pay for her time and conversation. She made friends with the club's sex workers and she became, by necessity, far less reserved than she had been as a teenager. This whole time, Barnett was still working on music. From the age of sixteen until the release of her debut album, she estimates that she wrote a song nearly every day for eight years. In 2006, she even began tentatively working with some local record producers, but emerged with only lacklustre demos and connections with producers who rarely contacted her again.

It was through the strip-circuit that Tahliah was, for the very first time, paid to sing. She appeared onstage at Soho's The Box, an exclusive and notorious club where she put on a faux-cabaret act, played to crowds of drunk, rowdy men and, on one occasion, Queen Latifah. It was a scary gig for a shy woman only three years out of college, but an invaluable one. Showgirls like her were expected to put together shows entirely by themselves, and Tahliah had no choice but to learn how to design a performance in totality: piecing together her own costume; arranging the lighting; choreographing the right dance moves to play seductress for an after-hours crowd. Cabaret forced her to emphasise seductiveness and she learned how to make that happen, performing 'I Put a Spell on You' to dropped jaws. The power which those performances granted electrified her and she decided that making music of her own was what she wanted to do for real.

Amid the club's social scene, Tahliah happened upon people who became essential in realising the ideas she would one day deliver on huge stages. One of the most crucial of these people was Carri Munden, the futurist designer and founder of the Cassette Playa fashion label who Barnett bumped into at a concert and recognised excitedly. Tahliah added her on MySpace and began messaging her (she didn't have a computer, so she'd go to the local Internet café to see whether she'd replied), and Munden (who was, at the time, styling the immensely popular Billionaire Boys Club), saw in that eccentric, geeky girl with a country accent a potential she wanted to help flourish. Munden introduced Tahliah to Sharmadean Reid (the founder of cult nail salon WAH Nails) and Grace Ladoja, who would go on to become the manager of huge Black British artists like Skepta and Naomi Cambell.

This circle soon started putting Tahliah forward to sing at shows at club nights in London and New York. It was at a WAH Nails party in New York where Barnett first performed simply as the nickname her friends had given her as a kid: 'twigs', with a small 't'. It was at another of these parties, thrown at a club, that she was introduced to Tic Zogson.

When he and twigs met in 2010, Zogson was an A&R for Young Turks, a label established within XL Recordings by Caius Pawson. The label was named after the dance parties Pawson used to throw in abandoned buildings around London as a teenager. One night in 2006, during a rave at an abandoned TfL building in Shoreditch, Pawson's party was raided by the police who seized everything he owned: his money, booze and sound system. Richard Russell, the founder of XL Records, happened to be stood at a pub nearby, watching and laughing as the chaos unfolded. Sometime later, he gave

Pawson a different suggestion: he should set up his own label within XL.

Once called Young Turks, now simply Young, the impact of the label Pawson established there cannot be overstated. One of the first bands he signed were The xx. He signed them when they were young and nobody else seemed to want to take a chance on them, but Pawson didn't simply want to sign artists, he wanted to develop them too. He built a £2,000 studio in the garage of the XL Records building for the band to practise in and – taking a leaf out of Malcolm McLaren's book, perhaps – introduced them to their fourth member: Jamie Smith (or, as he became known when he joined the band, Jamie xx). The band's catalogue is a story of mixed successes, but the impact of The xx on the aesthetic of the 2010s was huge, from the clean, typographic design of their record sleeves to the pristine production of their early hits. They were a new type of British indie band for the post-Test Icicles era, one which didn't much want to play the guitar anymore. In the wake of their colossal commercial success, Young went on to sign John Talabot, Kamasi Washington, SBTRKT, Sampha and, thanks to Zogson, Tahliah Barnett.

By 2010, twigs had returned to dancing properly, mostly as a way to pay the bills. Her agent helped secure spots performing as a backing dancer in music videos, at first for local acts like Lethal Bizzle and Dionne Bromfield, and eventually for bigger artists like Ed Sheeran, Plan B and Wretch 32. She earned around £200 per shoot. (You can see her acting as a blank marionette in the video for Jessie J's hit 'Price Tag'). She didn't relish the work and, eventually, she straight-up resented it. 'Do you think I want to be dressed up as a puppet?' she told the *Observer* four years later. 'As a doll, waving? No. But I was paying my dues. I'm sure Jessie J had to do rubbish jobs as well before she was where she is now.'

Young had just put out their first records – the debut albums by Holy Fuck and El Guincho – when Zogson met twigs in New York City. He was enchanted by the performance he'd watched her give, and suggested that she come to his father's house in Finsbury Park to work on music. Zogson introduced twigs to the Tempest, the legendary drum machine which allowed her to create instrumentals long before she understood how to program a DAW. (twigs later said that, without it, she wouldn't have bothered trying to start producing music at all). For the first time, she gelled properly with a producer, and decided to make an entire EP.

Before work began, twigs set herself the goal of producing one of the songs on the project in its entirety (that was, until the perfectionist kicked in, and she decided to co-produce them all). Just as she did when learning to dance as a kid, twigs began watching YouTube tutorials in her bedroom late at night, teaching herself Ableton's notorious complexities and calling Zogson at 3 a.m. when it broke, asking him why it was making strange noises. Within a single year, twigs managed to become proficient, and she emerged from months of work with four songs which felt ready. She decided to spend the Jessie J money on studio time, and recorded them in four days flat.

twigs uploaded this first project to Bandcamp and Tumblr in December 2012 and gave it a simple title: *EP1*.* She was twenty-four years old. twigs did not have a public presence at all. She had performed for most of her life, but not a note of her music had ever been released and so it could have sounded like just about any-

* Her first three projects were given such functional titles because of self-consciousness about her newness to professional songwriting. She felt even naming things was too premature. 'The second EP by twigs is called . . . *Solarisation*,' twigs joked to *Red Bull Academy* in 2013. 'Do you know what I mean? It's like: what are you on about?'

thing, from the punk of her teenage years to the smoky soul she performed in cabaret. It transpired to be far weirder than that.

So many of twigs' trademark moves are right there in the songs of *EP1* from the start; they're just more reserved and reticent. Not that reserved though. 'Weak Spot' opens with rubbery, thudding drum pads, skittish synths and a stiff, stilted hi-hat, ticking like a stopwatch. It's ominous but heads directly towards the strange when, one minute in, the instrumental cuts out and she begins to pant with what sounds like a mouth full of metal. Most of the song is delivered in what remains the softest vocal of her career. Until the final bridge, she's barely even singing, just whispering. It sounds like a piece of ASMR. On 'Weak Spot', that sensory pleasure involves a voice and a mouth. twigs is mixed so clearly you can hear her lips close, hear the saliva on her teeth. But beware the soft delivery. This is a bitter and threatening tune, sung from the perspective of a woman watching as her lover flirts with another woman. She aims her words not at him, but at her. 'Rolling on your back, pussycat,' she hisses, 'he's mine, swine / I dare you, do me like that.'

Throughout *EP1*, twigs sings in a way which makes Sade sound punk. Her voice is supple and airy, a softness which stands in sharp contrast to the moments of unnerving dissonance which litter these songs. Sometimes they come from her voice itself – like the stuttering 'I – I – I' which comprises the chorus of 'Ache' – and sometimes they're embedded in the sound design, like the hollow, clattering percussion of 'Hide'. As she put it to *The Guardian*, 'I love annoying sounds.'

It's no surprise. These colourful timbres are absolutely everywhere in the gothic pop she loved as a teenager, from the cold, snapping drums of Shakespeares Sister's 'Stay', the strange metallic bounce which opens Siouxsie's 1986 hit 'Cities in Dust' and, of course, all over Kate Bush's *The Dreaming*. There is none of the instrumentation of her stepfather's favourite music on the EP, no recognisable Afrobeat or jazz, but the disconcerting nature of these songs is made possible by the unusual syncopations and odd time signatures they're written in; the very things which make the likes of Fela Kuti so dynamic and off-kilter. It's more of an inherited philosophy because twigs' songs sound nothing like that music. In fact, they don't sound much like anything else at all.

Now that twigs is a known name – the kind of celebrity who appears on the cover of *GQ* and fronts Paris Fashion Week – it's near-impossible to articulate just how much of a mystery she felt back in 2012. She arrived at the exact moment when social media was allowing pop stars to become excruciatingly accessible to their audience, but twigs took the opposite route. At the start, it was impossible to find out who she was or where she came from. There were no tweets, no words at all, in fact. Her name – then only 'twigs' – was impossible to google. The few publications who wrote about her didn't even know whether she was a person or a band.

The cover of *EP1*, a plain white record sleeve, gave absolutely nothing away. twigs did release music videos for all four songs and appeared in each of them, but her body was distorted in strange ways: a dancing X-ray; a nude pair of legs with a bright red anthurium clasped between her thighs. These were unnerving accompaniments for sensual music, and made her even more baffling than if she hadn't released any visuals at all. Shortly after *EP1*'s release, twigs signed to Young Turks officially. Work on her second EP began quickly and, to help grow her sound, her manager suggested she meet with a budding producer in New York City. Things were about to get a whole lot stranger.

At the base of tree-covered Sorte Mountain in Venezuela, among 40,000 hectares of dense, virgin forest, in the otherwise unremarkable state of Yaracuy, stands a stone statue which looks completely out of time. The statue was carved in 1951 but it seems so apt for the concerns of this moment that the fact it was built over seventy years ago feels surreal. The statue, created by sculptor Alejandro Colina, was commissioned for the third Bolivarian Games by dictator Marcos Jiménez. The Central University of Venezuela, where it was first placed, rejected its design and consigned it to storage for decades, but, in 2022, a cultural heritage institute stole the statue from the university's storage and drove it to the foothills of Sorte Mountain.

The Sorte Mountain appears in no guidebooks. It is so remote that it is rarely even photographed. Every year though, tens of thousands flock to make the long journey to it through the forests to participate in a week of worship. Thousands of people – devotees of the religions of indigenous Venezuela – lie prostrate among the leaves, surrounded by candles and covered in wax. They sketch symbols in the mud, dance amid fire and bathe in the healing waters of the Yaracuy River. In mainstream Venezuelan society, the festival is remarked upon only in whispers, because of these acts' association with black magic.

These festivals have been a tradition for decades, but they hold a special power now given the presence of the statue, because it is a depiction of the object of their worship: the goddess María Lionza. The statue itself, as Alejandro Colina designed it, depicts Lionza as a razor-boned heroine, sat astride a tapir. In some drawings of her, she is soft and mystical, but Colina's depiction is far less delicate: he turned her into a titan, a bulbous warrior with grey skin taut around the crevasses of her swollen muscles. Massive, rippling quadriceps protrude like boulders, laid across the tapir's ribs. Her body is masculine in a Roman sense, with muscles so pronounced that they remind more of metal than flesh, but she isn't a male: her breasts are full and pointed, and in her hands, thrust straight up to the sky, is a woman's pelvis. In a time when, in the English-speaking West, strict notions of gender have been torn and scattered to the wind, the statue captures an idea about gender which seems so distinctly of the twenty-first century, despite it being born from the mythology of the fifteenth.

On the cover of Arca's 2021 album *kiCK iiiii,* María Lionza is rendered in digital form. This version, brought to life by code, is fleshier; the tapir stood on a plinth which sits in a vast cavern, sounded by smoke and streams of lava. She also has Arca's face. With this artwork and the five *KICK* albums in general, here the Venezuelan artist weaves a piece of her nation's folklore into her own fluid identity; an image of gender as complex as her own, presented in the shape of a figure people worship as a goddess.

When I think of 2014 – the year of Death Grips, Perfume Genius, Sun Kil Moon's *Benji* and Mac DeMarco's *Salad Days* – Arca is right there in the mix too. Without even knowing that the two had worked together, Arca always felt like she and twigs were kindred spirits. They were both mysterious beings: strange, faceless new talents who ran through boundaries of taste and genre. Arca took the trap sound of Atlanta hip hop and stretched it into strange, intense shapes: both garish and tender, both ugly and uncannily picturesque. In 2019, *VICE* named her the artist of the decade and hers was a name which made sense: from her 2012 EPs onwards, Arca's style leaked out in all sorts of unexpected places into the music of her generation and the next.

Alejandra Ghersi Rodríguez was born in Caracas in 1989, just a few months after Tahliah. Alejandra's family were rich. Her father was an investment banker who, in 1992, moved his family to America when he found work in New York City. When the family returned to Caracas six years later, the country was steeped in political and economic turmoil. Caracas was no longer the kind of place where children, even the children of the rich, played freely. Alejandra lived behind the walls of a gated community, attending the kind of private school where her friends rocked up with bodyguards in bullet-proof cars. Like twigs, Ghersi's bedroom became a sanctuary. She'd play with a blanket: wielding it like a cape when her mum was looking, turning it into a skirt when she left.

Like Devonté Hynes, Rodríguez owes her taste to an older sibling. As a kid Alejandra loved the Spice Girls and Nelly Furtado, but her older brother soon introduced her to the electronica being funnelled into America and the UK. Ghersi would take walks on the beach listening to Aphex Twin and Nine Inch Nails, getting lost in the glitches. She began releasing her own songs under the name Nuuro, instrumental music heavily indebted to Richard D. James, but with flashes of her own singing and pieces of acoustic instrumentation layered in.

Alejandra knew from a very young age that she was gay, but in college she got a girlfriend and began to address her love songs to 'she', hoping to pass as straight to the kids in class. It was a white lie, but one which Ghersi began to view as a great betrayal of herself, and one which had a long and profound impact on how she would present her art in the future. Nuuro began to gain some notoriety around Caracas, but Alejandra stopped releasing music, so ashamed to be making music for the approval of other people.

Her rebranding as Arca was tied closely to Alejandra's own self-acceptance. When she was seventeen she returned to New York to study. There, a shy and nervous teenager, she quickly came to be inspired by the icons of the city. One day, after spending hours sat in Chinatown café devouring a biography of Arthur Russell, she finally plucked up the courage to ask out a man she spotted on the Union Square subway. 'That was like jumping off a cliff,' Alejandra told *The Fader* years later. 'My survival instincts – everything I'd trained myself to do – were telling me not to do it, but something inside of me drove me forward.'

Around this time, Ghersi discovered GHE20G0TH1K: an underground club night which emerged in the wake of the financial crash. GHE20G0TH1K was conceived explicitly as an end-of-days party, replete with biohazard symbols, freakish costumes and soundtracked by garish, pummelling electronic music. It threw highbrow and lowbrow into a trash can, and set it on fire in a plume of confetti. DJs like Venus X, Shayne Oliver and Total Freedom were staples, artists who specialised in confrontational, kinetic dance music which influenced an entire generation of queer electronic musicians from Lotic to Rabit, Elysia Crampton and Arca herself. GHE20G0TH1K became famous among the fashion-conscious, multicultural, overtly queer community which had always existed in New York City.

Arca's sound as we know it was born directly out of those nights. Feeling liberated by her experience of coming out, Ghersi began to make music again in 2011, only now it contained far more of the open-eyed debauchery being blasted from Venus X's subwoofers. The music of her first two EPs – *Stretch 1* and *Stretch 2* – was far stranger than anything she'd made in Venezuela, marked by clattering percussion and strange, depleted synth patches. Her songs did something far more unsettling than even Shayne Oliver's shattered, maximalist remixes of Rhianna, reducing the kicks of dance music to ominous thuds and adorning them with spiralling, downtempo synth. Alejandra no longer sang but instead filled each track with fragments of voices, an attempt to find productive use for the ones inside her own head when her transsexuality was dawning on her: trapped between the person she was and the person her body suggested her to be. The effect of fragmented songs like 'Tapped In' and 'Ass Swung Low' is utterly bizarre: the sensation of pure paranoia captured in song.

In 2012, just months after she'd posted her first EP, Arca received an email from an associate of Kanye West's who asked her to submit some beats to put to the rapper. At the time, West was spending a great deal of time in Paris, drawing from the cold utilitarianism of various fashion houses and concrete Le Corbusier lamps. In the wake of the grand, chart-breaking opulence of *Watch the Throne*, West decided to shoot in a far darker direction for *Yeezus* and his team began scouring the web for pioneers of the digital underground. A raft of left-field, Internet-born producers got the call, from Evian Christ to Gesaffelstein and Glaswegian maximalist Hudson Mohawke (alongside a little outfit called Daft Punk). When she received the email, Arca made a point of sending only her freakiest shit, some of which laid the groundwork for 'I'm in It' and 'Send It Up', two songs which remain among Kanye's ugliest, and an apt soundtrack for an increasingly paranoid, ugly personality. A year after posting her music for free online, Arca's name was listed on that year's most talked-about LP.

Arca approached the beginning of her career exactly like twigs did: her unnerving songs made all the stranger for the fact they were presented without context online. Alejandra calcified her sound quickly, and 2013's *&&&&&* was a striking leap forward: smashing bright synths against lumbering drums and heavy, menacing dub. Soon after working on *Yeezus*, Arca was asked to DJ at the afterparties of Björk's *Biophilia* tour, and was soon invited to Iceland to work on her next album, the mournful, soaring divorce record *Vulnicura*. At twenty-five, Arca became its primary producer.

Aside from two enormous stars in Kanye West and Björk, the only other artist Arca agreed to work with in the first year of her career was twigs. They met over a coffee in New York

City. twigs' manager had sent an email to her with links to some of Arca's music, which she didn't listen to, but took the meeting anyway. At first, the meeting was incredibly business-like – twigs' worst nightmare – but Alejandra was disarming. They had, it turned out, a lot in common. They were both fans of dance and liked many of the same songs. Within fifteen minutes, they forgot that they were at a work meeting and decided that maybe it would be fun to make music together after all. In the studio they established a sense of mutual trust. For the first time, twigs was at ease with writing something on the Tempest, and allowing Alejandra to find the fifteen-second section which could be expanded into a song.

The first music that they made together – the songs which would become 2013's *EP2* – were the first I heard of FKA twigs. My first encounter was 'Water Me'. I remember it vividly. I saw the YouTube thumbnail before anything else. It was a picture of a woman's face, tightly cropped and set against a teal background; a simple image if not for the fact that this woman didn't look so uncanny. It was like she was a marionette. A tiny, open mouth with gap teeth and massive, teardrop eyes: big and oily black like a mollusc's. When the video began to play, that head started to rock from side to side, slowly at first, but gaining momentum with each passing second. It was an unnatural movement, rocking faster and faster until it grew manic, snapping across the screen in a blur. Once it calmed again, the woman wept a fat, silvery tear which slid down her cheek, performed a loop around her chin and dropped off her face entirely, only to fall back onto her own scalp. When it hit, it burst like a cartoon raindrop, and her eyes swelled even wider.

The music was no less disconcerting. 'Water Me' begins with an angelic, choral voice vamping up and down. It sounds saintly, but there's something uneasy about it too. There was that tapping, mechanical drum loop, and the voices rise and fall into nothing, making it sound like a machine *imitating* a human. Then twigs starts to sing. Her voice is delicate, so delicate that it feels like it would blow apart in a breeze. In the time of Rhianna and Adele's octave-shattering vocals, it was shocking to hear something so small. The words she sang expressed a vulnerability which matched her whispered tone. 'He told me I was so small,' she sings. 'I told him: water me.' I was sixteen years old, raised on Van Morrison and The Moody Blues. I didn't know that music like this was even *possible*.

twigs and Arca shared a taste for the weird, and the inexplicable details which enter their productions together and apart come from myriad sources. The frantic percussive arrangement in the breakdown of another *EP2* song, 'Papi Pacify', was inspired by twigs' teenage tap-dance classes. Her bias for low-end in her music, on the other hand, wasn't a matter of choice: listening to too much X-Ray Spex at high volume had given her chronic tinnitus, and made mid-range frequencies difficult to listen to, let alone work with.

Arca on the other hand drew several of her idiosyncrasies from the music of Venezuela. The way she programs sub-bass is inspired by the sound of the furruco, an indigenous drum played by rubbing a stick pierced through the skin of a large drum, creating a tone which is infrasonic and severe, just like the thick bass which quivers through the middle of 'Papi Pacify'. On the other end of the spectrum, some of Arca's most shrill moments are inspired by changa tuki: bright, frantic electronic music invented by the poor youth of Caracas to play at dance parties thrown in their slums. Changa tuki was politically demonised by Venezuela's upper classes and so never truly made it out into the wider world, but it was music Alejandra had partied to as a teen.

Arca works at a rapid pace, which suited twigs nicely. She was inspired by Arthur Russell's 'first thought, best thought' approach, and finishes songs in swift flashes of inspiration, happily trashing something which had taken five hours to make if it isn't coming together. While making *EP2*, breakthrough moments happened fast, after hours of achieving little. 'Water Me' was made at the very end of a session where Rodríguez and twigs had spent all day simply sat in the room, chatting and making beats. They had half an hour left before the clock ran out and so they started playing synths: twigs on the Tempest and Arca adding overtones. When the shape of the song was made, the words came quickly. twigs started each day by listening to 'Walk On By' by Dionne Warwick, reminding herself that one simple line could be as meaningful as twenty. With that song in mind, she began singing over the primitive instrumental and the whole thing was written in seven minutes flat. Then they put on a merengue tune and tangoed through the studio to celebrate. They hardly touched it again. 'Once I start to think about it,' twigs told *Red Bull*, 'it implodes on itself.'

EP2 brought twigs a new level of exposure, but she was determined to keep her process the same as it always had been. She continued to start each day attending a ballet class, before making beats in her flat, then heading to the studio. Over several months she invited a raft of collaborators to join Zogson and Arca to craft her first full-length record, among them labelmate Sampha, Devonté Hynes, Emile Haynie (the New York record producer who worked with Kid Cudi and who co-produced 'Runaway' with Kanye), Adele's producer Paul Epworth, and A$AP Rocky and Mac Miller's producer Clams Casino.

It was a formidable group, but twigs was careful that her style was amplified rather than diluted by her collaborators. She refused to work from any premade tracks and instead insisted on starting each instrumental from scratch in the room. Her collaborators were chosen to pick up the slack where her skill set was still underdeveloped. Sampha helped with the chords on 'Numbers', Epworth with the songs' structures. She asked each collaborator to pull from a sonic palette she herself had created, like synth patches she had created by reversing, tuning and warping hi-hats, and then layering them with other percussion. Across six months, she wrote dozens of songs, but only ten made the final cut.

LP1 was released on the 6th of August 2014. It was received euphorically by the music press. *Clash* and *TIME* magazine both named it the best album of 2014. The *Guardian* had it third, *Pitchfork* second (just behind the phenomenal *Run the Jewels 2*). Reading through contemporary reviews of the record is a funny experience: a legion of writers like myself desperately trying to work out how to actually describe the songs they were reviewing. If writing about music is like dancing about architecture, then reviewing *LP1* feels like doing a waltz to the Guggenheim. The *Guardian* (quite sweetly), called it 'a modern mess of sounds, that refuses to fit in anywhere'. Many others erred on the side of caution and imagined her songs as hypothetical collaborations. For *Stereogum*, the great Tom Breihan wrote that twigs' sound was like a world where 'Portishead's Beth Gibbons made a whole album with Richard D. James-era Aphex Twin'. He said that she had a distinctly 'British locution . . . of '80s art-pop types like Kate Bush or Talk Talk's Mark Hollis'. The *Pitchfork* review compared parts of her songs to Cocteau Twins and others to Tom Waits' *Rain Dogs*. There were, understandably, numerous comparisons to first-generation trip-hop: acts like Portishead, *Post*-era Björk, Massive Attack and MC Adrian 'Tricky' Thaws.

That explosive moment of pre-millennium, Bristolian magic is certainly the most astute point of comparison to the sound of twigs' early music (even though it's not a scene twigs has ever name-dropped herself). It too blended hip hop, dub, soul and electronica; acts like Massive Attack taking the pummelling beats of Jamaican-born sound system culture and slowing it down to a narcotic crawl. Some of the music from that era even features sensual, female vocals – like Tricky's 1995 masterpiece *Maxinquaye*, an album-length collaboration with Martina Topley-Bird, but the comparisons only go so far.

On one hand, *LP1*'s ten songs are like intricate, sonic sculptures. A track like 'Pendulum', for example, is so mind-bogglingly elaborate that it's hard to even understand how it works. It's stiff, tinny drums don't move in straight lines to create a rhythm: they rattle around the mix, floating in elliptical circles until a chorus emerges out of the ooze, ninety seconds into the track. 'Hours' sounds like a pop song trying to rev up, trying and failing perpetually to switch into a higher gear. Other tracks threaten to come apart at the seams: 'Numbers' feels like it was written inside a detuned piano; stabs of synths building and collapsing into silence beneath twigs' voice, opening up a gaping chasm beneath her.

The progression of each song is rarely linear either. Instead of hitting apexes, a track like 'Video Girl' – the closest *LP1* comes to a song which could conceivably sit in a top ten – actually loses its structure as it goes, stiffening up until twigs is just singing over the dismembered parts of her own song. There's plenty of music more chaotic than this, but *LP1* is somehow freakier than a lot of it because it often feels like the music is simply happening to the person who made it. A large part of this illusion was created by the utterly boundless things you can do with the digital tools like the Tempest and Ableton. Within the vast libraries of DAW plug-ins, each synthesised note can be tweaked and toyed with through layers and filters until it resembles nothing else before it, and each track of a song can be laced with these little, particular details if you want them to be. When twigs was making these songs, she dived deeper than ever into those devices. She worked until 3 a.m., tweaking individual moments for hours on end until each song was filled with details at a near-atomic level. The only way of making sense of a song like 'Kicks' is to realise that the synths were actually made from drums, and that some parts of her voice are layered in reverse.

Despite all of these unconventional things, what's remarkable is that *LP1* didn't become an onerous, avant-garde record. To this day I'm not entirely sure why all of its oddities don't make the album's style more off-putting than they do. My first guess is: it's fun. It's just straight-up entertaining to listen to someone work at this level of brilliance, hearing all of these strange details come together in interesting ways. Secondly, the album *is* full of little sticky hooks, they're just not always in the obvious places. Instead they're hidden in moments like the end of 'Pendulum' when she coos 'so lonely trying to be yoo-urs!'

twigs' presence is another of the album's most essential ingredients. In the midst of all of these ornamental constructions is Tahliah's voice and she acts as a rope, stopping all of these tunes spiralling out of control. Vocally she's a haunting presence, tightrope-walking between smoke and a breeze, tumbling around knotty beats and vamping tempos like only a dancer can. She would eventually flex considerable vocal power but on these early projects her voice often sounds on the point of bursting into tears. On 'Pendulum', she interrupts herself constantly, cutting off a breathy vocal with one which is ecstatic and clear.

The quality of her voice reminds me of the kind of sustained tension once perfected by prodigal pop star Aaliyah. By the time she died at twenty-two, Aaliyah already had several hit songs under her belt. What was so distinct about her voice though was that, even on her most bombastic singles, she refused to match Timbaland's explosive drums with vocal acrobatics, instead maintaining a simmering tension. twigs does exactly the same on *LP1*. It feels inherently intimate; a degree of expressiveness which contradicts the perception of twigs as a musician who makes cold, calculating music. Her performances could even be taken as a reaction *against* the vocal tinkering which became rife in the pop music of the twenty-first century. Sure, twigs' voice is often chopped and warped in impossible ways but her central vocal takes are often completely untouched, so pronounced that you can hear the breath leave her lips. It's the human and the computational. It shouldn't work, and yet it *more than* works: it's fireworks.

On *LP1* there are also thematic tensions which match the sonic contradictions: a pull, between passivity and exacting control. In the opening moments of the album, on the short but elegant 'Preface', there's something holy in the air. Her voice is the first thing we hear, singing daintily in a cavernous space. twigs' earliest experiences of singing in public were in gospel choirs and here it's like we're at midnight mass, candles flickering from their votives. 'I love another and thus I hate myself', are the words she repeats through the song. It's a fragile refrain, and one typical of that tension in full effect: love which comes at the cost of the self. It's the same sentiment which hit so strongly on 'Water Me', in those other lyrics: 'he told me I was so small / I told him: water me'.

In almost all music which deals with power and its sexual manifestations, it tends to be the artist bragging, but twigs acts differently. It's something I'd never really heard in secular music before: a degree of wilful acquiescence usually reserved for the religiously devout. In these songs she's almost pleading, and it's unnerving. How much of this is willing? How much of this is safe? It's a dynamic played out most explicitly on *EP2*'s 'Papi Pacify', a song which languishes in utter servility. In its music video twigs is wrapped in the arms of a much bigger man, his arm across her chest, his fingers prying open her mouth. It feels like you should recoil at the image, but her submissiveness is a paradox. How can passivity be passivity, if you're demanding more? The protagonist of these songs is not helpless or defeated at all, she's abdicating wilfully.

This dynamic is at the heart of *LP1*'s most famous single, 'Video Girl'. The song sees twigs reflecting on the jobs she worked immediately before making it as a musician: as a back-up dancer; as a cabaret showgirl, jobs where submissiveness and control go hand in hand. The song is a dialogue between twigs and a stranger, someone who feels like they know her simply because they once saw her on a screen. 'Are you the girl from the video?' This oppressive weight of expectation is central to the dynamic of most performances. You *are* the show, and yet many assume some degree of ownership in response. The art is theirs, isn't the artist too? twigs said that working the cabaret circuit made her feel like 'a lamb to the slaughter', but she soon learned how to turn watchful eyes back in her favour. As she got used to the work, she began ending her performances with a ritual. She'd seek out an attractive couple in the crowd and stride toward them, singing the final verse of the song directly to the man. She would lock her eyes on him until the tension became unbearable, and then, at the very last moment, turn to the woman, kneel, and kiss her hand instead.

This power, sexual power, is the flip side of *LP1*'s instances of excruciating vulnerability. Like all good writing about sex, none actually happens on the record. It's all in the promise. 'When I trust you we can do it with the lights on.' 'I could kiss you for hours.' In moments of songs like 'Lights On', when the chorus is wrapped up in a cacophony of clattering wood and noodling upright bass – all that dense instrumentation comes together in service of strong, sensual emotion, and no more so than on the album's third song.

I still find it hard to believe that real life human beings sat down and made 'Two Weeks'. This song is utter, distilled ecstasy. It's a vast, seismic pop song which makes pleasure feel like a death blow. It advertises its hugeness immediately, opening with deep, rumbling bass and another low, choral chant. More churches, more candlelight. Within seconds the song opens up, and I mean fifty feet wide. Hi-hats flutter and a synth enters which crackles like Tesla's coil. twigs sings softly. At the time, her method was to write verbosely and cut the lyrics down until only the most necessary words remained, and that pointedness is all we're left with. 'Suck me up,' she sings, 'I'm healing for the shit you're dealing / high motherfucker, get your mouth open, you know you're mine.' She sounds like she's about to steal your soul. Then the chorus hits, and it's pure bliss. A drum goes off like a bomb; a thick synth quivers like electricity searching for grounding. A cavernous voice repeats her words back at her. I think that, somewhere, I hear dolphins. 'Smoke on your skin to get those pretty eyes rolling,' she sings, 'my thighs are apart for when you're ready to breathe in.' Commanding is an understatement. 'Feel your body closing, I can rip it open . . . give me two weeks, you won't recognise her.' It's hot. Apart from Donna Summer's 'I Feel Love', it's probably the closest to actual pleasure I've ever known a song to come.

The music video for 'Two Weeks' is everything the one for 'Water Me' wasn't. Where that was an expressly intimate moment, this a grand, opulent tableau. The small, delicate marionette from the older song is recast as a high priestess, sat on a throne in a room made of gold. As the camera zooms out incrementally, the woman is revealed to be a giant; an emperor, surrounded by imps who are also played by twigs herself, each of them dancing frantically to please their queen. It's wild imagery, but what really makes these lavish, commanding scenes so compelling is the sheer scale of the contrast. This is the same woman that, a year earlier, had released 'Water Me', and moments ago had sung 'Preface'. The control she exerts on 'Two Weeks' wouldn't be half as effective if they weren't surrounded by the sound of joyful submission.

Fuck it, I agree with *Clash*: album of the year.

If, to new eyes, it felt like twigs was already a complete package by the time she arrived, then a significant part of that effect was achieved by the artwork which accompanied her first projects. The cover of *LP1* is a simple picture of twigs' face, but this no vanity shoot. Instead, her head sits on the cover awkwardly, like a misplaced toy. The middle of her face is dominated by a great, glossy bruise: a plum-colour shrink-wrap freezing her face in a permanent blush. Her eyes are bright and a little drained, looking absent-mindedly elsewhere. It's an image which puts an alien face to the weird, rootless sounds scattered through her songs.

This Grammy-winning artwork was made by Jesse Kanda, a multimedia artist and musician who twigs was introduced to by Arca. In real life, the Japanese-born Canadian cuts a gangly, wizard-like figure, often wearing dresses which trail around battered sandals, his long hair tied in tight, girlish ponytails. Alejandra and Kanda first met on the art forum DeviantArt when they were teenagers living on opposite ends of the American continent. When Ghersi began working on the first Arca *EP*, she thought of Kanda first, calling on him to produce strange, cartoonish covers for *Stretch 1* and *2*. In 2013, they moved to the UK together, sharing a flat in Dalston with a small Bengal cat named True.

It was Kanda who directed the videos for 'Water Me' and the other *EP2* track 'How's That'. In the latter, Kanda's changes to twigs' form are brutal. It begins with a model of her body which looks like it's been moulded from an oil slick, floating out in pristine whiteness. When the song begins, the body crumples like a carrier bag, torn apart and thrown around like tissue paper in a hurricane. It's a crazy video. Watching it unfold, it's startling to see a human form – imaginary or otherwise – subjected to such mutilation. It makes my own body feel very fragile indeed.

twigs had no real interest in portraying herself as beautiful. Not in the traditional way. The portraits of herself in her art were always versions of herself through the eyes of other people. 'Half of my life I've had people staring at me because they think I'm funny-looking,' she told *DAZED* in 2014. 'The other half of my life I've had people staring at me because they think I'm fascinating.' It was with an awareness that commentary on her music would be split between conversations about her art and conversations about her body that she started her career by presenting herself in such bizarre ways. 'Sometimes I look at someone like James Blake,' she continued, 'and I kind of envy the fact that he's a six-foot-two English guy and no one will say: "oh he's changed his T-shirt from black to blue".'

twigs' adolescent confidence as a performer did little to lessen a crippling lack of it whenever she caught her reflection. twigs has said that she would sometimes simply sit in front of the mirror and cry. Her self-consciousness was heightened by the fact of her being the only Black girl in a rural, Catholic school. On her first day a kid refused to hold her hand 'in case the brown came off' and, as she entered her teenage years the abuse became bolder. She remembered going to a hair shop in London for the first time when she was fifteen and feeling like she'd entered paradise. She found perfume and oils for her hair which she'd never encountered in rural Gloucestershire. She put her hair into plaits overnight and let the oil sink in, but when she wore them to school the next day, even her best friends began to laugh, mocking her and calling her greasy.

An obsession with twigs' race continued when *LP1* was released. Suddenly, her music began being described as R&B. 'When I first released music and no one knew what I looked like, I would read comments like: "I've never heard anything like this before, it's not in a genre",' she told *The Guardian* in 2014. 'Then my picture came out six months later, now "she's an R&B singer". I share certain sonic threads with classical music. My song "Preface" is like a hymn. So let's talk about that. If I was white and blonde and said I went to church all the time, you'd be talking about the "choral aspect". But you're not talking about that because I'm a mixed-race girl from south London.'

When she began dating the actor Robert Pattinson in 2014, fans of the *Twilight* films began flooding her social media with racist abuse. 'He was their white Prince Charming, and I think they considered he should definitely be with someone white and blonde and not me,' she told Louis Theroux in 2021. 'Whatever I did at that time, people would find pictures of monkeys and have me doing the same thing as the monkey. If I was wearing a red dress, they'd have a monkey in a red dress, or if I was on a bike, they'd find a monkey on a bike.'

twigs' reaction to this kind of abuse was to portray versions of herself in her art which expressed both extreme vulnerability and, especially later on, supreme strength. In the video for 'Pendulum', she's suspended mid-air in shibari (a type of Japanese rope bondage where you're suspended by your own body weight), only, in the video, it's her hair which binds her; extended to an impossible length and wrapped in knots around her body. These twisted visions of her body are expressionism but they were also reclamation: a choice to portray herself as she pleased, rather than in whichever way pleased other people.

Perhaps it was a product of a particular historical moment. twigs had pursued this idea separately to Arca and Jesse

Kanda – primitive versions of the body-warping she'd later pursue so elegantly, appearing in the Grace Ladoja-directed videos for *EP1* – but all three were young artists who happened upon it at the exact same moment in time, across three different continents. Artists had pursued these forms of expressionism in their visuals for decades: the character-performances of Gene Simmons; the album covers of Grace Jones and Alejandra's friend, Björk. In the early 2010s though, for the first time, the electronic music of the likes of Arca and twigs began to sound wild enough to match those complicated portrayals of the body, and present, holistically, a reality dictated not by the flesh but the mind.

Ghersi has stated that the sonic extremes of her albums – spacious at the same time as being devastatingly intense – are intended to create a discomfort which facilitates these boundary-breaking moments. 'If there's a really soft piece of music and then you're hit by a painful explosive sound, your brain does this funny somersault trying to make sense of why this happened,' she told *Vogue* in 2014. 'At that very moment your brain is malleable. When you're uncomfortable, that's when you learn something new about yourself. That was my only goal.'

After collaborating with twigs, Kanye and Björk, Alejandra began work on the first albums of her own. In their Dalston flat, she and Ghersi worked separately, vanishing into different rooms and diving into separate projects, but, naturally, their ideas began to bleed into each other's. Alejandra began to craft music which interrogated the unease which she felt with her body and gender, while, at the same time, Kanda became interested in the power of flesh. He began to create 3D drawings of grotesque and tactile creatures whose eyes glint like a human's do, but whose limbs were stripped bare or blown up into bright red suits of rippling fat. These impossible creatures were crafted out of the very real textures of muscle and skin. Bodies are painted the colour of pus and blood; limbs adorned with organs, with arms shaped like fallopian tubes. Like an Edwardian provocateur teasing her audience with the skin of an ankle, these bizarre beings turn a spotlight on a squeamishness inherent in us all: a discomfort with the ugly and our hidden insides.

Kanda's creatures appeared on the covers of many of Arca's early projects. *Xen* – her debut – features an imagining of a character which had existed in Alejandra's life since she was a child: the name she used for her imagined, female self when she still very much presented as a male. On the LP's cover, Kanda creates a flamboyant, ivory-pale creature with wide, oily thighs and pink, pin-prick nipples. 'Everyone is simultaneously attracted to it and repulsed,' Ghersi told *DAZED*. 'I can't imagine him representing her in a more accurate way.'

After *Xen*, Alejandra worked prolifically, indulging provocative side projects like a swirling remix of 'Hips Don't Lie' and, on 2017's self-titled record, returning to singing for the first time in a decade. It was in 2021 though that she finally fulfilled a promise she'd made to herself as a teenager in Caracas: that she would never compromise on herself again. She proved it on a gargantuan scale.

Arca's five-album *KICK* series began in 2020 and ended in December 2021, when Rodríguez released the last four albums all at once. She doubled the length of her discography in a single day. Spanning three hours in length, the series was an outlandish proposition even for an artist who, the year prior, had released a hundred remixes of a single song. Each of the five *KICK* albums indulges different avenues of Arca's ever-expanding trajectories. Among them are her most accessible album, and her least. *KiCk i* is a direct (if vicious) pop record and *KICK ii* is filled with music to vogue to, defined by pounding, strutting reggaeton. But then there's *KicK iii*: a nasty, pummelling album in a discography already filled with plenty of disturbing material. Drums pound and scatter like on a footwork record. Shots of thick bass interrupt every fragment of a blissful moment. It's an unrelenting thirty-six minutes where jabbering beats, spasming synths and electronically butchered vocals smash into each other, bounce off the walls and try to chop each other's heads off. If all albums sounded like this, then music would be hell but, luckily, there's only one *KicK iii*.

KICK wasn't just a series of albums though. Inspired by the epic speculative fiction of Octavia E. Butler and Richard Wanger's enormous opera cycle *Der Ring des Nibelungen,* the albums were an exercise in extreme world-building. Arca replaced Jesse Kanda's bodily portraits with entire science-fiction vistas created by Frederik Heyman, with Ghersi's body central to every one. On the cover of *KICK ii* she's spread-eagled, shooting lasers as robots hack at the flesh of the clones around her. On the shoegaze-y, queer-centric *kick iiii*, she's as big as a Sphinx, being pieced together by cranes. Metal melds into flesh, the body knows no end, and the difference between a girl and a boy seems as relevant as the distinction between a gnat and an ant.

It's on the cover of the fifth *KICK album*, *kiCK iiiii*, that Arca depicts herself as María Lionza, the stolen statue at the base of Sorte Mountain, with a woman's pelvis raised above her rippling shoulders. It's an apt and historically loaded image, one which brings into question the modern hysteria around gender fluidity. In truth, Lionza presented a similar vision to Arca's, five hundred years before she was born. It's no wonder she was drawn to her, perhaps even shaped by her. Unlike the statue and the myth, though, Arca's fantastical music carries another meaning: the implication that, perhaps, these outlandish, fantastic worlds are, in some ways, also true-to-life depictions of herself.

*

Things changed quickly for twigs after *LP1*. The album itself was nominated for a Mercury Prize. When 'Two Weeks' was released in June 2014, it briefly rose to number one on Billboard's Trending 140, knocking Pharrell's 'Happy' from pole position. On her first North American tour, she sold out Webster Hall and played the show with both David Byrne and A$AP Rocky stood among the crowd. She received her first producer credit, helping to write and featuring on 'Ouch Ouch' by Chicago rapper Lucki Eck$. In November 2014 she made her US TV debut on *The Tonight Show Starring Jimmy Fallon*, a stunning performance where she wore gold body armour and danced around a sculpture made of air.

Word spread fast. On an episode of Snoop Dogg's *Double G News Network*, he and T-Pain discussed their three favourite albums, and T-Pain named *LP1*. He struck up a friendship with twigs, for no other reason than to learn her process. When Kanye West debuted his Yeezy Season 3 collection in 2015, he pronounced that he cared about two guests only: 'please invite [Louis] Farrakhan and twigs'.

Exposure didn't equate to wealth. In the summer of 2014, she was both appearing in *Vogue* and asking her dad for £50 a week. Then came accusations of theft. For the first two years she was releasing music, she did so simply as 'twigs' but, in April 2014, just before her first headline performance in the US, she was hit with a lawsuit. The claim came from a pair of twins from Ohio who recorded cutesy covers of The Kinks and made swing songs about blueberry jam. They did so, crucially, under the name The Twigs, and they held the trademark.

Barnett had reached out to them after they first issued a complaint in 2013, hoping that they could co-exist, but the sisters declined. To rectify the situation, she changed her name to 'FKA' twigs. This does not stand for 'formerly known as'. Instead, she simply typed some random letters on the keyboard. At first she landed on 'AFK' twigs, until a friend informed her that, on Internet message boards, 'AFK' stands for 'away from keyboard'. She swapped the letters around, and FKA stuck.

Despite her growing fame, twigs remained an insular person. When she was doing noisy bar work a friend brought her a 'twigs' necklace as a joke so that, when the punters asked for her name, she could simply show them the necklace and point. She was so focused on music and dance that she paid very little attention to her contemporaries at all. Charmingly, when asked at the Mercury Prize about her fellow nominees, she said that she hadn't listened to any of them yet, but was definitely going to. At busy parties, she was usually the first to leave.

If this personality seems at odds with her choice of career, then that's exactly how it played out when public interest in her skyrocketed. twigs soon developed a reputation for being a somewhat tricky interviewee. She often resented having to explain her art to journalists. In an extended profile with *The Fader* in 2014, she continually pulled out a disposable camera and started taking photos of the interviewer, offering it as gift at the end of their meeting and explaining that she felt uncomfortable with the entire thing being about her. 'If this is what being an artist is,' she told *Complex* in 2015, 'I'm just not really sure this is for me. This is horrific. I could be doing dance class right now.'

In 2014 twigs had met Boots – the Roc Nation producer named Jordan Asher Cruz – at a bar. Cruz was in the midst of a major career breakthrough after helping to produce Beyoncé's 2013 self-titled LP.* A complete unknown, he'd been living in

* *Beyoncé* helps to make the case that 2013 was truly the beginning of twenty-first century music. It was a commercial behemoth and a solid record, but its greatest legacy was inventing the 'surprise drop': the idea that a major artist releasing a record without warning could be an even greater marketing coup than months

his car only four years earlier but, within seven days of the album's release, there had been 452 million Google searches asking who he was. Barnett was one of the few people who knew the answer to that question. In fact, he'd reached out to her shortly after they met and for months, she'd avoided *him*. One day though, when the media cycle became too intense, she finally decided to reply to his email. Within hours she was on a flight to New York City and hadn't told a soul. Straight away, they began work on her new EP.

M3LL155X was released on the 13th of August 2015, almost exactly a year after *LP1*. Work on the songs was mostly finished before that album even dropped, coming together quickly in a spree of furious, unexpected creativity. Her third EP is testament to the succinctness with which Barnett can deliver complex emotions, feeling as rich in only five songs as many albums do across ten. It was also her most ambitious work to date, spanning genres and being released with a complete short film, which she directed herself.

'Melissa' (as the title is pronounced) was, to twigs, what *Xen* had been to Arca: a name she put to her feminine energy, as a means of separating it from herself. Through the film which accompanied the music, twigs depicts this femininity in specific, rarely seen ways. How often, for example, do we see an elderly woman in the way we do at the start of the film: not sweet nor fragile nor as an object of pity but as a powerful, menacing force. In near-total darkness, French designer Michèle Lamy leans into the frame, luxuriating in the light of a bulb which extends from her scalp like an anglerfish, and

of advance promo. Only a decade later, the idea already sounds quaint. There are still plenty of surprise drops, major label or otherwise, but they don't make the same impact today; truly, they're just normal. Liberated from the confines of printing CDs or records in advance, music can now be released any time, any place.

then swallows it whole, teeth bared and cackling. Then there's the pregnant woman, which twigs transforms herself into while 'In Time' plays, dancing furiously at the camera until her waters break. The waters take the form of neon paint, which she proceeds to dance in. In another, she even becomes a sex doll, a sad polyurethane blow-up with her own face, singing sensually as a dopey looking man approaches the bed. 'Love me rough,' she mouths. 'I'm your doll.'

'I'm Your Doll' is the only one of the hundreds of songs twigs wrote in her teenage years to see the light of day. When she heard back the demo as an adult she was shocked at what she'd written. 'I realised that I'd been brainwashed and preconditioned to write a pop song and write it from that point of view,' she told *Complex* shortly after the song's release. Remade as an adult, the version which appears on *M3LL155X* continues a theme of wilful submission which she'd indulged since 'Water Me': a degree of surrender which, backed by the heaviest, most industrial tones she's unleashed to date, feels genuinely voyeuristic and nasty.

But *M3LL155X* also evolves these ideas further. On 'In Time' subjugation actually becomes self-affirmation over the course of a song; two sensations she had previously performed only separately. At the start of the track, it's clear that the protagonist is in an imbalanced relationship, one where she is far more committed than her lover. Through most of the song she repeats 'you've got a god damn nerve'. At first it's delivered with vitriol, as part of a verbose, half-rapped chorus. At the song's climax though, something changes. Out of nowhere, she delivers that line completely differently: as a long, beautiful note, right from the base of her gut. It's not a small shift; it's the sound of a scorned person declaring: no more.

Two of *M3LL155X*'s songs were born explicitly out of experiences twigs had in America after escaping the music press. She became, for a few months at least, a New Yorker. There, she continued to do what she'd done in every other city she'd ever lived in: she danced. After becoming infatuated with krumping in her early twenties, in New York she also became obsessed with voguing, and started to compete in the kind of Ballroom contests frequented by figures who appear on Blood Orange album covers. She became a regular at Vogue Knights, one of the city's most popular competitions, and made friends with dancers like Jamel Prodigy who helped her up her game when she faced up against rivals. She wasn't given special treatment. Just like anybody else in the room, she'd take the spotlight and, if she flopped, she got chopped. She relished becoming a student again. 'I just respect its honesty,' she told *i-D* magazine. 'I respect that no matter who I am, if I don't train and I go and dance, I'm not gonna get my 10s.' 'Figure 8' is named after a lesson Prodigy taught her: that every twisting movement in voguing revolves around the figure eight.

To this day, dance and dance choreography are central to twigs' identity as an artist. It's pretty normal to tune in to a clip from a festival performance or a spot on late-night television and see her demonstrating three disciplines at once; to find her standing at the front of a stage singing softly amid billowing smoke only to drop into a formation with a gang of male dancers behind her, leading every move. It's not abnormal to see her wrapped around a pole, slowly opening her legs until they form a perfect line, all while continuing to sing. It's not strange to see her dressed like a Roman soothsayer, carefully running a sword along her body, and then striking an attack pose, puncturing the air with the point of the blade.

Of course, it's also not normal at all. I've seen stars perform on huge, arena stages, and watched them struggle to keep up with posses of professional dancers, allowing them to do all the moving on their behalf. There are many spectacular performers who are able to make the audience feel like the show is just for them, or play their instruments like they're extensions of their limbs, but we don't necessarily expect them to dance so brilliantly, so compellingly, that it could be a show all on its own. In videos like the *M3LL155X* short film, or the Congregata tour which followed it, twigs alone has made the utterly exceptional seem predictable, turning her body into spectacular works of art in the process.

The exacting discipline which makes these eclectic talents possible is evident in every aspect of twigs' career. Across her first ten years in music she released only fifty-five songs. Between her first album and her second, there was a gap of five years. Even when projects did arrive, they were succinct. In her search for perfection twigs has shelved entire albums, and left material with the likes of Oneohtrix Point Never and SOPHIE – pioneers many artists long to enter the studio with – unreleased.

M3LL155X's lead single – 'Glass & Patron' – was immediately twigs' most upfront to date; the first of her songs which you could actually imagine making people get down in a club. But don't mistake that for conventional. It opens with the soft, fragile sound of chimes, chopped and stretched for twenty seconds before another instrument even enters the fray. When it does, it's twigs' voice. 'Do you have a lighter?' she sings softly, as a humming, abrasive chord begins to blare. 'Am I dancing sexy yet?' The song tackles the same tensions inherent to acts of performance which appeared in *LP1*. 'I wait all week for a moment's break / Away from being told who I am.' Just as it seems like the song will continue to linger in this haunting moment, a chorus emerges, out of nowhere. The synth grows, amassing scale and intensity until it spasms completely, and then, suddenly, where there was once no rhythm at all, there are drums. 'One, two, three,' she counts, her voice glitching around the mix. 'Hold that pose for me.'

That count is straight from New York City Ballrooms: it's the way MCs often end a round of competition, to give dancers a chance to bask in their applause. Each time twigs says it the song staggers to a halt, the drums drip out, and the loop restarts. This creates a tension; like it's holding back, waiting to play. A nervous energy accumulates. Her first verse reappears but sped up, her words becoming frantic and demented. With each repetition, the instrumental becomes more layered. Ghostly voices join the chant, and the dynamic begins to tilt. 'Shut your eyes and feel the rush,' she urges, her questions becoming commands: 'will you fuck me while I stare at the sun?' Any illusion of serenity pretty much dies with that line. The synths blare, percussion rattling like a ticking clock. Before our very eyes, the song has turned into dance music. The whole thing is a remarkable tease, a slow crawl which becomes a thunderous rush in its final minute. You can see the cameras flashing, beads of sweat flying. It once came on while I was on the exercise bike and, by the time it faded into 'Mothercreep', there was a puddle beneath me on the floor.

As she fostered her talents, twigs acquired dance partners, and soon set about putting them at the forefront of her work. Jamel Prodigy appears in the music video for 'Glass & Patron', dancing on a bizarre forest catwalk alongside a troupe which also includes members of Wet Wipez, a krumping crew she'd befriended in London. Prodigy praised her for doing what other artists who'd been interested in queer subculture had failed to. 'At the time, [Madonna] didn't really celebrate, say, Jose Xtravaganza the way she needed to,' he told *VICE* in 2015. 'twigs allows me to have a voice . . . She wouldn't want it to seem like she is the vogue mother. She understands that she is still a student.' In her early music videos twigs was noticeably alone, but in the video for 'Glass & Patron', she was surrounded by a crowd. The balance of power in her songs was beginning to tilt.

In 2012 twigs was working as a backup dancer just to pay the bills, but only three years later, she had become a professional dancer; a performance artist; a director, producer and musician of some considerable acclaim. She continued to do the only thing she'd ever known: work diligently, and incessantly. In the twelve months after the release of *LP1* she toured the UK, the US, Europe and Australia. She performed twice at Coachella and then began touring again, putting on a series of shows she called Congregata, which she designed with Alexander McQueen and which featured meticulous group choreography. In July she staged *Soundtrack 7*, a week-long residency at the Manchester International Festival where she allowed the public to watch her create and film a new dance piece each day for a week, which was then turned into a film.

At the start of her career, twigs manifested a prolificity which seemed superhuman, especially given the physical nature of her shows. But events beyond her control were about to stop everything in their tracks. twigs had released four projects in three years, but her next album would take four more to complete. At times, she even began to doubt whether she'd make another at all.

In 2016, twigs performed a series of seven shows across Russia, Norway and North America titled Radiant Me², which seemed to be the start of a new era, debuting three collaborations with Oneohtrix Point Never and SOPHIE. That same year she released the airy, gushing single 'Good to Love', another false start which remained a loosie. Things began to stall.

The truth was, twigs had come to resent the expectations which *LP1* had placed upon her. Her music had been detailed and labyrinthine: that's what she was known for, what she was *acclaimed* for. But even as she began to crave something different, she found that producers were just presenting her with work which felt like more of the same. 'I wanted something simpler, something honest,' she later told *The Guardian* in 2019. 'It felt like I'd made this ornate golden birdcage, and everything was so intricate, like tapestries and beading and beautiful wirework . . . I was like, "oh my gosh, this is actually a nightmare".' The recording of new music was complicated further when her personal life descended into turmoil. Her engagement to Robert Pattinson ended in 2017 and twigs experienced a heartbreak which she described as 'all-encompassing'. Shortly afterwards she became, for the first time in her life, dangerously ill.

Her second album, the record which would eventually be named *MAGDALENE*, was a reaction to both of those things: an ornate, emotionally upfront record, rich, for the first time, with acoustic instrumentation. Although she had been searching for several years, she eventually discovered the sound she'd been looking for in the space of a single day. It began with two of the greatest musical minds of their generation, sat in a studio, jamming.

'Thousand Eyes' – the opening song on *MAGDALENE* and the first written for it – happened quickly. When twigs began working on new music, her label Young reached out to renowned electronic artists for her to meet with, as they had done with Arca. SOPHIE and Oneohtrix Point Never were two of the names they approached, and another was Chilean-American producer Nicolás Jaar. twigs asked whether he wanted to meet her in the studio.

Despite the detailed, tactile textures of his music, Jaar is somebody who works fast, and believes in the honesty of improvisation. (In 2012 he launched *From Scratch*, a live concert series in New York where he sampled only records he had purchased earlier that day.) They met in the studio together one day in 2017. As they chatted, twigs' dog Solo loitering around their feet, Jaar began to play the sombre, dainty piano part which would become the 'Thousand Eyes' central motif. twigs, who professes to begin singing almost intuitively to just about anything, started to improvise on top of it. 'If I walk out the door, it starts our last goodbye,' she whispered, eyes closed. 'If you don't pull me back, it wakes a thousand eyes.'

Within twenty minutes the core of the tune was written and, by the end of the day, a version of the song close to what we hear at the start of her second album was complete. It was passionate, and concise. twigs and Jaar were delighted, and she knew where she wanted to go next.

It will always be a mistake to conflate an artist's lyrics with their literal reality, but it's hard not to assume that simple lyric she wrote for 'Thousand Eyes' is about the end of a romance, and the intense public scrutiny which followed. In 2020 she wrote that the title 'refers to the chorus of people who have an opinion on the choices made in one's life'.

Indeed, there is no group of people on this planet more shamelessly relentless than the tabloid press, and that press took an intense interest in twigs' life when she became engaged to one of her generation's most famous sex symbols. Looking back, the images which were taken of them, photographs snapped as they walked down the street or left the back entrance of a club, are excruciating in their intrusiveness. The *Daily Mail* began writing articles with headlines including 'Braless FKA twigs leaves little to the imagination in flirty frock as she takes her tired pet pooch along to lunch date'; pieces which (as they tend to for so many young, female celebrities) luxuriated in the sexualisation of a person doing something as ordinary as walking their dog. For the non-famous, it's hard to comprehend the horror that this must inflict upon a person, let alone someone as infamously reclusive as twigs; but it's all there in 'Thousand Eyes', simply and honestly, just as she longed for it to be.

When you play 'Thousand Eyes' after *M3LL155X*, you can literally hear Nicolás Jaar arrive in twigs' world. If those earlier songs were like ornate birdcages, then Jaar's sound, though equally synthetic, feels far more fluid than that. In his world, every sound has weight and each element emerges organically from the other. The timbres he laces into a song trigger a gravitational response. In 'Thousand Eyes', when horns begin to blare, little shards of sound splinter.

The song begins with the most intimate sound in music: a solitary voice, singing in a void. twigs repeats that refrain softly, high in her register, as if the words are drifting out from her throat. But quiet sadness soon transforms into explosive devastation. Blasts of horns shatter the church-like calm and twigs' voice responds, becoming tense; panicked even. As twigs delivers a gorgeous falsetto in the song's third minute, her voice breaks into pieces and each fragment melts into the other, like rain trickling down concrete stairs. The song's low-end begins to rumble, like the earth itself has vanished beneath her. The instrumental morphs into a splintered cacophony so exhausting that the final minute of the song seems to exist simply as a cool-down: the last siphoning of gutted adrenaline.

Eventually, Nicolás Jaar became *MAGDALENE*'s most overarching collaborator. When the record was done, he and twigs sat in a studio as the songs were mixed and mastered, refining every detail. Yet still, when her label released a press release which listed him as an executive producer, Jaar asked for it to be corrected, saying that it was a misrepresentation. 'There's some truth to the fact that, at the very end of making that record, she and I were going through every single song and honing them in,' he told me via video call, 'but I saw the final track-list and realised that the vision of the record was twigs' specific vision. At the end of the day, she was the producer and I didn't feel comfortable taking credit. I was working on a lot of things which already had an incredible, beautiful trajectory before I ever was involved.'*

Nicolás is a particular and idiosyncratic writer, but *MAGDALENE* remains the only record he has produced for another artist. He was born in New York to Evelyne Meynard, a dancer, and Alfredo Jaar, the famous Chilean photographer and architect. Across the 2010s he became one of the decade's most eclectic and astounding new voices. He spent his childhood between Santiago and Chile's dominating colonial power, America. With Palestinian ancestry on his father's side, he emerged from a distinctly New York scene to become an ethnographer of the sounds of Latin America and the Middle East. 'His music is so familiar to anyone who has grown up listening

---

* In the spring of 2023 I spoke to Nicolás to ask about his experience working on *MAGDALENE*. He was warm and passionate, but bristled at artists like himself being referred to as 'producers' at all. 'What is the song?' he asked me. 'The song is a central kind of melody and lyrics, right? This is, in most Western conceptions of what a song is, the way that the voice is singing and the piano and the melody and the notes. But, for example, percussion is left completely out of that. You could say, "oh, you could have any beat on top of that, that doesn't matter, that's not part of the song . . ." That's an extremely particular way of understanding songwriting. To this day we believe that a drummer would never be a writer because he or she didn't play any notes, which is wrong. Every single drum sound is a note, it's just that we have a certain conception of the notes. You asked me what production versus writing is and I don't see them as that distinct. Every single sound that you could produce is going to have notes, is going to have overtones, and it's a kind of hegemonic decision to say: those are not notes that count. It's a particular system that decides that.'

to folk music from the Global South,' said Pakistani-American singer Ali Sethi. 'I kept hearing it in random places. On a rooftop in Lahore one rainy night, some guy who was passing out was playing [Nicolás] on a loop. I was in Istanbul and I heard the azan from a mosque and then afterwards I heard some music and was like, "that's Nico!", and of course it was.'

Like twigs, Jaar was a teenage prodigy. He released his first EP on the label Wolf + Lamb in 2008, when he was only seventeen. Listening to it now, that music doesn't feel like it was written by a teenager. There was no EDM era in Jaar's career. Those first releases were incredibly elusive, more akin to cult Portuguese composer Nuno Canavarro than David Guetta.

While Jaar was a student in New York, he became enmeshed in the city's burgeoning left-field electronic scene. Wolf + Lamb's founder, Gadi Mizrahi, suggested to Jaar that he start adding 4/4 kick drums into his songs to give the people something to dance to. It was a new direction for Jaar but not an alien one, adoring as he was of fellow Chilean producer Ricardo Villalobos. Before he was even of drinking age, and with tunes like 'Time for Us' in hand, he began to perform live sets at Wolf + Lamb's legendary Marcy club nights at the Marcy Hotel.* But Jaar always seemed an uncomfortable fit, even among that more cerebral crowd. 'Back then everything DJs were playing was 128 beats per minute,' Mizrahi told the *New York Times*, the stuff [Nico] was doing was almost half that speed.'

Jaar's debut album was the first taste of what he was truly capable of. Released in January 2011, *Space Is Only Noise*, is about texture above all else. Sometimes the songs groove, sometimes they simmer, but each of them possesses a fascinat-

---

* Not a hotel at all, but a stripped three-story building which they turned into a rave spot.

ing, detail-driven tension. The songs are often moulded around specific worldly timbres, like the sound of cascading ping-pong balls on 'Colomb'. Basslines sound like rubber; songs are built around the sound of trickling water. Jaar's voice often hovers above it all, pitched downwards and whispering incantations. It's music full of inherent contradictions – the sort often hastily labelled 'intelligent dance music'. The album *is* intelligent, but it's not academic. It's about sensory pleasures above all else. Songs like the 'Problems with the Sun' are legitimately funky, just filtered through a woozy, golden-hour daze.

From this record onwards, Jaar's music splintered in a dozen different directions. In 2012, he started both his label – Other People – and the band Darkside, a project which somehow finds a middle ground between blues, funk and sweet, blissful ambience.* In 2018 he released a slick, soul-sampling house album under the alias Against All Logic; a surprise success given the fact that he released it, at first, with no mention of own name.† In 2020, he turned that moniker into something far angrier with the album's sequel; songs like 'Deeeeeeefers' being close to industrial music in their pummelling ferocity. Listening to *Against All Logic 2017–2019* felt like watching Muhammad Ali go at Joe Frazier in Manilla: a sophisticated fighter turned into a battering ram; a calculated artist going absolutely buck-wild.

In 2016 he released a triptych of albums, the most famous of them being *Sirens*. It's an album which, like *Freetown Sound*, deploys a tapestry approach to personal history; featuring both Chilean instrumentation and Spanish, the native tongue of his

* Their first actual release appeared online a few months earlier under the name DaftSide, a brutalist, album-length remix of Daft Punk's *Random Access Memories* entitled *Random Access Memories Memories*. (They're that kind of band.)

† The same cannot for said for 2014's harsh, dissonant *Ancient Astronaut*, which few have heard to this day.

mother. The percussive 'No' is a direct allusion to the 1988 Chilean referendum, where 'no' meant a rejection of the brutal, US-backed dictator Augusto Pinochet, and 'yes' represented an embrace of democracy. Jaar's music, often wordless, challenges our idea of the kind of music which can be expressly political in this way.

Another record in his triptych was *Pomegranates*, a collection of instrumental tracks he compiled from various ambient sketches he composed in hotel rooms, studios and airports. He arranged them into a makeshift soundtrack for *The Color of Pomegranates*, an experimental Soviet film about an Armenian poet, Sayat-Nova, which was already forty-one years old.

The album, which he released for free in June 2015, is vivid in a way I can only describe as visual. It's an electronic record filled with acoustic instrumentation like a rich, bluesy piano. Each of its twenty vignettes have such a remarkable sense of place and time which are so evocative of specific moods and eras and places that they conjure, through sound alone, pictures in the mind. 'Pass the Time' immediately brings to life a lonely traveller with a ragged bag strewn across his shoulder, making his way down a winding desert path. 'Near Death' seems to capture a sun-baked person, crawling along the floor, grasping for a well they'll never reach. 'Muse' feels like an entire funeral procession within a song: the procession, the flowers, the coffin; everything. It's astonishing, disorientating art. Out of all of the albums I name in this book, I've listened to *Pomegranates* the most, just throwing it on and letting it fill up the room.

In 2020 Nicolás released the grand, majestic *Telas*, which had the same effect as the small fragments of *Pomegranates* on a far broader scale. I asked Jaar about these two records – two of his least known – and he lit up, saying that they are the ones he's proudest of. Despite the existence of albums like *Sirens* – which have a specific, vocalised philosophy – I think they are also his most meaningful. 'What I gravitate to in regards to purely instrumental music is that it says things in another language. I think that other language is really, really, really necessary. Unfortunately, people – journalists particularly – need things to hold on to and so that kind of music doesn't seem to hold so much for people. It ends up sounding like the most pretentious music, despite the fact that it's often the most honest.'

It may not be a fashionable moment for it, but the time-tested idea that instrumental music is capable of not only conveying emotional truths but political ones is at the heart of Jaar's approach to songwriting. Much of his discography is filled with inexplicable feats of sound design like the ones which unfold in the closing moments of 'Thousand Eyes'. Because of their creaking, organic quality, many of them sound more like chemical reactions than carefully constructed stems. It's a dazzling illusion. I asked him about the philosophy of that sound, and why he keeps so many of the cracks and strains present in his instrumentals when so many artists choose to polish theirs out.

'For me, I want to hear the machine working,' he told me. 'I want to know what is there, and also what is there but not shown. I want to know the labour that is written down on paper and I want to know the invisible labour that has taken place too. In the past twenty or twenty-five years, since DAWs started becoming a predominant way to make music, they started finding ways to stretch music . . . If you want a drumbeat played at 120BPM to be warped to 140, you can do that. Most of the time, when changing the actual time signature of a sample, you can decide to make that change as non-recognisable as possible and say "hey, look at this magic trick!" Often I choose to say: no, this is not a magic trick. There's a machine working here and I want people to hear that machine as much as possible.'

*

Even after the breakthrough of 'Thousand Eyes', twigs' work on her next record was quickly set back by a series of misfortunes. Even while she was making that song, she knew that there was something wrong with her body: a crippling pain in the middle of her stomach. She shot a video where she was voguing and she remembers the choreographers getting frustrated with her stalling the entire time, calling her lazy and moaning that she was always going to the toilet.

'My whole life, I'd never been called lazy,' she told *The Guardian* in 2019. 'It made me break down.' She ignored the pain for as long as she could bear it but by the time she called her father to explain, she could hardly sit upright. Her dad insisted she take herself to a doctor, and she was diagnosed with fibroids: non-cancerous growths which develop in the womb, and which Black women are especially susceptible to.

In December 2017 twigs underwent laparoscopic surgery to remove them. She had six fibroids in total, and they were large. 'The size of two cooking apples, three kiwis and a couple of strawberries,' she wrote on Instagram. 'A fruit bowl of pain every day. The nurse said that the weight and size was like being six months pregnant.' For twigs, daily, ritualistic training had always been a form of meditation. Losing both her health and her ability to move broke her confidence, and she was left feeling lonely and directionless.

As always, work was twigs' salvation. She hurried her return. At the start of 2018, director Spike Jonze called her up and asked whether she would be interested in starring in an advert for the Apple HomePod, scored by a song from Anderson .Paak. twigs was only four weeks out of surgery and said yes, thinking that the ad would take some time to make. Instead, Jonze asked her to fly out the following week.

Jonze is the man who made Christopher Walken rock out to Fatboy Slim and had a human bloodhound stroll the feet of New York for Daft Punk, so the finished product was no Skoda advert. In it, twigs plays an office worker who trudges to her apartment after a day at work, and turns on the HomePod to unwind. As she begins to dance she realises that her limbs can control the very fabric of reality, and as she moves, she turns her flat into a playground: extending sofas, raising tables, turning walls into tunnels of many-coloured light. It's exciting, silly and chaotic, and it was agony to make. twigs had been told not to walk for six weeks after the surgery, and yet here she was, dancing. 'I looked like death,' she told *i-D*. 'I looked disgusting. I wasn't supposed to be moving. And Spike's like, "Okay, so we're gonna play the song and I need you to dance around your living room to it." I was fully going for it and literally feeling like my uterus was gonna fall out. I didn't tell them about the surgery or that I had all these stitches in my bellybutton . . . It was grim.'

While recovering from her surgery twigs had become fascinated by a piece of history which had always intrigued her: the life of Mary Magdalene. Even while she was in the studio recording 'Thousand Eyes', Nicolás told me that she was reading a book about her.

twigs' interest in the Apostle of the Apostles began at her Catholic school in Cheltenham where, unsurprisingly, she heard her name often. Even as a teenager, she felt wary that the stories she was hearing might be dictated by the perspectives of men. twigs had, like many of us, known Magdalene simply as a disciple of Jesus and a prostitute but, as she read more about her, she discovered that she had been much more than that. According to the Bible, Magdalene was Jesus' closest confidante; she was a herbalist and healer and it was her wealth which funded his travels through the Middle East. The idea that the truth of her life had been twisted through the ages until she became nothing more than a follower of Christ struck a chord with twigs.

'No matter what you're doing or how great your work is,' she told *i-D* in 2019, 'sometimes it's as though you have to be attached to a man to be validated. I'd felt like that at times.' Through realising the distance between the perception of who Mary Magdalene was and the historical truth, the saint became, for twigs, what Julius Eastman had been to Devonté Hynes. She was a guiding light; a figure whose story was corrupted by a history written by its winners, and whose power was overlooked for reasons she herself understood well.*

MAGDALENE, it should be said, is *not* a concept album about its namesake, but researching the saint's life did unlock a chain of thought which unfolds throughout the record. twigs was fascinated by the dichotomy of a woman who has two legacies: as a prostitute, and someone with access to the divine. In the story there is, after all, both extremes of the traditional conception of femininity: the virginal and the impure, the sinful and the saintly. It was a dichotomy and

---

* It transpires that even the notion of Magdalene as a prostitute is false, a misconception set in stone by one man's blunder. In 591, Pope Gregory I gave a speech where he somehow confused Mary Magdalene with Mary of Bethany, a barely-referenced 'sinful woman' from the book of Luke. In an age of widespread illiteracy, the words of the Pope mattered a great deal and that mistake stuck as truth, making the image of the 'virgin whore' synonymous with Magdalene's name until 1969 when Pope Paul VI formally rescinded his predecessor's error. Regardless, it's very hard to imagine such a false image persisting about someone who funded Jesus' expeditions, served as his confidante and was (so the story goes) the first to lay eyes upon him after his resurrection, if that person had been a man.

an illusion twigs had encountered as a shy, introverted girl performing on the cabaret stage, and one she had written into the songs of *LP1*, which veered between the extremely passive and sexually dominant.

'I recognise myself as both of these things,' she told *NPR* in 2019. Mary Magdalene isn't present in every song, but her myth haunts the album like a holy ghost. In the portrait which adorns the LP's cover (a digital painting by Matthew Stone, the man who photographed twigs for her first magazine shoot), twigs lies baroque and resplendent, but the visage is not a literal one. Like the statue of María Lionza, twigs' muscles are masculine and rippling, her body laid out like a lion in repose. But this is a fragile portrait of a powerful person. The paint which comprises twigs' body is flaying, peeling away and leaving nothing but vacant space beneath. Even her eyes have been stolen, replaced by only mottled specks of colour. It's art which matches the music, and across her second album twigs adorns herself with supreme power, while reckoning with emotional devastation.

MAGDALENE is a document of a period in twigs' life which she was leaving behind as she was recording it. twigs even called her manager in tears one day during the making of the record, suddenly realising that she was making an album full of songs about heartbreak which she'd have to live through night after night on tour. Following her fibroid surgery, she settled in LA and began a period of extended solitude. 'I was in a sad place, mentally,' she told *NME*, 'and I didn't want to come out of it. I don't have many friends there, and wasn't communicating with my friends or family. I just went and locked myself off.'

She replaced the outside world with an obsession with defunct fashion label Gunne Sax, who made dresses inspired by the American Gothic era: all laced bodices and puffed sleeves. They were rare and expensive but she went to a vintage fair and came across one – a white, medieval dress – and lived in it for weeks, wandering around Los Angeles, looking like a prairie maiden. Eventually, she returned to the studio and began to record again, picking up the ornate, piano-led sound she'd forged on 'Thousand Eyes' a year earlier. It was around this time that she wrote 'cellophane', another song which would set the tone for the record to come.

It's hard to overstate just how strange it was to hear 'cellophane' in 2019, three years after FKA twigs had last released a note. Her music was, so far, defined by those ornate, electronic constructions, but 'cellophane' is startlingly bare, lit by some soft beatboxing which feels like a waning heartbeat. Recorded in a time of solitude, it's a desolate, lonely song; perhaps her saddest. She had been vulnerable before, but here she sounds like a small child, thrust under a spotlight, singing to empty stalls. She gives a vocal performance which is dexterous but deceptively so, like Roberta Flack on 'The First Time Ever I Saw Your Face'. She's in total control, scaling from a soft, breathy soprano into a searing falsetto seamlessly. She stays true to the linguistic concision which had served her well on *LP1,* sticking to short and cutting phrases. 'Why don't I do it for you? / Why won't you do it for me / When all I do is for you?' There's a world of pain in those three variations on the same seven-word question: the pain for a love unrequited, and of a public life which demands the world. The take we hear on the record is the first she ever recorded, and she was crying as she sung it.

Around the time she was writing 'cellophane', twigs filmed her parts for the music video of A$AP Rocky's 'Fukk Sleep', an ominous, slinky cut from his austere third LP *Testing,* on which she appears. In it, she and Rocky – dressed like *Blade Runner* extras – smash up a bodega and terrorise the diners in a high-class restaurant. Then, as she delivers her verse, she pole-dances. When she was nineteen and working as a hostess in a gentlemen's club, a stripper taught twigs her first pole move: a back-hook spin. At the end of 2016, she sought out pole-choreographer Kelly Yvonne with plans to incorporate pole dancing into an ad-campaign she was directing and became immersed in the process. After finishing 'Fukk Sleep', she decided that the video for 'cellophane' would be based entirely around a pole routine, and not just a pole routine, but one enacted so virtuosically that she could pass as a goddess. It would have been easy to hire a stunt double or edit around her flaws, but instead twigs began taking pole classes, practising every single day for a year until she felt she was ready.

After reading about the deep connection between Black artists and Chinese martial arts (which had been at the foundation of hip hop's most famous Clan) twigs also took up wushu taolu, the sporting variety of an ancient Chinese martial art which involves artful performance with a razor-thin jian sword. twigs named hers Lilith. Wushu was the ideal counterweight for her training on the pole because it requires the body to stay low to the ground and weighted in the pelvis. twigs hired a vocal coach too, to help open up her voice after the strains of surgery, resulting in the lower, stronger tones she delivers across *MAGDALENE*. Before long, she was being coached in three disciplines, all while working on her second album. She was committed to a degree that any reasonable person would find maddening.

Efua Baker, twigs' fitness trainer, told the *New York Times* that 'people are quite confused, especially men, by [twigs'] two completely different energies': her soft demeanour and her immoveable dedication to discipline. In school and throughout adolescence, these two archetypes – the athlete and the artist – are framed in diametric opposition. In a way though, training the body and writing a song are two variations on the same sheer feat of commitment: the pursuit of something ludicrous and painful, and the will to get there regardless. In *What I Talk About When I Talk About Running*, novelist and marathon runner Haruki Murakami put the physicality of the creative process into words: 'writing novels, to me, is basically a kind of manual labor. Writing itself is mental labor, but finishing an entire book is closer to manual labour.' No other living musician better embodies this reality than FKA twigs, who uses her body to translate the emotional toil of her songs into physical feats which can be witnessed on a stage.

When speaking to the press, twigs' choreographers went to great lengths to emphasise just how committed she had been to her training for the 'cellophane' video, and how much exertion the filming actually took. For the four-minute clip she was on the pole for eight hours, holding her body weight most of the time, absorbing the bruises which are unavoidable in a discipline where metal and skin are in permanent tension. To get to the point where she, as a novice, was able to conduct the magic trick of total ease and smoothness, twigs worked with her choreographer to select specific moves it would be realistic to master in such a short window, and decided how many hours each one would take to learn. If a trick required thirty sessions, then she booked out thirty hours. In the two weeks before the video shoot, twigs stuck to her schedule meticulously, more like a boxer training for a fight than a singer preparing to film a music video. Even when she pulled it off convincingly, Kelly Yvonne stressed the enormity of the task. 'Don't let her fool you,' she told the *New York Times*. 'It was easy for *her*. But it's not easy for the average person. I've coached over a hundred dancers and I've never seen anything like her.'

The 'cellophane' music video is a masterpiece. It begins with twigs, dressed in fur, peering at her spotlight from behind a curtain. Things become surreal the second she brushes her way onto the stage. We hear the cheers of an audience, but there is none, and the pole waiting for her in the middle of the crescent seems to stretch higher than it should be able: straight up into the sky. twigs drapes her coat on the floor and struts across the stage in nothing but a bikini and a pair of colossal stilettos. We can hear them tap like a sword upon glass as she makes her way towards the pole. She grabs the metal and leans away from it, writhing at the hips, dropping to the ground until her eyes are level with the camera and she's crawling on the woodwork. As she manoeuvres further upwards she climbs, absurdly, into the clouds themselves. Then she is approached in the sky by a metal-masked creature: her own visage depicted in mottled brass. Upon placing her heel in its mouth it splinters, and she spirals towards an unseen underworld, finishing the song's haunting final moments writhing in clay-red mud.

Andrew Huang's direction is so perfectly attuned to the music that it's easy to forget just how abnormal what we're seeing really is. Firstly, there's the cultural contradiction. Pole dancing is a type of performance usually disregarded as the stuff of strip clubs and the lurid, HBO shows which are set there. Here though, twigs uses that pole as a display of total female ascendancy. But this isn't straightforward empowerment. Even more strange is that this scene, the epitome of grace and physical strength, is scored by, of all songs, 'cellophane' – a tragic ballad, filled with utter self-deprecation. Taken as a whole, it's a glorious alignment of cinematography, physicality and music, but it's also a rebuttal of the idea of artistic accomplishment being equivalent to personal zen. To sing a song about being a failure 'whilst doing these amazing tricks on the pole,' she told *i-D*, 'there's almost something humorous about that.'

*

With her health on an upward trajectory, twigs spent several months recording the album across New York, Los Angeles and London. More than half a dozen names are listed as producers and co-writers on the record: Nicolás Jaar, Noah Goldstein, Michael Uzowuru, Skrillex, Koreless, Benny Blanco, Cashmere Cat, Sounwave, Jack Antonoff and Oneohtrix Point Never. Any project shared between so many names has the potential to veer into chaos, and so twigs was determined to make a record which still sounded distinctly like her despite the idiosyncrasies of her many collaborators. As such, she made sure to work only with people who were capable of being totally egoless; willing to see their ideas dismissed or discarded. Given the fact that most of her chosen collaborators were also male, she needed them to access their feminine sensibility too.

twigs isn't trained in any musical instrument so she recruited people who were virtuosic with theirs. She would sing them a melody or a rhythm, and they would help her translate it with their playing. Sometimes, these requests were nebulous. For 'mary magdalene', she asked Koreless to create the effect of witches burning at the pyre; for 'mirrored heart' she requested a synth which sounded like it was crying. It inspires a fun game of wondering what twigs might have asked for in the record's most sonically acrobatic moments, like three minutes and fifty seconds into 'sad day' when the song's drop seems to pause-stumble backwards in mid-air. A gymnast falling down a well? A scene from a *John Wick* sequel set in outer space?

twigs would sit in a room and develop ideas with one artist and then pass each song, like a little parcel, from person to person, having them change it as they went. Sometimes a whole song would be revised, other times she'd add just a single note. 'mirrored heart', for example, started with a guitar riff she suggested to her childhood friend Cy An, which she began singing over. To that Koreless added the deep, squelching bass which intensifies as her falsetto plummets. Then she took the song to the studio of producer Rick Nowels (who had credits on songs with the likes of Madonna and Lana Del Rey) just to use his vintage amps, running the song through them again and again until the synths sounded like a spasming heart.

MAGDALENE was released on the 8th of November 2019. The most noticeable thing about it, at first pass, is just how beautiful it is. There are a few albums, released over the last ten years – like Björk's *Utopia* and Arooj Aftab's *Vulture Prince* – which just absolutely luxuriate in prettiness and splendour, and I would absolutely put *MAGDALENE* among its ranks. On the third anniversary of its release, twigs released a perfume of the same name, and I can't think of a record better suited to be turned into a scent.

twigs' wish to deliver something as straightforward as beauty was born out of an intensified creative process. In 2014, twigs had told *Rolling Stone* how she approached songwriting on *LP1*. 'I put in everything I can think of: everything, everything,' she said, 'until it's just a massive wall, sometimes with no BPM, no structure, nothing. Then the next day I'd go in and just chip away at it, and keep on chipping.' On *MAGDALENE*, she pursued this process of reduction further than she ever had, until some of the songs, the likes of 'daybed' and 'cellophane', make her earlier songs feel claustrophobic by comparison.

This preference for quiet, and a newfound focus on her voice, helped her to deliver the kind of emotional directness which she desired from the outset. What's most striking about *LP1* or *M3LL155X* is their aesthetic: these strange sounds and textures, and the way her voice finds a place among them. With *MAGDALENE*, what's more impactful is the absolute directness with which its author captures the torments of her life. The sheer directness of her words reminds me of songs from the crooner era, when it feels like there was less of an inclination to couch a pure sentiment in floridness. 'I'm never gonna give up / Though I'm probably gonna think about you all the time,' she sings, over a coughing, splitting synth. 'For all the lovers who found a mirrored heart / they just remind me I'm without you.'

MAGDALENE is an album with a clear centrepiece and, unusually, that song features one long instrumental break in place of a chorus. 'mary magdalene' functions as the album's spiritual heart, a dive into mysticism which gives the biblical and mythological allusions scattered through the record a point of context. In the lyrics, twigs alludes to the mythology of womanhood; of sex, or seduction, and of motherhood. 'A woman's hands / So dark and provocative' she sings in near silence. 'A nurturing breath that could stroke / Your divine confidence'. She promises to lift us higher. She calls herself a 'creature of desire'. She threatens to 'do it like Mary Magdalene'. Then, around two minutes in, the song erupts into something stunning; a long, languorous melody which unravels like a spool of thread. It returns in greater force after the second verse, a wash of taut, spiralling notes which drive through the sound of a crackling flame, exploding upwards and carrying the ghost of her voice with it. Somehow that moment, in combination with her words, delivers all of the promise of the first verse; all of the passion and the mystery and the pain.

Unsurprisingly, 'mary magdalene' was the album's hardest-won song. Dozens of different iterations existed, from pulsing electronica to a slow balladic version. The song was stuck in a state of arrested development for months, until it was solved in a single night at Electric Lady Studios. twigs and Nicolás Jaar were sat at Prince's old mixing board, its surface still painted purple, listening to what they had. A caffeine-wired Jaar asked her to give him a moment, and went about overhauling the entire instrumental section in a flurry, finding what twigs called 'a hardness in air' that she'd been seeking for months. As she watched him work, she stayed utterly silent, terrified that she might break the spell if she even dared to move.

The album's track-list shifted constantly before it was finalised. Nicolás told me that, for a long time, 'cellophane' was the opening track: a tonal shift which would have changed the mood of the entire album to follow. One single was such a late addition that Jaar wasn't even aware of its existence until he saw the final track-list online: the song 'holy terrain', featuring Future.

For that collaboration, twigs contacted the rapper directly, by text. She was nervous and so, when he messaged her back immediately, she threw her phone across the room in a panic. His was the first guest vocal to ever appear on an FKA twigs album and, despite feeling intimidated, she still made sure that she got exactly what she wanted out of him. The song was, like most of the rest, a long work in progress, and it was Skrillex this time who was essential to making sense of the chaos: spending two days piecing together all of the song's 200 individual parts, including warped strings, ad-libs and a Bulgarian folk sample. When the song dropped as a single, two months ahead of the album's release, it was divisive. Haunted by the likes of Kendrick Lamar rapping with Maroon 5, hip hop features still carry – for many millennial music fans – the implication of a pop artist trying desperately for a hit. Unlike when K.Dot teamed up with Adam Levine though, Future actually sounds like he's trying.

In the 2010s, Future (born Nayvadius DeMun Cash in Atlanta) became one of the most inconsistent and yet undeniably influential, voices in rap. At his least inspired, Cash is a monotonous presence on the mic: a purveyor of empty debauchery whose woozy, lean-steeped flow so easily tips into tedium. At his best though – on 'Codeine Crazy' or 'Purple Reign' – the opposite becomes true, and that messy delivery becomes captivating: a gruff, ragged flow almost bluesy in its sombreness. It's for that reason that Future slips so well into *MAGDALENE*'s eclectic canvas. On an album about womanhood, he's the only male presence. His bars latch onto the record's fascination with duality from a macho point of view. Here he's not a Gucci-obsessed addict (as he is on his worst songs) but a tragic figure, aware of the impact of his vices but too infatuated to step away from them. 'He's just talking about his downfalls as a man: how he's sorry and asking for healing,' twigs told *i-D* in 2019. 'I love sad Future. I love when he gets emo, when he expresses himself.'

The rapper's mournfulness stands in sharp contrast to twigs' presence on the song, a successor of sorts to 'Two Weeks' where she frames her sex in biblical terms: 'I'm blue when the moon hits my skin right / Hot pink when you open up my sweet thighs.' It's a statement of dominance which offsets the heartbreak which runs throughout the record. 'daybed' is another more blissful spot; the slowest song twigs had released since *EP1*, and a rare moment of emotional tranquillity. The word 'daybed' seems pulled straight from the Victorian era the Gunne Sax dresses she collects so strongly evoked. She plays a lady in waiting on the song too, reclining in onanistic perpetuity as her home gathers dust around her. 'Fearless are my cacti,' she sings, 'friendly are the fruit flies.' It's a liberated image and a decadent one (that kind of permanent rest is, after all, a luxury of the rich) but, as with the solitary dance of 'cellophane', it's a lonely picture too.

Loneliness is at the heart of the album's best song too. At only three minutes and forty-five seconds, 'home with you' is one of the LP's shortest tracks yet somehow feels like the record's most sprawling. It feels like it contains every sound and mode from across the record within the space of a single song. *MAGDALENE* is a wonderful album, but you only really need to listen to 'home with you' to understand it.

It begins with a snarl: twigs at her most spiteful and vengeful. Throughout the recording of the album she used a vocal processor called a TC Helicon, and, on 'home with you', it shapes her voice into a throaty snarl. It was the closest she'd ever come to straight-up rap. 'How come the more you have / the more that people want from you?' she drawls, jaw hung loose. It's sinister, one of the most ominous moments of her career, but it doesn't last. All of the clipping and the sub-bass and the Helicon snarl vanishes, in an instant. Suddenly, her sweet, blissful voice is back in full flight, and suddenly she's full of empathy, like someone who has finally confessed a fatal weakness. 'I didn't know that you were lonely' she sings. 'If you'd have just told me, I'd be home with you.' A rich, acoustic piano picks up beneath her. Towards the end of each rapped verse, we can hear the effect waning and the spite fading with it. 'Mary Magdalene would never let her loved ones down,' she sighs.

The two contradictory modes of a person which are examined throughout all of twigs' work are present most explicitly in 'home with you', rubbing up against each other. After that fleeting moment of connection, she vanishes again. She snarls, drums start to thump. But it's a resistance which she can't maintain for long. In the song's final act, the buzzing electronic components fade away and the song is fully, completely transformed into a gushing proclamation of devotion. It's a soaring ballad in an ANOHNI and the Johnsons vein; twigs is running across fields towards the object of the song, wind in her hair, a huge grin on her face.

When I was a teenager, I was lonely often. I'd spent my childhood so content with my books and my music that, when puberty hit and I looked around my classroom and realised I didn't have a single friend, it caused a kind of panic and depression which took me years to shake. Loneliness is an acute and rare kind of torture because it's the only form of pain which it's impossible to share, caused cruelly by the very lack of somebody to share it with. It wasn't until 'home with you' that I'd ever heard anyone put that feeling into song. The rush which arrives at its end, the way twigs' voice lifts until it's an ecstatic cry, bathed in strings and fluttering clarinets, is a big, gushing, tidal wave of connection: 'I didn't know that you were lonely' she soars, 'If you'd have just told me . . . I'd have told you I was lonely too.'

In November 2019 I watched twigs perform her *MAGDALENE* tour at the Brixton Academy in London. It was one of the final concerts I'd see before the pandemic swept the world a few months later, and I sat in the velvet stalls oblivious to the fact that, when it was over, I wouldn't be able to see live music again for two years. twigs' show wasn't a 'gig' of the kind I was used to seeing often: it was a *performance*, proper and true. The tour's set list was fixed every night of the tour, which enabled twigs to plot a show with theatrical scale. She wielded a sword and tap-danced, sometimes in baroque dresses, sometimes hardly in anything all. In moments it felt like being in a Ballroom for Vogue Knights in New York City; other times it felt like being in a ballroom in eighteenth century France. twigs' expressed aim for the tour was to produce Gesamtkunstwerk – a 'total work of art' – and she delivered on that promise. To see one person achieve so much – to dance spectacularly while singing those eerie, labyrinthine songs, which she'd written too – was one of the more spectacular things I've ever seen.

One of the most enduring notions in popular music is the veritable bad-assery of the (mostly male) musicians who spend their careers doing high-quality drugs and desecrating themselves in ways which are public, gross and *totally awesome*. The legacy of Tommy Lee and Keith Moon and Axl Rose persists far beyond rock music. One of the most embarrassing musical moments of the 2010s was the sight of rapper-turned-pop-punker Machine Gun Kelly, dressed like Johnny Rotten, rocking out to his own music on the table of an Interscope boardroom, diligently avoiding all the coffee cups scattered around him. Green Day promoted their dire 2020 LP with a poster which read 'no features, no Swedish songwriters, no trap beats, just 100% pure, uncut rock'. Liam Gallagher still draws crowds in their millions just by swearing a bunch of times, wearing a parka and cracking out milquetoast versions of Oasis' already-milquetoast hits.

In my time, I've sat through several music-industry-type events, listening to critics be met with murmurs of concerned agreement when their idols float the notion that 'rock 'n' roll is dead'; that new music is dull and pedestrian, and that my generation is simply too scared or too Instagram-obsessed to take up the mantle of rebellion. These are places where 'teenage girl music' is still used as a pejorative. I think what the people who hold those sorts of opinions tend to overlook, however, is the fact that in the 2010s, rock 'n' roll (or at least, their vision for rock 'n' roll) is actually just pretty fucking boring. There is nothing interesting or exciting about getting your cock out onstage, I'm sorry. That vision of radicalness in music was already in terminal decline, and artists like FKA twigs helped to bury it once and for all.

The *MAGDALENE* tour was every bit as draining as twigs had feared. She had just left a relationship which she described as physically and emotionally abusive. When the first COVID-19 lockdown hit, she had no choice but to return to her London flat. Forcibly halted by the pandemic, she began to enjoy simply living, and not having to find a way to turn each new experience into a song. She just called her friends on FaceTime, being goofy and being mates.

One of the people twigs spoke to during that time was Pablo Díaz-Reixa, who goes by El Guincho. Díaz-Reixa was already on Young's roster when Tic Zogson signed her, and had since become Spanish superstar Rosalía's primary collaborator. After meeting once in person, they struck up a friendship in the lockdown over video-call. As two musicians, they couldn't help but begin to send each other little ideas for songs. twigs began to think about embarking on a new approach to songwriting, one which captured the feeling of friendship and fun she was relishing in that moment. It would be music for people to bond over, like the mixtapes she'd made on cassette for her friends as a teen. She had, in short, decided to make a pop album.

If *MAGDALENE* can feel, at its saddest, like a wake held in the midst of a collapsing empire, then 2021's *CAPRISONGS* feels more like a night out in Shoreditch. Released in January 2022, it's the sound of twigs throwing her doors completely open: to dance music, to pop music, and to a dozen new collaborators. It's exactly the kind of album you wouldn't expect an artist like twigs to make, which is ironic, because twigs says it's the closest to herself. 'I just love the getting-ready process of going out,' she told *The Guardian* in 2022. 'I love deciding what you're going to wear. I love having your friends over and having a couple of drinks, and everyone making the sink really messy. I love the cab ride. I love not being able to get a cab. I love getting into the club. I love not getting in the club. I love the anticipation of it almost more than I love being there.'

CAPRISONGS, an album made almost entirely over the Internet, is far from a complete about-face. It's still meticulously crafted, just this time around much more commonplace things, like voice-notes and cassette tapes. Listening to it feels like you're in a stranger's living room, drinking cheap booze with its songs playing from a tinny speaker on the table among phone chargers and rolling papers. We hear snippets of twigs and her mates talking on the sofa, discussing their star signs and gassing each other up.

CAPRISONGS feels like a packed room too. It's an album full of voices. The artist who used a single guest vocalist across her first five projects suddenly decided to stuff her sixth one with some of that year's biggest names, from The Weeknd to Daniel Caesar, from Coventry rapper Pa Salieu to Walsall singer Jorja Smith (who twigs also found out was a distant cousin). On 'papi bones', twigs pays tribute to her Caribbean roots, making a dancehall cut ready for a West Indian club. The songs bristle with the energy of a playlist, different sounds and cultures bouncing off and enriching one another.

The whole thing, from front to back, is just a stupid amount of fun. The music is a pretty big shift for her, but somehow these bright, sunnier songs don't abandon the idiosyncrasies or the sonic weirdness which made her so compelling to begin with. I love the moment at the end of 'oh my love' when the chorus breaks into a chant and it sounds like noughties indie-pop band The Ting Tings. You can almost picture twigs and her mates in the studio with their arms around each other, chanting the hook. I love the twitchy horns on 'papi bones', and how much Shygirl seems to relish slotting in among them as they rise to such a fever pitch it feels like the speakers might blow. I love the chorus of 'jealousy' because it sounded so good when I heard it at a bowling alley with my mates. I love the moment at the start of 'darjeeling' where she raps 'Crystal Palace, brap-brap-brap' because it's cute and ridiculous, and Unknown T kills his verse, riding over a beat which mixes UK drill with something ethereal and elfish.

twigs does seem, even here, to be legitimately incapable of making songs which don't at some point transport you up onto an alien spacecraft, and so we still get moments like 'meta angel', where the first word of the chorus seems to set off an alarm made up of only that syllable, or on 'lightbeamers', where she sings so ludicrously high that her face must have turned blue behind the mic. (That song is adorned with some dainty string arrangements by Marius de Vries, who worked on Bjork's classic 'Venus as a Boy'). Even 'minds of men' and 'thank you song', the two weakest tracks twigs has ever released, are welcome; they add to the general sense of freewheeling looseness, and a party tape needs breaks as much as bangers.

On the cover of *LP1*, released when she was twenty-six years old, twigs appeared like an alien doll, her face made of polished wax. Eight years later, on the front of *CAPRISONGS*, she is stood, fresh-faced, in a park in east London; fur hat on, flexing her grill to the camera. Her music will endure for a very long time, but nothing will replicate the feeling of following the journey she embarked upon across the first decade of her career; a remarkable transformation from an anonymous weirdo to a consummate, virtuosic performer. A woman in her mid-thirties making music about her home and her mates, maybe a little more like us than we thought and seeming at ease with herself at last.

One of the first things I noticed when I pressed play on the video for 'Water Me', almost ten years ago, was that twigs' eyes, big and round and wide, looked just like *The Scream.* In fact, if you hung the covers of twigs' projects side by side in a gallery, then you'd have a series of self-portraits, lined up on the wall. Like Edvard Munch and all of the other expressionist painters of the early twentieth century, FKA twigs' music is self-portraiture too. Her work, like Munch's vision of himself looking over a Norwegian fjord, renders in sound the subjective self in exaggerated, spectacular ways.

twigs' work goes against the grain of a world the people of the nineteenth century couldn't have conceived of; one where the tools of digital alteration can be used to eradicte imperfection, and commit acts of moral deceit. twigs never liked doing things that way. In the grimy opening verse of 'home with you', when her voice is still twisted into an electronic rasp, she snarls an interesting line: 'I've never seen a hero like me in a sci-fi.' At first glance, those words could be getting at what Ashlee Haze was saying in her poem about Missy Elliot on *Freetown Sound*; but really, she was talking about a more precise philosophy.

'I am powerful and independent,' she told *The Guardian* in 2019, 'and incredibly vulnerable and sensitive. As a woman of colour, this idea that I need to be a Nubian Queen all the time is very stressful. I do find it problematic to always feel like your icons are always strong and always okay. If that is somebody's idea of "slaying" . . . it's wildly off the mark.' Existing as it does in this kind of status quo, twigs' music beings to feel extraordinarily subversive. She and Alejandra Ghersi use the same tools of digital alteration which are typically deployed to conceal blemishes to emphasise the ugliest parts of her body and the vulnerabilities of her mind instead. It reminds me of Nicolás Jaar's thoughts on digital manipulation, and the choice an artist makes to either manufacture an illusion or expose the reality beneath. After a career begun in anonymity, twigs' revolutionary idea was to reveal that her alien art was no magic trick at all, but a portrait of humanity at its ugliest and most sublime.

APPLE MUSIC

SPOTIFY

3. DANIEL LOPATIN / ONEOHTRIX POINT NEVER

Oneohtrix. One-oh-trix. The tip of the tongue taking a trip of three steps down the palate to tap, at three, on the lips. It's a strange word. An impossible word. The *one* and the *oh* meld awkwardly in the mouth, and the *trix* feels like it has no right sitting there at all. In a world where success is dictated by search hits and virility, it's an unintuitive, almost self-defeating name for a musical outfit. In my experience, it provokes that distinct reaction we English-speakers reserve for names we don't recognise or understand: to run away, or mispronounce wilfully; approximating the syllables as revenge for the inconvenience. But 'Oneohtrix Point Never' isn't really an alias at all. It's a memory.

There's nothing in Daniel Lopatin's life older than the memory of music. He was born in the summer of 1982 in Winthrop, a suburban town in rural Massachusetts with a population of a few thousand. His parents were musicians, émigrés from the Soviet Union who flew six thousand miles to settle in the Puritan state at the height of the Cold War. His mother taught piano and, back in the USSR, his father had been part of a small outfit called The Flying Dutchman, where he played drums and a pitch-black polyphonic synthesiser called the Roland JUNO-60. His father – Leonid Lopatin – had kept that synthesiser with him, and it sat in their suburban home. It was through this instrument that Daniel first discovered all the ways which you could play with sound.

Even when it wasn't being made, music filled the Lopatin house. The jazz fusion of Herbie Hancock and Chick Corea; British rock eccentrics The Beatles and Manfred Mann.

Once settled, Lopatin's parents became involved in that most American of professions: home computing. As they played their part in a technological revolution, new machines began to enter Daniel's childhood home. 'It was a Unix-based computer,' he remembered to the *New Yorker* decades later. 'I had never seen anything like it. It looked like the monolith from *2001* . . . It was beautifully designed, it looked like a crazy black cube. It was connected to a 28.8kbps modem, and it got me on the Internet . . . Computers all the time and music all the time. That explains everything you need to know about me.'

As Daniel was driven around Winthrop's maple-lined streets, his window-gazing was scored by something more involuntary: the radio. The early '90s were a different time, one where FM ruled the airwaves and, in America, local stations shaped each state's musical and cultural identities, leaking from car stereos and supermarket tannoys. In Greater Boston that dominance was asserted and reaffirmed by one jingle: a cooing chorus of voices singing deliriously 'Maaaagic One-Oh-Six Point See-ven: WMJX'. It was a motif repeated ad infinitum, every ninety minutes or so; the coo of a cereal commercial, jutting into the atmosphere.

It was this jingle, for Boston radio station WMJX, which came to mind in the mid 2000s when Daniel was about to upload the first synthesised music of his own. Instead of simply stealing the theme tune he took the words and smudged them, like a half-remembered thought: turning 'Magic One-Oh-Six Point Seven' into 'Magic Oneohtrix Point Never'. Before long, the 'magic' vanished too, and he was left with the floating half of a bastardised phrase, Oneohtrix Point Never: a snippet of a memory of a jingle from the '90s.

It might not be ready-made for googling but 'Oneohtrix Point Never' is an incredibly apt name for the music of Daniel Lopatin's career. His work sprawls in myriad directions under a number of different aliases, from film scores to production work and ten studio albums, each distinct from the other. Sometimes he created cosmic soundscapes using his father's JUNO-60, other times writing haunting, hyper-referential records inspired by everything from New Age cassette tapes to the music of TV commercials. Across mediums though, much of his music shares a common interest, a quality right there in the process which made his name: the warping effects of time and the mind.

It's a feeling each of us recognise. A song which doesn't sound quite the way we remembered it. A chorus or a melody once heard fleetingly on a stereo, scratching away like an itch on the brain. A love song from the 1950s which, filtered through layers of time, now sounds eerie and sad. It's also a feeling which is becoming a smaller part of our lives. Software developers know that forgetting can be an agonising experience too, and have filled our smart phones with technology which tries to act as a corrective: reminding us of a song or a celebrity or a record, sometimes from a poorly whistled facsimile alone. But that sensation remains in the music of Oneohtrix Point Never, written into his songs from the point of inception.

In the late 2000s, Lopatin finished college and decamped to a flat-share in Boston. He took a job at a textbook publishing company in Massachusetts and immediately experienced the weight of American corporate existence pressing down upon him. 'I was nothing,' he told the *New Yorker* in 2023. 'I was a piece of furniture. I could just feel the life draining out of me.' Lopatin set about keeping his sanity the only way he knew how. Trapped at his desk five days a week, he had no access to the sophisticated synthesisers with which he wrote the music of his college years, and so he was forced to take a more rudimentary approach. Using a free audio editing program he downloaded to his desktop, Lopatin spent his hours manipulating sound in only the ways the rudimentary software allowed him: deploying lashings of reverb, and sequencing staggering, repetitive loops of sound. He was inspired by the aesthetic of the American power ballads which filled the radio stations of his youth, but he presented them as haunting, melancholic snatches of half-forgotten songs.

Lopatin uploaded his creations (which he christened 'echo-jams', or 'eccojams') to early YouTube under the name 'sunsetcorp'. Titled things like 'A6' and 'B4', the eccojams were makeshift music-making, but their haunting qualities soon caught on. Soon dozens of acts like Infinity Frequencies and Macintosh Plus were making their own music which bastardised the aesthetic of commercial pop music and paired it with deeply unfashionable imagery inspired by video-game loading screens and billboards for make-up brands and cars. These artists sought to mimic an effect only the passing of decades can usually muster, turning commercial or utilitarian art into trippy, fantastical dreamscapes as if being misremembered by the mind. It was a style which eventually became quite a hit (among the terminally online of 2009), and the movement was soon christened 'vaporwave'; an apt name which riffed on a computer industry term for software which is unfinished or unreleased. Some critics interpreted these songs as damning critiques of consumer culture, others took them to be loving reappraisals. Daniel considered it a kind of folk music.

In 2009 Lopatin signed to Mego, an Austrian electronic label with a devout cult following. First they reissued Oneohtrix Point Never's first three straight-to-cassette albums as the exquisite compilation *Rifts* but – when it came to make his first original record with them – Daniel thought to apply the logic of vaporwave to a far larger canvas. Made with a band of his high school friends, Lopatin described 2010's *Returnal* as his 'Rousseau record', referring to a dead French painter and unlikely kindred spirit of Tumblr users of the twenty-first century. Henri Rousseau was renowned for paintings like 1910's *The Dream*: naïve and garish depictions of tropical jungles and far-off lands which he – a travel-averse city dweller – had never actually seen with his own eyes. Rousseau had only ever seen the vistas depicted in his works, rich with lotus flowers and exotic birds, in the artworks hung in the galleries of Paris. His own paintings were, in short, depictions of depictions.

Just as he had filtered the qualities of brash popular music through great swamps of reverb, Lopatin became fascinated by this other kind of distortion of the mind. He set about attempting to do with the synthetic notes produced by instruments like the Akai AX60 and the Roland MSQ-700 what Rousseau had done with oil on canvas.

'It's a hyper-realised vision of open spaces based on "inauthentic" scenarios,' he told *The Quietus* in 2010. 'In other words, I'm not inspired by the Serengeti, I'm inspired by world-music depictions of African expanses, and the sort of false authenticity of those depictions.' As pursued on *Returnal*, these experiments sound like rich and vibrant music being bathed in a thick, smothering haze. 'Pelham Island Road' sweats with the heat of '80s synth-pop and yet nothing, from the arpeggiated synthesisers to the sounds of busy treetops, moves like it would in a pop song. Instead, the playing oscillates and drifts, simmering without climax. On 'Preyouandi', pristine, synthetic timbres feel like they've been pooled into a petri dish and left to bake in the sun. Much like our memories, these are not really true representations of anything, but rather the idea of them, shaped by the mind.

*

When I first encountered Oneohtrix Point Never, he seemed like the kind of artist whose album reviews tended to come with references to critical theory, and a diagram. Even as his reputation has grown, that impression of Daniel Lopatin has never truly abated. He spent the early years of his career floating between various independent labels – Arbor, No Fun, Editions Mego, his own Software – but, even by the time he signed to the legendary Warp Records in 2013, his increased profile seemed only to make famous his reputation for obscurity. It's so much the case that the cover of 2013's *R Plus Seven* (a room of grey, geometric oddities which better resembles a maths textbook than conventional album art) is still used in memes among music fans as a placeholder for music which is pretentious, obscure and kind of sex-free.

In any other era Daniel Lopatin would have probably stayed that way: a beloved but rarely listened-to artist whose music was ready-made to be rediscovered several decades later. It is proof of the cross-pollinating nature of the modern music industry, then, that this didn't prove to be the shape of Oneohtrix Point Never's career at all. He is – out of the five artists who comprise this book – absolutely the most obscure and niche among them, and yet he's also by far and away the most popular, because, in 2019, Lopatin became the go-to producer for one of the most popular musicians on the planet.

At the start of 2010, Abel Tesfaye was releasing music in much the same way that Lopatin was. He uploaded his music, for free, to YouTube. Tesfaye was born in Toronto in 1990 to two Ethiopian immigrants. He was smart, fluent in French and Amharic, but school was an ordeal. He was badly bullied and resented being sent back there each day. When he was seventeen, Tesfaye dropped out and lashed out, moving from his mother's house to an apartment with friends. There he began abusing drugs and alcohol and spent time in jail and on the street. It was a project of pure hedonism which would one day become the subject matter of his music.

Somewhere among the vices, Tesfaye found his way into music. If you know one thing about him, it's that Abel Tesfaye can *sing*. Like Celine Dion, another Canadian superstar, he receives less credit than he probably should for this because he does so effortlessly. Tesfaye has a delicate, feminine voice, the kind which expands as simply as gas does. When he was a teenager though, he didn't have a clue what to do with it. Tesfaye always had an inclination towards music but he channelled it into projects like The Noise: a double act he'd started with a friend which performed chintzy R&B in an Usher-type vein.

One day, sat at a house party, he met the producer Jeremy Rose. Rose heard him sing and proposed a different route, playing Tesfaye an instrumental he'd made on Ableton. It was an R&B song, undeniably, but a skeletal one; ice cold and with great voids where, on a pop song, strings would rush in to fill the space. Rose suggested they team up for a dark R&B project built around songs like those, and Tesfaye began to write with those ideas in mind. In August 2009, he uploaded three of those songs to YouTube under the name 'xoxxxoooxo'.

It didn't take long for The Weeknd to become a pretty big deal. He released three mixtapes in 2011, beloved by DIY R&B which set blogs ablaze and earned him a contract with Universal Records. By 2014, he was already playing in stadiums around Europe and North America and, in 2015, his album *Beauty Behind the Madness* yielded two Billboard number ones and a placement on the soundtrack for the first *Fifty Shades of Grey* movie, no less. Its follow up, *Starboy*, featured production from Daft Punk and was certified four times platinum. Abel and Daniel Lopatin began their careers operating in near identical ways, but The Weeknd had become the antithesis to Oneohtrix Point Never: an example not of how the Internet could disseminate outré ideas but how it could birth superstars too.

After *Starboy*, Tesfaye took his time writing his fourth album *After Hours*, a record which took him to new heights of commercial success and critical acclaim. To that point, The Weeknd had been fairly derided, critically; his early mixtapes were praised, but he'd quickly become like *another* Canadian: Justin Bieber, the kind of pop star who was invited to headline the Kids' Choice Awards. *After Hours* was something different: jagged, propulsive synth-pop in the vein of Depeche Mode, rather than Bieber. The album had 'Blinding Lights' as its lead single, a song which remains the best-performing song in Billboard history. By 2024, The Weeknd had sold 75 million records worldwide, vaulting him into rarefied air.

The change to The Weeknd's sound was born, in no small part, thanks to the presence of Daniel Lopatin, who was brought into the sessions late to work on synths. His presence is felt immediately on a song like 'Until I Bleed Out', a track which deploys the choral, gleaming arpeggios which had appeared on his own *R Plus Seven*. Three writing credits on *After Hours* turned into an executive producer role on its sequel, *Dawn FM*, where Lopatin co-wrote half of the songs.

Together, Daniel and Abel formed one of the most electric and – frankly – unlikely partnerships in all of pop music. In 2021, Tesfaye asked him to serve as the musical director for The Weeknd's Super Bowl half-time show: an artist renowned for repurposing the deluge of American culture being handed the keys to its biggest night. The performance – delivered among a hall of mirrors before the eerily deserted stands of a Florida stadium – was a creative peak for the traditionally crowd-pleasing event, and Lopatin had the kind of audience few artists ever attain.

This sequence of events could only really happen in the streaming era, where the space between the mainstream and the underground is smaller than it has ever been. In another time, Oneohtrix Point Never might have been deemed a sell-out; but instead of ceding one role for another, he retained his status as a cult artist at the same time as being part of a massive commercial enterprise, with few people seeming to find a contradiction between the two. Beyond The Weeknd, Daniel has now toured with Nine Inch Nails and produced for David Byrne. He has collaborated with pop stars from Charli xcx to FKA twigs, and has produced era-defining scores for films starring Robert Pattinson and Adam Sandler. An exploratory, conceptual artist and a pop producer, all at the same damn time. That's why I decided to speak to him.

When Daniel and I spoke at the beginning of 2024 he was preparing to embark on an international tour behind his tenth studio album, *Again*, which had been released the previous September. Work on that record began just as he turned forty and, in order to make it, he did something he'd intended to do for some time: he left New York for good. 'I was in the city for fifteen years, but every time I wanted to make a record I had to leave,' he told me. 'That's been something bugging me about my life for a very long time. I come from a rural suburb. I don't think they're the greatest places on earth but they happen to be where I can hear myself think.'

The first place Daniel transplanted himself to was an isolated home buried in the forests of upstate New York, a modernist marvel sat stubbornly among the trees. 'It was completely sweating and falling apart, an overpriced Airbnb rip-off,' Lopatin said. 'But, in retrospect, it really did do the trick.' In late 2022 Lopatin had shut himself away there to work on his next album, projecting *Twin Peaks* onto the wall obnoxiously large as the owls circled the spruces outside.

Again is a boon for a book like this because it's a record about an era of sheer musical discovery afforded by the new-found access granted by existing online. To make it, Lopatin thrust his mind back to the early 2000s, when he was nineteen and studying at Hampshire College. 'It was a very, very exciting time,' he told me. 'When I went to college, there was an iTunes network set up between all of the different computers, so all of the students had immediate access to each other's music. They were becoming friends through this thing! I would be like 'who's this guy Pepe Lopez, who has Danny Wolfers' Belgian techno on his computer? Who is Legowelt?' So I'd find Pepe* and tell him I'd downloaded all these Legowelt records onto my computer. That was a *huge* revelation because the guys Pepe was into, I loved. Suddenly *I* wanted to be Danny Wolfers. That turned me on to everything, but there was a camaraderie too. It was a very social thing for us.' This kind of immediacy is commonplace now, but Lopatin and his friends were doing it at a small liberal arts college almost a decade before social media gained any real import.

Daniel spent his teenage years moonlighting in noise-rock groups and jazz-fusion groups, but it was at Hampshire College that he began to write the kind of synth-based music which would eventually define his sound. When students dropped out, Daniel and friends would find their abandoned dorm rooms and lock themselves away with typewriters and speakers, filling the room with techno while writing automatic poetry.

Oneohtrix Point Never's albums make a lot more sense once Lopatin explains the kind of music he was devouring

* Not a metaphor: real guy.

during those formative years, music which came in two distinct, discrete forms. The first was the glitch music which was becoming prevalent in that era's electronica: records like Fennesz's *Endless Summer* (which took bright guitar melodies and warped them with twitchy manipulations) or Ryoji Ikeda's '+/-', a highly abstracted breed of electronic minimalism based around a limited palette of sine-tones, half of which are almost beyond the range of human hearing. The other was the (slightly) less niche, post-rock wave of the 1990s. Albums like Godspeed You Black Emperor!'s *Lift Your Skinny Fists Like Antennas to Heaven* and Swans' *Soundtracks for the Blind* which dealt, antithetically to Ikeda, in sheer, lumbering cacophony. 'Those were the things which were happening when I was first using computers: the two poles of my music imagination,' he told me. 'That really messed with my mind when I was starting to do the thing.'

Daniel's musical discovery was aided by a professor who quickly discovered his student's very specific style and set about feeding it. 'He felt like he understood that my music wasn't experimental: it was too pleasant somehow,' Daniel remembered. 'He wanted to show me examples of composers who were also towing that line. He gave me records from the Lovely Music catalogue: Robert Ashley and David Behrman. It was 2002, so *Disintegration Loops* had come out, and he gave me all four CDs of that too.'

Indeed, William Basinski's *The Disintegration Loops* is one of *the* passed-around records of the early twenty-first century, so much so that it was still making the rounds in that way a decade later when I was developing the same kind of appetite. It was music which had been made almost entirely incidentally. In the early '80s, Basinski had begun making minimalist music from the feedback loops created by reel-to-reel tape decks. Two decades later, he rediscovered those experiments and tried to digitise them for posterity. When he did, he realised that the magnetic strips were peeling off the tape and crumbling. As it did, the music which was being recorded to his laptop was decaying too, becoming more broken and fragmented as the loops spooled on. The end result of that happenstance are *The Disintegration Loops*, a kind of organic decomposition which would be near impossible to replicate by will. It's the melancholic feeling of time passing, in musical form; the sound of worldly artefacts dissolving before your very ears.

Basinski's *Loops* left a great impression on Daniel, and it wouldn't be a leap to say that many of his more abstracted moments have been attempts to recreate the effect by hand. 'With *Again*, I wanted to make a record in praise of that period in my life,' he explained. 'It was this very abstract autobiographical idea. Who was I at the birth of my desire to do this? I think it's important to get in touch with that person while making any project because that's the pure artist; but in this case I decided to stay there a little while and make a portrait of that person.' Lopatin committed to the idea fully, even recording voice-notes from that kid in college directly to his adult self.

Excitement defines every inch of *Again.* It's an album which bristles with that sense of pure, unfettered discovery. Different sounds and different timbres bounce off one another, often within a song. Arpeggiated synths give way to luscious, gushing strings. Choirs enter at will. The title track begins like a painting; bright, pristine sine-waves knocking up against the open vocals of a computerised voice, before rumbling arpeggios enter the fray followed by cellos, which grow in size until they dominate the mix. 'Krumville' bursts into the Midwestern emo which was flourishing in Massachusetts in the '90s. On 'Memories of Music' a crackling electric guitar solo rips a simmering ambient track to shreds.

The album features some of the very musicians who Daniel became besotted with in those Hampshire College years. Jim O'Rourke plays piano on 'Again'; Sonic Youth's Lee Ranaldo slathers his guitar over 'Memories of Music', and Jamie Stewart of Xiu Xiu lends 'Krumville' its fragile, mournful chorus. Despite the meticulousness which must have characterised its composition, *Again* still plays out as if these shifts are happening according to some mysterious, unknowable pattern. It's a trick which happens in plain sight. Each song tends to end in a very different place than its beginning, but it would be hard to point to the moments when things changed. The record feels like the sounds of Lopatin's college iTunes account, bubbling way in a primordial sludge.

Not only was Daniel ahead of his time when it came to online music discovery, he was also among the very first to use computers as a means to create and promote music in a recognisably modern way. 'Around that time, eBay popped up!' he told me. 'I discovered that Roland made a dedicated sequencer called the JSQ-60, which recorded your notes in real time and played them back as if it was looped or sequenced, and that helped me realise . . . oh my god, I can make Legoweldt records now!' he laughed. 'I got the sequencer from eBay, the inspiration from Pepe's iTunes shared folder and I started recording my music right onto a computer. The world had suddenly become a reference library.

'MP3 blogs started showing up around 2005 and you could submit your music to them. There was one called *20 Jazz Funk Greats*, run by Robin Carolan.* Robin was the first person to ever publish me online. I made a MySpace page at some point, much to my chagrin. I did it because my friend got very upset with

* Carolan would go on to run London and New York label Tri-Angle Records, who would sign the likes of Forest Swords and The Haxan Cloak.

me that I wasn't advertising my stuff and wasting my talent. It turns out it was very good for a private person. I'm gregarious and happy but I really don't like to socialise at things like parties, so the Internet was an amazing way to have it both ways. I relished the opportunity to be alone *and* with others. I gave myself the alias Magic Oneohtrix Point Never and made the page look like my music. It had a picture of a couple from the '80s in silhouette on the beach, looking at the horizon next to some evil thing. Everything was: make your own shit, do it yourself.'

Daniel didn't just post one album to his sparkling new MySpace page, but a trilogy of them: a loose, imaginary soundtrack to the life of a lonely spaceman. The first was 2007's *Betrayed in the Octagon*, followed by 2009's *Russian Mind* and *Zones Without People*, where the astronaut pens the score for his own death. It's evocative imagery, but the music doesn't need it. Those early albums were pure imagination, born of Lopatin's mission to dive deep into the instrument which sparked his childhood imagination: the Roland JUNO-60. The trilogy was the result of hours upon hours of experimentation: noodling with arpeggiators, creating loops out of simmering drones or bubbling chords, then feeding them through his laptop and messing with them all over again.

In his commitment to the one instrument, Lopatin was – like the lonely astronaut – quite adrift from his contemporaries. In fact, in 2007, the sound of the JUNO-60 really couldn't have been more *unfashionable*. While various corners of electronica plunged into harsher, colder forms of techno, and others constructed intricate, frantic glitch music, Lopatin's reference point was the music made by the synthesiser adopters of the early '80s: the cosmic epics of Vangelis, easy-listening music and New Age meditation tapes.

'I [never] limited my interests to the music of the '80s,' Lopatin told Emilie Friedlander in 2023, 'but I was dedicated to it. I felt that it was a renaissance period for the instrument I was obsessed with, and I wanted to hear every single colour of the rainbow from the great origin story of the consumer-level synth.' A song like 'Months', which opens *Russian Mind*, is music which wouldn't sound out of place in a Norwegian spa; far warmer than sharp sine waves or furious breakbeats. Moments of serenity like those were set against the likes of 'Laser to Laser', pulsing tracks where arching arpeggios are set against slow, drifting backdrops. These pure, synthetic textures had become *démodé* but those timbres of pure, colourful synthesis often had a drifting, melancholic effect. In his later film scores Daniel would revisit the idea: deploying the sound of New Age pan flute tapes to create a sense of low-lying dread, as if that degree of serenity could never be trusted. I asked Daniel about where that inclination came from.

'You're asking about the origin of my interest in seeing New Age music as intrinsically anxious?' he laughed. 'It was just a hunch! I became obsessed with synthesisers at a pretty young age which meant that, by the age of fifteen, I'd exhausted all the classic synth records I could find. First it was jazz fusion, then totemic synth artists like Vangelis, then techno, then it was all this experimental stuff . . . I just rinsed it all. At some point, you think "I want more". You're like a drug addict and, like a drug addict, you start hitting the dustbin, literally: the Salvation Army CD bins. It was a whole new world. Who's Andreas Vollenweider? Who's Steven Halpern?* But, ultimately, it was all because I was so obsessed with electronic texture and sequenced, arpeggiated music that I had to hear every single piece of it in existence to make sure I wasn't missing any overlooked gems. I found fantastic, incredible records

* (A Swiss harpist and one of the founding fathers of New Age respectively, in case you were wondering.)

from people like J.D. Emmanuel, which do much more than they have a reputation for. He didn't even really make New Age music at all. Over time I was able to see this picture of a period which involved ideas of hypnotic music and see them for what they really were, which were often quite different to what they were supposed to be.'*

Much of the music Daniel makes seems to emerge from the idea of finding something beautiful or profound where you wouldn't necessarily expect it. Like Devonté Hynes, many of the records Daniel would go on to make challenged broadly held preconceptions about some types of music being more valuable than others inherently. On *R Plus Seven*, Lopatin left both the Internet's sonic detritus and his beloved JUNO-60 behind him, instead making a record from MIDI synthesisers and keyboard presets. These are foundational tools – synthesisers which emulate acoustic instruments; keys you press to produce the sound of an entire choir – but musicians would usually bury them among more organic tones before presenting them on their records. On *R Plus Seven* though, Lopatin has them take centre stage.

For a time, some people assumed that Lopatin's music was either parody or an academic exercise. No idea seemed to irritate him more. 'I like the idea of crass things, but it's not a fucking wink at the audience,' he told *Resident Advisor* in 2013. 'It's more: let's deal with characterising our struggle

* Ironically, in the late 2000s, a new wave of music called 'cottagecore' emerged which explicitly sought to revive older electronic instrumentation as a rebuttal of the hyper-progress of the present. With the release of *Rifts*, Lopatin found himself being mentioned alongside the likes of Emeralds, Stellar Om Source and Blues Control as those reviving once-passé serenity sounds. Ironically, Lopatin had been fascinated by those sounds from the time his parents were still packing his lunches, and he did not share cottagecore's Luddite pretensions.

with crass things. If I stopped at simply satire . . . personally I'd find it very unsatisfying.' Instead, Lopatin confronted fashionable sounds and the ones considered clichéd, and tried to divorce them from their cultural connotations. As he wrote in an essay about the easy-listening saxophonist Kenny G: 'frameworks of taste rely on dumb and great things to exist in concert with one another.' On *R Plus Seven*, when he deployed a synthetic pipe organ, he was playing with the cliché of a timbre like that as much as the instrument itself. As Daniel was eager to point out to me, it wasn't necessarily the case that the records he discovered in his great dive through the archives were always *good*, but that doesn't mean they were without purpose. 'The main thing I realised listening through all of these old library records – all of this crazy, zonked-out, wonked-out hippy stuff – was that most of it wasn't doing a very good job at what it was supposed to be. The bill of sale was that you've purchased something to relax to but – through the process of time chipping away – many of the recordings had an amateurish, humorous quality to them. The alchemical twist was time. The inescapable shadow of the unconscious. It makes things interesting and beautiful and frightening. Eventually, when I started to develop my own music, I thought that those sounds could be a reflection of the fact that my own personal attempts to be a "mindful person" have never really worked for me. I'm wound like a cable on a bridge.'

In 2011, Daniel released what many consider to be the definitive Oneohtrix Point Never LP: *Replica*. It was his most explicit investigation into the transformative power of time. On it, he made a sharp turn away from his first four albums – defined by heavily synthesised, completely original soundscapes – and brought the vaporwave method into the world of Oneohtrix Point Never. On *Replica*, the sources which influenced him were not pop songs but television adverts from the '80s and '90s which had been crammed en masse into endless YouTube playlists. The results were a fascinating experiment: taking the sonic palette of that turbo-charged moment of all-American consumerism and turning them into something mournful, and just a little out-of-time.

Replica is an album which doesn't age. It's nearly fifteen years old now, but it would be impossible to pin it to the year it was made in because its source material was already decades old. 'Up', for example, bounces New Age drums around the same clipped sound of a man declaring 'up!', repeating and repeating until his voice is swallowed in a tide of spasmodic noise. Earlier, 'Power of Persuasion' centres around the kind of oscillating piano you could imagine scoring the demonstration of a new operating system; but Lopatin lets the melodies wander, dissipating like mist into different corners of the mix. These melancholic tunes feel like something which might be heard drifting from a gramophone in a wartime ballroom. We're used to knowing the origins of the sounds which reach our ears, but these songs disenfranchise them, leaving a strange, implacable mystery in their wake.

One of the most notable qualities of *Replica* – one of the reasons the album continues to age impeccably – is that the music recreates an experience which is increasingly lost to us: having a fragment of a melody rattling around your head which you can't quite put a name to and have no means to identify. Now that frustrating phenomenon is easily cured, but that's not the natural order of things. Once upon a time, before the age of infinite access, those songs would have remained that way, remixed and reshaped by our firing neurons as years drew on. *Replica* takes us back to the time before, making the sensation of forgetting concrete.

In case it's not already readily apparent: the music of Oneohtrix Point Never is *steeped* in the past. In 2011, while writers like Simon Reynolds feared that immediate access to old music was leading to a stagnating culture, no artist was delving in as excitedly as Daniel Lopatin. He was, in 2009, even completing a library science degree with the expressed intention to become an archivist. On his blogs, he wrote about the power of what he termed 'ecstatic regression'. Back then, he was even interviewed by Reynolds in his book, *Retromania.* In it, Oneohtrix Point Never was framed as a counter point to the thrust of the book's argument. I asked him, in 2024, whether his thoughts on the merits of the 'radical forgetting' which Reynolds proposed had changed.

'I think that, no matter which way you go, you end up modern,' Daniel told me, after a pause. 'Forcing yourself on an amusement park ride through the past, or the future . . . you still end up right where you need to be. Retro-mania goes back far before the 2000s. There are people inclined to think about the past more than others but I think doing it's always in service to existential comprehension. It's not about "times were better then", it's just inevitable, and unavoidable. It's why people sit down with a rabbi or a priest and ask: what does the Book say? What did our ancestors do which can help me see what's going on right now? I'm looking for certain kinds of patterns which should explain what I should be doing.

'Progress is not simple either. Look at movies! I agree with Martin Scorsese: Marvel movies are simply not doing the same things which films do, and that's a big problem. And how do people make films which aren't superhero movies right now? They have no choice but to do it cheaply and simply, but by doing it that way, if the story is good, you should be able to show unbelievable transcendence on film just using shadows, or faces. Is that regression, being more human and using less computers? It seems to me that, today, that would be progression. I think part of being a responsible artist is realising that you're standing on the shoulders of giants and that you shouldn't belittle or look down on the past. Instead we should try to understand their contemporary situations and, ultimately, borrow from their incredible repository of tricks.'

Much of the writing about leaving the past behind was based around an urge to imagine a collective future beyond capitalism. I told Daniel that it was striking to me, then, that so much of it reminded me of something else: the arguments of technocratic billionaires Peter Thiel and Mark Zuckerberg, and their insistence on moving fast and breaking things.

'That's exactly right,' Daniel said. 'The thing about regression which is interesting is that you realise not everything has to progress in the way that Western society says it does. It doesn't have to follow that strange, prescribed, accelerated-progress idea. Clearly it doesn't because we've taken so many steps backwards as a society by following that highly technocratic path. It's hard to argue against the fact that a lot of us are kind of braindead zombies now *because* of that thinking. That seems like inertia to me, not progress. Thank god that people were inclined to preserve so much over thousands of years, and maintain their archives and their texts. Thank god we have that huge body of work on a purely informational level, which can then be transmuted into knowledge through this amazing alchemical process which is us and our automata, us and our machines. We're really doing alchemical work with the past. That is highly mischievous, highly human work and it's really cool to me.'

'I always think about Peter Bogdanovich's movie *Targets*,' Daniel continued, biting down on a breakfast bar. 'The opening scene is Boris Karloff watching himself in a film as a guy from the 1940s, but it's 1968. Certain things remain very Karloff-y, but he's gotten older. Some things ripen and age well and gain wisdom, and other things just cannot withstand the pressures of time. I think there's something very interesting in doing the same thing in music: taking something which was once considered vital in some way, or even futuristic in its time, and seeing how it fares in the present. Dressing them up and playing with them like dolls. That's all I'm ever doing. I'm just having fun.' After releasing *R Plus Seven*, Daniel opened these conceptual wormholes wider and applied these same tests of time inwardly, upon his career and the music of his life. When *Again* was released, Lopatin announced that it was the concluding chapter in an unplanned triptych which enacted these tests upon three separate moments in his life.

The first was 2015's *Garden of Delete*, an LP Lopatin deemed his 'version of a rock record'. It was 'set' in his teenage years, when his career could have easily gone in the direction of the nu-metal and grunge played by his high school bands. Lopatin built an entire world around the album. Through tweets and blogs and websites, he concocted a wide, messy backstory involving a spotty teenage blogger called Ezra and a fictional grunge outfit named Kaoss Edge, a band which had its own website and extensive discography. On the page were MIDI files which fans could download, files Lopatin claimed Ezra had been given on a USB stick by a visiting alien and from which he'd constructed the album. It was, to say the least, a lot.

'Putting together the lore of *Garden of Delete* was the most satisfying thing I've ever done,' he told me. 'I worked with a graphic designer who I'd stay up very late with in Ditmas Park [in Brooklyn], eating butter chicken at five in the morning making these very bizarre things. We'd always see the sun rise. He's some kind of insomniac and so I had to adhere to his schedule. I did all of the art with my best friend Shaun. Everyone involved was so talented.'

Garden of Delete stands out as Oneohtrix Point Never's wildest, most abrasive moment. The serenity of records like

Returnal had been replaced with the jagged edges of grunge and metal; the music of his teenage years blasted through an electronic prism of Daniel's making. He made the record after supporting Nine Inch Nails and Soundgarden on tour in 2014. After experiencing one of Trent Reznor's shows, he quickly realised that he needed something more thrilling and harsh to satiate the band's more sadistic devotees. In response he wrote a thirty-minute set of what he called 'hard rock cyberdrone': barbarian music designed to jolt and pummel the audience.

The raw animalism of cyberdrone helped him to finally understand the EDM scene which had swallowed electronic music whole just as his career began to gather steam. He embraced it, working the drops of dubstep into his music alongside the serrated edges of grunge guitars; sounds which took him straight back to his early years, to bands and artists he had dismissed as a synth-obsessed teen. (When he first purchased a Soundgarden CD, he went back and traded it in for Rush.) On *Garden of Delete*, Lopatin made a maze out of this previously discarded music: the nu-metal, grunge and EDM. The album has the palette of an '80s slasher: littered with huge choruses, growled vocals and trance swings, offset by acoustic bass and sudden ambience. Daniel intended the bewildering chaos of the album to channel the discomfort of his teenage years; an oozing, pugnacious sound which matches the seething chemicals of a pubescent brain.

Daniel followed *GoD* with *Age Of* in 2018, another conceptual album designed to tackle the political divide emerging in America following the election of a populist president. In 2020 though, Lopatin returned to his trilogy of abstract autobiographies, and released a self-titled record (of sorts): *Magic Oneohtrix Point Never*. On *Magic*, Lopatin reached all the way back to the time of the jingle which inspired the name; the age of the radio. He set about making a punchy, fifty-minute

LP like the iconic albums of the era, using the genre-spanning structure of radio stations to interrogate his own life as an avid listener of music.

'We had really good college radio and freeform radio in Massachusetts,' he told *The Guardian* in 2020. 'I loved that you could go in one swoop from hearing Charles Mingus to Anal Cunt to Phil Collins . . . I thought, what happens if I take a power ballad and infect it with things that don't really belong, within my own false memories?' Listening to his music in the time of *Replica*, it was utterly inconceivable that a Oneohtrix Point Never LP would one day contain a power ballad, but that's exactly what we get on *Magic Oneohtrix Point Never*, and it's delivered by one of my generation's biggest stars to boot.

In between records, Daniel had met Abel Tesfaye, and The Weeknd lends his voice to 'No Nightmares', a soaring ballad where Lopatin's arpeggiator uplifts Tesfaye's immaculate vocals. It's a song set within the realm of Daniel's tastes, but it's also delivered fairly straight, only once drifting into simmering digital abstraction. Abiding by the brief he's set himself, much of *Magic* walks that line closely. Songs drift close to clear-eyed pop, but they're smeared with the haze of a waking dream. The music also revisits moments throughout his career, blurred together where entire albums once divided them. The beautiful spring melody of 'The Whether Channel' sounds like New Age bliss, until it breaks into a warped verse from Virginia rapper NOLANBEROLLIN. The elegiac 'Long Road Home' is a hall of mirrors Kate Bush song, replete with warm, gratifying strings and vocals by Caroline Polachek, whose gorgeous voice is slathered in distortion and chopped to pieces.

'I've never worked in a room with Dan, we've only ever worked together remotely,' Polachek told me. 'In some ways I'd consider him to have the total opposite process as Dev.

He's the most Machiavellian artist I've ever worked with,' she laughed. 'He knows exactly what he wants from his collaborators and he wants that on his own terms, uncompromisingly. I think he's much more what we expect of a traditional auteur. I feel a real carefulness around the people he works with, because they really enhance the meaning of his own work, like The Weeknd bringing in this aspect of modern tragedy. Everything is doubling down on a gesture he's already decided upon.'

Magic Oneohtrix Point Never articulates the paradox at the heart of much of Lopatin's work. He is meticulous in his composition – Machiavellian, even – and yet all of that meticulousness is devoted to the feeling of something happening completely organically, as if his songs hadn't been arranged by anybody at all. *Magic*, for example, feels like a compilation of songs we might have once known, now half forgotten. As an FM announcer declared on 'Cross Talk II': 'somehow the music we grew up listening to doesn't relate to our adult reality.'

It's no wonder then that Daniel bristles at the idea of 'radical forgetting' because so much of his work is tied inexorably to using music of the past, idiomatically, to locate the modern.* 'I'm a sponge, and I love culture and the process of soaking it in,' he told *Tiny Mix Tapes* in 2009. 'I don't understand people who refuse to listen to music while they're recording because

* Aptly, some artists have already begun to use the aesthetic of *his* past ideas to make their own. British band Saint Etienne formed in Croydon two decades before Daniel made his first eccojam but, in 2020, lead songwriter Bob Stanley became infatuated with vaporwave and suggested the band base an album of original music around it; only, instead of using reference points from Japanese and American culture (as was the norm), they would draw from the cultural detritus of England instead.

it stifles their creativity. I'm more in the Burroughs camp of everything as a mimetic virus. I enjoy getting that bug.'*

Indeed, Daniel suggested to me that much of his entire career has been, in effect, a prolonged investigation into the very first music which entered his ears. 'My dad had a synthesiser. Not a keyboard or piano but a synthesiser,' he told me. 'Those years were so formative, and the music from that time was so intense, that I might never get past it. For me, it was the birth of excitement. That's a pretty crazy thing to happen to you, and I may always want to go back to that place.'

As Daniel's career progressed, the volume of ideas he presented within his music quickened. His records were always conceptual, but albums like *Replica* and *R Plus Seven* tended to riff on a single idea throughout. By *Magic Oneohtrix Point Never* and *Again* though, different aesthetics began to meld at a blistering speed. Where *Replica* once felt like a walk through the graveyard of commodity culture, Lopatin's style evolved to reflect the sensation of the modern world: a relentless inundation of information, being thrust at us at great speed.

This artistic development aligns with the way culture developed across the 2010s. When Lopatin began doing it in the early 2000s, MP3 crate-digging was still the remit of Internet hobbyists and true music nerds. Now though, all of us consume entertainment like that every single day: screens within screens, in thirty-second doses, filling every incidental

---

* Making use of the music of the past had been part of Daniel's personal history long before he was even born. In 1969 his father's band won over a crowd at a music competition in Leningrad with a ripping rendition of a Manfred Mann classic. 'In the Soviet Union it was way more rare and based to cover Western songs than write originals,' Lopatin told the *LA Times* in 2016. 'Ingenuity was measured by how close you could replicate illegal jams.'

pause with pure, furious input. That's how records like *Magic Oneohtrix Point Never* and *Again* feel, jolting between one idea and the other: a dozen fleeting, contrasting sensations at once.

During our conversations, several times Daniel expressed admiration for *The Art of Noises*, a 1913 manifesto by Italian futurist composer Luigi Russolo. In it, Russolo argues that the human ear was, in the fledging twentieth century, evolving into something new. He said that the beauteous pastoral music of recent centuries was losing import in the industrial age, and that people's ears were becoming accustomed to the harsh mechanical noises of urban places. As such, he proposed that musicians should help to create rhythms and timbres which better reflected this brave new world, and even – over 110 years ago – suggested that electronic music could be a way to do it. Russolo invented, in short, noise music.

Just as Russolo intended to introduce the sensation of the new world into music, perhaps Oneohtrix Point Never's sound developed in a similar way. In the re-examining of his musical life, particularly the beginning of hyper-consumption in the early days of the Internet, Lopatin's sound has evolved to reflect our own brave new world: voluminous, eclectic, and mixed up in the mess of our overstimulated imaginations. 'There's a Philip K. Dick quote that I love that I've been thinking about,' Lopatin told *Flash Art* in 2021. '"The symbols of the divine initially show up at the trash stratum". For me, what he's saying is that if you remain enchanted with the world, then whether you're in the gutter or however bad the smell is, it's still going to be really interesting because you're alive; because you're there to bear witness.' 'Tales From the Trash Stratum' was released as a single, with Elizabeth Fraser of Cocteau Twins, in September 2021.

Because of this new style, Daniel suggested that the amount of time it takes to appreciate his albums might have grown as his career progressed. An LP like *Again* is overwhelming at first, or even *under*whelming, as much of the immense stimuli which come at us often is. Over time though, all of the album's parts become more tangible, and more thrilling as a result. I asked Daniel: in a songwriting sense, how do you make an album like that without everything becoming utterly incoherent? Is it done through retrospective editing like a collage might be, or does he emulate a collage in his approach from the start?

'I don't like highly incoherent music either,' he answered, after some consideration. 'I never try to punish somebody by making something which would annoy or irritate me. I find all of my albums coherent but, increasingly, I allow myself to leave the song and go somewhere else before it's even over. I allow myself to make odd decisions in terms of contrasting elements in this way and that way, but I always think of each song as a place – it might have other dimensions and pocket universes – but each song is a place; ticking away, doing its thing. I think that's where the coherency comes from. There's always a return. That's why I called the record *Again*! I've always loved thinking about the return, and the loop. It's the same idea as waking up every morning. There are certain things we're used to and give coherency, and yet our days might be completely insane. Across a lifetime . . . well, it's hard to even imagine. In both life, as in music, there's coherency but there's also a sense of being orphaned in a completely confusing universe. All of that happens at the same time. That's how I write music. If it gets too off the rails I don't like it, but if it stays on the rails too much it becomes ordinary and I get bored. I have to see what's around this corner, or the next.'

As we spoke, one thing which became apparent was that Daniel likes to understand things through the lens of cinema. His allegories were filled with allusions to film; to auteurs and actors and directorial styles. He was inspired by the 1942 horror film *Cat People*. He compared his career to that of spaghetti Western pioneer, Sergio Corbucci. At one point he showed me his cap, which had 'Directed by David Lynch' sewn in a florid font. It was hardly surprising, then, when Daniel began scoring films. He began in 2013, when he composed the soundtrack for Sofia Coppola's *The Bling Ring* and Ariel Kleiman's *Partisan*. Then, in 2015, he met two brothers from New York known as the Safdies.

Propelled into film young by their cinephile father, Josh and Benny Safdie had already begun building a reputation as two precociously talented directors by the early 2010s. From *Lenny Cooke* (a documentary about a failed NBA prodigy) to *Heaven Knows What* (a drama about two homeless heroin addicts), their style aspired to near-unfeasible levels of realism. Born and raised in New York, their lens was affectionate and unforgiving, lingering on the dilapidated, ugly corners of the city absent from the likes of *Sex and the City* or *Succession*. Casting largely non-actors and shooting often from a distance like they were spying on their own protagonists, the Safdies' films are among the few fiction films I've ever seen which aspire to realism and almost pull it off.

Daniel Lopatin had been aware of the Safdies from social circles in New York, but it wasn't until they began work on the thriller *Good Time* that they approached him to work together. 'I briefly worked at a video store in Little Italy,' Josh Safdie told me. 'A CDR sat on the player with the name of a friend who I used to cruise to electronic music with. This was probably around 2008. Track twelve took the shop into a new place. The arps flew. I texted my buddy, "who's track 12?" . . . he wrote back "oneohtrix". It was one of those words that you read but don't say aloud in your head . . . more like an image. The track was called "Betrayed in the Octagon". I thought it was a cool heady title. When I was looking to fully embrace scoring a movie, I instantly thought to reach out to Dan . . . With a name like Oneohtrix I didn't really know what to expect and for one reason or another I didn't think to google him. He showed up wearing a Boston Celtics hat, which was alarming, but I instantly felt like I was in an infinite hang session. Dan is a very deep guy and yet everything is possibly a joke . . . arriving at deep thought together is funny for some reason.'

Good Time was going to be the Safdie brothers' first genre film; an experiment because it starred a proper, known-name actor in Robert Pattinson, then not far past his days as sexy vampire Edward Cullen. What Daniel wrote for *Good Time*, and their Adam Sandler-starring thriller *Uncut Gems*, are not conventional film scores of the 2010s at all. Absent was the symphonic bombast of Hans Zimmer or the brooding iciness of Lopatin's old touring buddy Trent Reznor. He had written pure, unadulterated prog; engaging in neon-coloured synth-worship to an extent he didn't even indulge in back at the start of his career. Set against the unvarnished realism of the Safdie's work, it's a startling combination. This was the kind of stuff Eduard Artemyev deployed for other worlds in grand, cosmic science fiction, but Daniel set it against the scaffolded streets of the city. *Good Time* and *Uncut Gems* are both excruciatingly tense films; the spectre of death looms constantly over the heads of both of their desperate, blagging protagonists. In this context, the pulse of Lopatin's JUNO-60 suddenly feels like the sound of the blood pumping around their brains.

'Dan's music is very emotional, very nostalgic, while also being futuristic, dystopian, romantic, euphoric and melancholic,' Josh enthused to me. 'It also has a pulse, most of the time almost literally. We both look at the score as music to listen to. That's why I was so into his music when I first heard it. It was like the score to a movie which didn't exist. I think that's also why we really wanted to credit him as OPN on the *Good Time* score. I was proud to be part of an *album*. We're both in search of some destination outside time and place. We're both very serious people but also entirely interested in the moment and getting lost in it. We also both suffer from anxiety, and music – in particular electronic music – can tap right into that, both good and bad.'

The power of Lopatin's scores was due, in no small part, to his and the Safdies' attention to the unconscious effect music has on the way the viewer absorbs their images. 'Some of my favourite stuff wasn't the cues, but the sound design operating on a subliminal level,' Daniel told the *Fader* in 2017. 'A car's going underneath an underpass . . . how can we activate that strip of highway? What can we do to make it seem like the highway's electric, like it's alive? We put in sonic moments tethered to certain objects in the frame, and panned them in a way which was relative to the movement of the object on the screen.' In *Good Time*, one piece of the score is even written in the key of a hydraulic lift Pattinson escapes into. This quality, this effort to reach out and create a reaction in the listener, is one Lopatin tends to call 'physicality'.

'When you're siting in a movie theatre and your body's completely still, that's not exciting,' he told me. 'Because of this, I want a score to have muscularity to it. I want that in my records too. The main purpose of easy listening and New Age music, for instance, is to put you at complete ease, but that means there's a kind of interesting physicality at play because it's trying to literally change how your body feels. That's more physical to me than most pop songs.'

I asked him to define what exactly it was he was aspiring to by pursuing this inclination. 'It's about how much emphasis you put on certain sounds and how much of the music is jutting out and biting you and doing things to shake you out of your comfort zone,' he told me. 'I believe in music which has animacy, it has a life of its own, music which is as close to being alive as it could possibly be. Some people do that with melody. Duke Ellington. Beethoven. On notated sheet music, Beethoven could create highly embodied, highly physical responses with melody alone. I can't do that, I'm a schlub. I make computer music, and so my melodies are basically crash test dummies which I need to animate with all of the tools at my disposal.'

This animating quality appears in Daniel Lopatin's studio albums too, in the dissolutions which occur across records like *Replica* and in the flitting universes indulged in by albums like *Garden of Delete* and *Magic Oneohtrix Point Never*. It's a quality best demonstrated in 'A Barely Lit Path', the final track from *Again* and perhaps my favourite Oneohtrix Point Never song to date.

It's a song which begins as a ballad. Throughout his career, Lopatin has had a habit of recording lyrics and then mangling or processing the words so much that you can hardly tell they're language at all. Here though, his voice is loud and clear, albeit warped with an electronic rasp like Laurie Anderson's on 'O Superman'. As Lopatin sings, a bright chorus swells beneath him. The second his final word fades, a radiant, stuttering arpeggiator pulse erupts out of nowhere. It's one startling moment followed by another when, thirty seconds later, that arpeggiator is replaced by a gorgeous, soaring string section (arranged by British composer Robert Ames). It's in a moment like this where Daniel's words like 'jutting' and 'biting' make complete sense, because every move is startling, at the same time as being utterly compelling. Strings like those had never existed on any Oneohtrix Point Never's album before, and Lopatin adorns them with the sounds of his universe; synths stuttering and straining and spiralling, building until the point where it threatens dissonance, but dissonance isn't what arrives. Instead, a chorus of real, angelic children's voices rush in, and the song goes fully baroque, with harps fluttering away in the background. Later those voices take an ominous, downtempo turn, snapping into a final passage where a synth growls like a cock-rock guitar solo, until vanishing into smoke. It's a music which embodies the concept of the entire record: sheer discovery, like a ship arriving to shore.

The Safdies were just two of the many generational talents Daniel bumped into across his career, from ANOHNI to David Byrne. I asked him which of them, if any, had the greatest impact on the way he made his own music. After pausing to think, he gave me a surprising answer.

'I was with André 3000 once,' he told me. 'It was on a James Blake session, it wasn't for my own stuff, but the day had nothing to do with recording anyway. We were just sitting there, speaking to each other about music and life. As we talked, there were these loops we'd made playing incessantly in the studio, over and over. Eventually I got to watch this poet write his verse to them. I experienced the same thing with Ishmael Butler.* It took both of them an enormous amount of time but also . . . it was a day. A day for André and a day for Ishmael. But they were both sitting there, trying to work on what was going on with *me.* They were trying to document what was going on with me as a producer and as a person and it was just so *present.* It was the closest thing I've seen to a painter painting something from scratch, and that really messed with my head because I don't work like that. I don't do *anything* like that. After seeing them do their thing in that way, I think I slowly began to change. Now, when I'm the one

* Butler is the genius MC who fronted the radical '90s jazz-rap outfit Digable Planets and later, in the 2010s, Shabazz Palaces. Together Daniel and Ishmael released the song 'The Rapture' in 2017.

coming into a studio, I try to channel André and Ishmael and gauge what the person is about; to see whether we should even be there at all. If nothing happens then nothing happens but it's a day, no more than that. It's work, because you're not just hanging out, but it's completely inter-personal.'

Indeed many of Lopatin's collaborators attest to the deep sensitivity of his music; like Nicolás Jaar, challenging the notion that electronic music is somehow more calculated or less emotionally driven. 'One of the greatest parts of collaborating with Dan is that like myself, he sees work as a deep communication between two people,' Josh Safdie told me. 'A lot of my fondest memories of producing the two scores we've done together come from the middle of the night when we decide to pull up a YouTube video and decide to score that instead. When I'm with Dan, I feel like I can create music and that's the most powerful part of the collaboration. I think that lies in his desire to understand people and get on the same page.'

When Lopatin first met the Safdie brothers, they realised they *did* have a great deal in common – from a passion for film to a love of Alice Coltrane – but all of their work, despite existing in seperate mediums, contains one distinct strain which is more abstract and idiosyncratic than simple taste. Because, yes, the Safdies' films *are* committed to realism, but that's not enough to make them great. Alongside the naturalistic style with which they're shot, *Good Time* and *Uncut Gems* also contain an aspect of the surreal. It's there in the neon colours which coat Robert Pattinson's face; it's there in the opening sequence of *Uncut Gems*, which zooms through the inner prisms of a black opal stone and out through Adam Sandler's colon. It's there in the intrusive, proudly synthetic score Daniel pairs those images with too.

'That kind of sonic language makes New York feel like this bioluminescent, science-fiction, sentient being,' Lopatin told *Pitchfork* in 2017. Like the Safdies' films, Oneohtrix Point Never's studio albums often sound pretty fantastical, even though their reference points are usually absurdly everyday: TV commercials, USB sticks, radio stations, albums downloaded off LimeWire in a Massachusetts dorm room . . . I asked Daniel whether, if you're seeking to astound, you need the presence of the mundane as much as the surreal? (This is when he showed me his David Lynch cap.)

'I think that's exactly right,' he said. 'I think that's what makes David Lynch's work so successful and why, to me, it's so absolutely beautiful. He's often actually thinking in a very ordinary way; this beautiful, literary approach to everyday people and everyday things. The difference with Lynch is that he then drives deeper and deeper into those surfaces until he's doing some kind of unconscious work, some alchemical thing down there in the depths of himself *through* these normal things. That's where you get this dance. You realise that everything is capable of being interesting, that enchantment should be located everywhere, if it exists at all. At the end of the day, an artist is just a highly sensitive antenna for the stuff which otherwise just gets overlooked. Life is difficult and complicated for most people and not everyone has the inclination or time to peer under every rock, but the artist does. That's what we're supposed to do. For me, if I just had to drum it up from within, I don't think that would very interesting. Instead, I like to start from something regular, some chintzy sound or somebody else's idea of a good time and go about re-enchanting them.'

It was through Daniel's work on *Uncut Gems* that he first encountered Abel Tesfaye. As testament to how quickly The Weeknd accrued lore around himself, Tesfaye appears in the film as a younger, blog-era version of himself. When he was shown cuts of the film, Tesfaye was stunned by Daniel's music. He had heard Oneohtrix Point Never's music before but, set against the underbelly of New York, he understood it for the first time.

Tesfaye invited Lopatin to LA late into the *After Hours* sessions. 'Illangelo* would be in there doing arduous stuff at the eleventh hour, and I'm popping over there like Kramer saying, "Hey, I just fucked around with some synthesizers!"' Daniel laughed to *GQ*. Despite the fucking around, Abel and Daniel stayed in touch. Lopatin appeared with Abel to play 'Scared to Live' on *Saturday Night Live*, and the superstar somehow became an incredibly unlikely advisor – and executive producer – for *Magic Oneohtrix Point Never*. 'It was obvious that he's someone I can really rely on when it comes to honest feedback,' Daniel told *GQ*. 'I love his perspective because it's so wildly different from how he's in the world musically, and that means a lot to me.'

It turns out that becoming a close collaborator to one of the most listened-to pop stars on the planet does wonderful things for your exposure. After co-writing half of *After Hours*' successor – *Dawn FM* – Lopatin's songwriting was soon circling around the planet on The Weeknd's post-pandemic world tour, a proper, old-school pop spectacle where a masked Tesfaye strutted around a metallic, post-apocalyptic cityscape. The tour took him to many of the biggest stadiums on the planet.

I asked Daniel a question which can be asked of only a handful of living people: how does it feel to have your work heard by millions upon millions of people around the world? He laughed, and surprised me again. 'There's times when it hits me and it's completely strange,' he said. 'But it was always something I wanted. It wasn't somehow outside of my comprehension when I was beginning making those cassette tapes. It was always the end goal.' This isn't exactly the answer you

* Regular Weeknd producer and mixing engineer.

expect to hear from a man whose very name is synonymous with difficult, conceptual work, but it became apparent over the course of several hours of conversation that that wasn't how Daniel viewed his work at all.

'I want to communicate effectively to as many people as I can, without making any major sacrifices,' he said. 'Oneohtrix Point Never is one of those things which many people may know about at this point but that doesn't mean they like it or care,' he laughed. 'It's just my thing, and when it's my thing people seem to like it a whole lot less than when it's part of some other, more clever person's thing. I can help those people out though. I'm *happy* to help those people out, because I love to reach a lot of people and get outside myself. I have certain skills and I'm not opposed to dividing them up. I don't want to hoard those things, I want to see what happens when they bump up against other people's.'

Daniel's attitude is indicative of the type of culture we now find ourselves in, deep into the streaming era. Across the course of the Internet age, old values around what constitutes authenticity – be it certain artists themselves or the sound of a pipe organ produced by a Japanese synthesiser – have been shattered by platforms which expose the short distance between pop and the underground.

As someone who was still at the tail end of puberty when many of those brilliant, outré voices like Oneohtrix Point Never were emerging, it has been fascinating to watch them populate the aisles of award-winning, Grammy-night pop music while continuing to pursue challenging, progressive careers. In 2023, Danny L. Harle of London collective PC Music was the lead producer of Dua Lipa's top ten single 'Houdini', and Jam City, the British producer who entered the 2010s making think-piece spewing records about dubstep, produced Olivia Rodrigo's enormous second album *GUTS*.

Lopatin was pretty unequivocal about the fact that, not only is it a good thing, but that it's also (whisper it) the way it's always been. 'We never wanted to be somebody's secret,' he told me, speaking of the wave of electronic artists he came up with. 'We didn't. I also think people would be surprised just how adventurous some major figures are, who you might presume are not. Things are mixed up now, in a really beautiful way. That world which I came from, where there was a very strict divide between what was considered academic or gate-kept music, has imploded. That began with cassettes tapes and home audio: being able to dub records, and make your own ones at home; do sound/unsound experiments, and mimic stuff which was once highly specialised. That changed our relationships to those things, and I don't have any moral judgement on it at all.

'It's through that process that we get someone like Jim O'Rourke. Jim is viewed as being on the fringes . . . but is he? He produced Wilco and Sonic Youth and Stereolab. I think it makes things really, really interesting because it used to just be accepted that music on the fringes had a depth to it which other music just doesn't possess; and people analysed art on those terms. Now though, there's been a general deepening, which should put everyone on alert. We have to think about shallowness and depth without those easy things we used to hold on to, like how niche something is or isn't. We have to find new ways to determine what's interesting and why.'

You don't head into a conversation with Daniel Lopatin without an awareness that you're likely to leave it with various facets of culture mixed up and flipped upon their head. That is, after all, what Oneohtrix Point Never's music has been doing for two decades and counting. Even still, there was one persistent theme of our conversation which I didn't anticipate: an insistence Daniel made, time and time again, that he doesn't view his music as difficult at all.

At one point in our conversation, I raised the comment Nicolás Jaar made to me about the philosophy of his style, where he said he wanted his music to show the labour of his work. I asked Daniel if he felt the same way and, for the first time in our conversation, he bolted upright in his seat. 'I don't want the labour to be present,' he told me with a grin, 'I want to be Walt Disney! I want you to go on a magical, wonderful ride. I absolutely appreciate that perspective but it will only take me so far. I'm looking for a kind of deeply embodied, deeply mysterious experience which no amount of technique can provide. I want nothing about me to be remembered, just the experience of the thing. If I've made a theme-park ride, I've done my job. Then I can go on and make the next one.'

APPLE MUSIC

SPOTIFY

4. THEBE KGOSITSILE / EARL SWEATSHIRT

Has any genre of music ever been declared finished quite as often as hip hop has? If rock 'n' roll was invented in 1951 – with Jackie Brenston, His Delta Cats and a broken guitar – then it took almost fifty years before Marilyn Manson declared 'Rock Is Dead' in a song. Rap, on the other hand, was barely out of its first golden age when Nas named an entire album *Hip Hop Is Dead*. That was 2006 and, by the end of the decade, plenty of others joined to lay flowers at its gravestone.

In 2009, the *New Yorker*'s chief music critic Sasha Frere-Jones penned a public service announcement of his own, titled 'Wrapping Up: A Genre Ages Out'. In it he observed that the blues-based swing which had always underwritten hip hop's various permutations was being edged out by the thudding pulse of European dance music, leaving even the shining lights of the genre – like post-retirement JAY-Z – playing catch-up to a new zeitgeist. Regardless of the somewhat dubious dynamic of a middle-aged white man encouraging a Black art form to shut up shop and head on home, his claim was met with much agreement. One month later, Simon Reynolds concurred in *The Guardian*, but contended that it should have been called sooner, at the release of *Hip Hop Is Dead*, or earlier, in 2004.

'By any sensible metric, rap has slipped hugely from where it was when this decade began,' Reynolds wrote. 'It's not dominating the pop charts anymore and neither is it irrigating the mainstream with new beats, styles, and slanguage. It's not producing major album-length statements, give or take an *808s & Heartbreak* . . . it's not even coming up with compelling new personalities . . . judging by its output in recent years, it's become a deadening force: as a listening experience, but also as something that maintains a deadlock on the musical imagination (and personal ambitions) of Black American youth.'

It's always easy to take a potshot at someone from the past prophesying about the future, like laughing at novelist George Gissing, who made the claim that the invention of the aircraft would make war impossible back in 1903. I've done the same plenty of times, I'm sure we all have. I used to think Sheck Wes was going to be a generational star. After 'New Rules', I remember thinking that Dua Lipa would be a one-hit wonder. It's why, in these very pages, I talk quite exclusively about the past, because guessing the future? That's a dangerous game.

On the other hand, there's wrong . . . and then there's *wrong*. In the 2010s, hip hop reached new heights by just about every conceivable metric. In the summer of 2015 rap became, for the first time since its inception in the mid 1970s, the most listened-to genre of music worldwide. Its new biggest star, Drake, garnered the most top ten hits of all time, beating Madonna by twelve. Many of the genre's most beloved albums, from *My Beautiful Dark Twisted Fantasy* to *Piñata* and *To Pimp a Butterfly,* arrived in the decade following Frere-Jones' proclamation. Hip hop (always a limited term for an entire musical cosmos) continued to spawn new permutations at a ferocious clip, from drill to cloud-rap to plugg. The characteristics of these styles leaked into genres far beyond those featuring MCs: jazz groups like BADBADNOTGOOD and Sons of Kemet translated the percussion and bass of hip hop instrumentals into the basis of a modern jazz revival, and electronic artists from Flume to Flying Lotus took rap's roots in dance music and applied it to theirs. In the 2010s, hip hop was everywhere, and its influence trickled into the tributaries of almost everything.

To be generous to those who forecast hip hop's demise (the fact one of the greatest rappers to ever pick up a mic was among their ranks certainly helps), the noughties ended with a whimper rather than a bang (JAY-Z's *The Blueprint 3*, to give it a name). Lil Wayne had spent several years declaring himself the greatest rapper on the planet, only to fudge the victory lap with the uneven *Tha Carter III*. Unlike the '90s, rap in the new millennium had been dominated by the various dance-driven crazes of the Dirty South, but what had begun with New Orleans bounce and crunk devolved – like the imitators of 'The Twist' and 'The Mashed Potato' in the early '60s – into a game of dance first, song second. One of the most popular rap songs on the planet was Black Eyed Peas' 'I Gotta Feeling'. When I listen to that song, I also get the itching feeling that maybe music in general might need to call it a day.

In one sense, 2009 did indeed seem to stand as the last gasp of a distinct, older era of rap. Raekwon released a sequel to one of the most beloved Wu-Tang solo albums in *Only Built 4 Cuban Linx . . . Pt. II.* Against all odds, it was killer. MF DOOM released what would be his final solo album, as did Mos Def. Eminem made it clear that his untouchable run was over with the influential dud *Relapse*, and kicked off a still-unbroken cycle of releasing albums which sought only to apologise for the last one.

If you were looking in the right places though, the groundwork of rap's renaissance – commercially and artistically – was already being laid. Mobb Deep's one-time producer The Alchemist had begun a path into the underground. Kid Cudi's *Man on the Moon* was released that year: an emotionally overwrought record where electro-pop and psychedelic beats laid down the road for kaleidoscopic, post-genre madness like Lil Uzi Vert's *Pink Tape* a generation later. The same month Reynolds said there had been no major new personalities in rap, Tyler, the Creator posted *Bastard* on his Tumblr, and two fresh Young Money signees called Drake and Nicki Minaj had just released new mixtapes, readying the stage for rap's imperial age.

If 2009 was a crest, then the following two years were a tsunami. Nobody knew exactly what Kanye West was cooking up, holed away in Hawaii with some of the best songwriters on the planet, but *My Beautiful Dark Twisted Fantasy* ended up fulfilling an archetype of rock which rap had so far resisted: the big, expensive, statement album. *Enter the Wu-Tang* wasn't that, nor was *Madvillainy*, but Kanye had finally made rap's *Dark Side of the Moon*. On it, several world-famous rappers delivered the best verses of their careers. There was a song with Elton John on backing vocals. It was the kind of album nobody could have seen coming.

Just as a superstar like West was changing conceptions of what a hip hop record could even be, an influx of young names began releasing a bevy of records which matched his opus in creativity and vision. In 2010 alone we received Kendrick Lamar's *Overly Dedicated*, Big K.R.I.T.'s *K.R.I.T. Wuz Here*, Danny Brown's *The Hybrid*, Roc Marciano's *Marcberg*, Flying Lotus' *Cosmogramma*, Waka Flocka Flame's *Flockaveli* and Earl Sweatshirt's *Earl*. The following year was even crazier. There was Frank Ocean's *Nostalgia, Ultra*, A$AP Rocky's *Live. Love. ASAP*, Death Grip's *Exmilitary*, Childish Gambino's *Camp*, Future's *Streetz Calling*, JPEGMAFIA's *JOECHILLWORLD*, Shabazz Palace's *Black Up*, ScHoolboy Q's *Habits & Contradictions*, Ab-Soul's *Longterm Mentality*, Meek Mill's *Dreamchasers*, Drake's *Take Care*, Action Bronson's *Dr. Lecter* and J. Cole's *Cole World*.

Most of those names had a totally different sound then, but many would overlap in various forms and combinations over the decade to come. It was all kinds of remarkable. All of these total unknowns – the artists who would dominate the genre and the radio for the next ten years and beyond, who would release masterpieces and twist hip hop into new sounds and shapes – had emerged from absolutely nowhere, in the space of two years flat. Aside from the band boom of the 1960s, I can think of little like it in the history of music. In retrospect, maybe making big statements at the precipice of something as unprecedented as that was just really, really bad luck.

Most of my musical life has been defined by rap, likely in no small part because I started tuning in just as the artists I listed began to break. I remember reading Kendrick Lamar's name for the first time, rather unglamorously, on the iTunes cover page, advertising *good kid, m.A.A.d city*'s deluxe edition. I was probably looking for the new Tame Impala or something, but that image – just a warped fisheye of a 1996 Chrysler Town & Country, idling beneath a clear sky – was too intriguing. At that point Dizzee Rascal's *Tongue n' Cheek* was probably my favourite rap album, so I think I was expecting something a little like that. I didn't get it. I got a movie instead.

Kendrick's first album on Aftermath and Interscope was so verbose – each song so vivid and distinct – that I felt the need to understand it better. I watched a review for the album by the YouTube channel *Dead End Hip Hop* – five guys from Atlanta picking apart the details of words I could hardly hear – and came to realise that rap is a competition, and that Kendrick Lamar was winning. Before long I was playing *GTA V* in my room for hours on end, listening to every album they reviewed on repeat, luxuriating in the ones I loved; trying to understand the ones I didn't. I cried to Ab-Soul's devastating 'The Book of Soul'. I went on a bloody rampage to Killer Mike's

R.A.P. Music. Aesop Rock and Kimya Dawson's *Hokey Fright* showed me that rap could even be *Juno*-level twee. Finding these MCs when I was young and following them as they each evolved has been the most fun I've ever had listening to music. '[Hip hop] is ravenous,' John Cale told *The Guardian* in 2024. 'Rock music just doesn't do that any more and neither does the avant garde. Hip hop is the new avant garde'.

Twenty-first century rap music deserves an entire tome of its own but, in lieu of that, this chapter will centre around one artist who, remarkably, operated in the midst of not one but two of the most thrilling scenes in the genre's recent history: Earl Sweatshirt. Before we get to him, we must first tell the story of Odd Future, a collective of skateboarding, graphic-designing, punk-loving teens who were idolised and derided in equal measure. Theirs is a tale as old as rap: a group of kids from the city who got together to write rhymes and piss off their parents. On the other hand, and against all imaginable odds, they also happened to produce not one, not two, but three generational stars. The way they went about producing and releasing their songs could have only existed in their unique moment in musical history, where technologies of art and access to art enabled them to become among the first home-grown superstars of the Internet age.

Shortly after Odd Future disbanded, Earl drifted in another direction. He became involved in a countercultural wave of rappers who took hip hop to strange, uncharted waters: from the postmodernism of JPEGMAFIA to the psychedelic expressionism of Danny Brown. His music tied together stories of disparate cultural pockets: an avant-garde collective from Brooklyn, a producer from hip hop's first golden age and Billy Woods, one of the greatest rappers to every touch the mic. All of these voices coalesced into an amorphous scene which forged a new kind of psychedelia from the surrealism of everyday life. This was a true countercultural movement but one which, for some time, seemed to go mostly unnoticed; like if the hippies didn't have a Woodstock, if disco didn't have Studio 54. From Mac Miller to Vince Staples, from the Alchemist to Kendrick Lamar, Earl Sweatshirt's career *is* the story of rap's second golden age, and living proof that hip hop isn't dead yet.

Part 1 (MySpace Radicals)

Sydney Bennett took a while to find her instrument. She began taking piano lessons when she was four, but rarely practised. She tapped away at drums and picked at her mum's guitar, but neither stuck. Things only changed when she and the family began taking trips to visit her uncle. Bennett's mum was a city clerk, her dad the owner of a manufacturing company in China, but her uncle, Mikey? Well, he co-wrote 'Mr. Loverman', with Shabba Ranks.

When she was young, Sydney's parents flew her and big brother Taco from South Central LA to Jamaica to visit him. Mikey Bennett took her out to his studio in Kingston and she would sit opposite the mixing desk, watching him work. Sydney stopped wanting to simply listen to music, and began wanting to make it instead. After watching her uncle do magic with all of those blinking buttons and sliders, the studio itself became the first instrument which Sydney completely, unabashedly, fell in love with.

Openly gay from a young age, Sydney felt like a total outsider in high school. She left her first school after only a year and a half, and her parents sent her to the Hamilton Music Academy instead – a big, proper, Californian performing arts school near Castle Heights. She kept up the piano lessons, but loved the music-tech classes most of all, and began bingeing beat-making tutorials on dial-up Internet when she got home from school. When she was fourteen, her parents let her build her own makeshift studio in the guest room of their house. She was still shy – her brother christened her 'Syd The Kid', because she stayed looking young even as she aged – but Sydney wouldn't stay lonely for long.

It's easy to forget just how huge MySpace was. Now, it's little more than a digital time capsule – the subject of Internet memes for nostalgic millennials – but in the first decade of the twenty-first century, it was *the* place to vanish online. Each one of the five artists of this book began their careers posting music there. MySpace launched in 2003, around five months ahead of Facebook, and for the first four years of Zuckerberg's baby's existence, it remained the most popular social networking site in the world. Because the best way to post music to the platform was via YouTube links, it was pretty essential to the success of that website too. By 2006, it surpassed Google as the most visited website in America. It was so big that, in 2005, its CEO turned down a chance to buy Facebook.

At fifteen, Sydney was on MySpace a lot. She would dig for songwriting tips and interact with other teenagers making music and posting it there. Little scenes emerged, half of them existing solely online, and soon she was speaking to kids from local neighbourhoods who wanted to lay down raps. On message boards, Bennett was well aware that she had two stand-out qualities: she had a studio, and she was a girl. One of the people this caught the attention of was Matthew Martin, an Atlanta-born college freshman who posted MIDI-made, cosmically obsessed soundscapes to his page. Bennett messaged him, praising his work, said that if he ever wanted to work together, he could come by her studio, which she christened 'the trap'.

Martin was heavily into the deep soul of Earth, Wind & Fire and the Isley Brothers, albums his dad would always play around the house. When he turned seventeen, YouTube became his record collection, using the vast doors of the Internet to stumble upon potent instrumental music like Kyoto DJ Tomoyuki Tanaka's Fantastic Plastic Machine, and he saved $2,000 just so that he could set about making music of his own. He began posting his own nu-jazz songs to MySpace, shamelessly ripping off the Gorillaz by creating The Super 3: a fictitious band starring Matt Martians (himself) and two imaginary avatars he named Betty Vasolean and Yoshi Jankins, Jr. One day, Martians received another message, this time from a profile called 'imaginace'. The profile was filled with images of burnt-orange clouds, watermarked with a distinct mission statement: 'Creativity is rare. Dreaming is bliss. Imagination is novel. Music is love. Odd is our future.' At the top, a name: Tyler, the Creator.

Tyler Okonma was a pretty loud presence online. By the time he and Martians began messaging in 2007 (often going under the name Ace the Creator) he'd already amassed a small following among the weirdo kids of MySpace. At school, Tyler had almost no friends. He'd been to twelve different schools in twelve years and, like most kids who arrive one month and leave the next, he was a perpetual outsider. It didn't help that he was a Black kid who loved to skateboard, enjoyed collecting pictures of Sid Vicious, and whose favourite film was *A Clockwork Orange*. He didn't tell people at school that he rapped but some of them found out anyway. One kid walked up to him in senior year and starting to rap Tyler's own song back at him. 'Stop!' he said. 'It's awkward.'

Ever when he was small, Tyler was obsessed with music; not only the sounds of songs but even the ways album were presented. When he was a toddler, he'd pull the artwork out of CD cases and create track-lists for imaginary albums of his own. He was a loud, goofy, extroverted kid with the obsessiveness of a dork. His first verses came early too: he started rapping at seven, to the second half of Black Eyed Peas' 'Positivity'. Tyler had an uncanny ability to remember the dates his favourite albums were released, the track numbers of his favourite songs, and the seconds and minutes when the details he liked most kicked in. When he was twelve he started making instrumentals on his computer and, two years later, began to teach himself piano.

When he was fifteen, Tyler sketched two fat, Homer Simpson donuts on the back of his notepad, in the shape of an O and an F. He liked the look of them, and began to draw them on every piece of clothing he owned. He dreamed of putting together a loose collective under that name – Odd Future – inspired by groups like A Tribe Called Quest and the Soulquarians. At first, Odd Future was going to be a magazine (Tyler was a big fan of titles about his endless hobbies, from the skateboarding magazine *Thrasher* to dispatches from the world of rap, like *The Source* and *URB*), but it soon became about music. He already knew who to invite.

Tyler had a tendency to collect the rapping, beat-making teenagers in his vicinity like Pokémon. He knew of an eighth-grader who was the son of JAY-Z's bodyguard and could rap well. He went by Casey Veggies. He knew Left Brain and Hodgy Beats from the skate park outside his grandma's house, where he was living at sixteen after his mom left for Sacramento. Together they formed MellowHype, the gruff, weed-toting duo who were the first of Odd Future's many sub-groups and aliases. Tyler brought his friend Davon, who chose the name Jasper Dolphin, to be their hype-man. He messaged Matt Martians on AOL Instant Messenger and told him about Odd Future too. In turn, Matt told Tyler that he knew some-one with a studio and that, even better, she was a girl.

Before long, Syd's parents' house was being bum-rushed by teenage boys. With her cropped hair and T-shirts, she looked almost indistinguishable from them. Before long, Syd was engineering every Odd Future song. 'I'll never forget being around Syd for the first time,' Martians told the *Fader* in 2019. 'I was like, man, this is like the chillest girl I've ever been around. She was around so many crazy personalities but was just this calm in the middle of the storm . . . She was the person that created our fake promotional website so that the places which posted about us would take us seriously.'

Tyler became wrapped up in his new crew's lives. For three years, he'd slept on the floor of his grandma's house, sometimes with no food to eat at night. The guys' various homes became a refuge. 'I'd sleep over at their houses and they'd cook and shit, that would be like my family,' he told *SPIN*. 'I try to give back because when I didn't really have shit, they was always there . . . Anybody in my camp, even if they didn't really do shit for me then, I just try to look out for them.'

The first way Tyler looked out for his friends was by doing what he'd spent his whole life practising for: making albums. In March 2008, Casey Veggies posted *Customized Greatly Vol. 1* on DatPiff and MySpace, while he was still only fourteen. It was the first Odd Future release. Tyler joined him on a couple of features and laced him with the beat for 'One': an airy sample of 'Huit Octobre 1971' by Cortex, an idea he likely grabbed from Madlib's beat for MF DOOM's 'One Beer'.

The group's first mixtape, *The Odd Future Tape Vol. 1,* was uploaded in November 2008. Just over an hour in length, nobody apart from the MySpace nerds who already had Tyler, the Creator's profile on their radar really heard it. Many of the group's most charismatic rappers – Mike G and Earl Sweatshirt included – were yet to join, so there's plenty of Hodgy Beat's cumbersome drawl and Casey Veggies, sounding still very much like a teenager with his pen. Even then, Tyler stood out above them all. Tyler wasn't exactly proficient but he was lyrically audacious enough to stay captivating. A student of rap, even though he'd later deny being one, he finished the tape with a call-out track. He shouts out his favourite albums, a startling list for a seventeen-year-old who was releasing EPs called *I Smell Panties*, which included Sade's *Love Deluxe*, Jamiroquai's *A Funk Odyssey*, Clipse's *Lord Willin'*, Herbie Hancock's *Flood* and Stereolab's *Chemical Chords*. It's a sweet moment from a kid who had never previously been serious on the mic. (Of course he finds time to also thank 'Hitler, Mussolini, Stalin, M'butu' and 'all of the porn in the world'.)

Tyler obviously thought that two of the songs from *The Odd Future Tape* were worth keeping, because they appeared on his first solo mixtape too. Work on *Bastard* had begun in 2007 when he was sixteen. Half of it was made with GarageBand stock sounds. He recorded 'Pigs Fly' on a staircase, whispering into a mic, because his grandma was asleep in the next room. They shot the music video for 'VCR' in Jasper's parents' basement, trying to be as quiet as quite as possible as they filmed a scene of him seducing a sex doll. He released it on Christmas Day 2009, as a morbid joke.

It's fair to say that *Bastard* is nobody else's idea of festive fun. By that point, Tyler had developed a taste for the abominable. Back then, Odd Future used homophobic slurs like they were definite articles. *Bastard*'s cover was a photograph of a bunch of schoolkids, bathed in blood red, with pentagrams etched onto their foreheads. The tape revels in sexual and physical violence. The first lyrics on the album are 'this is what the devil plays before he goes to sleep'. If Tyler's first songs did receive the response 'you really shouldn't be saying that', then, as surely as the rising sun, this teenager's response was: 'Watch me.'

In 2011 *NME* reported that, on *Bastard*'s follow-up, *Goblin*, Tyler raps a homophobic slur or gag 213 times in a little over an hour. Women got it even worse. On 'Sarah' a prom date goes wrong, and Tyler's alter ego takes her to a basement, rapes her, kills her and eats her. 'Sarah' is as fictional as a Tarantino film but, in terms of gender, the violence tends to be pointed one way. Unlike a great many inarguably bigoted MCs (take a listen to Ice Cube on 'Black Korea'), it's pretty clear what these teenage boys were doing.*

In a particularly bizarre cultural moment, in 2012 Odd Future appeared on BBC's *Newsnight*, interviewed by the especially fusty Stephen Smith. 'What about your lyrics,' Smith asked, 'what are you saying in your lyrics?' 'Nothing,' Tyler responded, a glint in his eye. 'Just stuff to piss old white people off like you.' That was certainly part of it. Why does the rebellion of teenage boys so often manifest in ugly bigotry against marginalised groups? Well, that's one for the psychologists, but there were real-word consequences of his lyrics. In 2015, the Australian feminist organisation Collective Shout succeeded in getting his tour cancelled in their country. Bans from New Zealand and Britain soon followed.

It has been bizarre, in recent years, to see a new generation – who began listening to Tyler with records like 2019's *IGOR* – discover that this is how his career began. By the 2020s, Tyler, the Creator has come to symbolise the complete opposite of the

---

* Much of Odd Future's inspiration came from their documented fandom for Eminem, a rapper who did, after all, release songs on hit albums where he shoves the mother of his child into the boot of his car and murders her in the woods. If armies of concerned parents emerged at the turn of the millennia who were worried about the influence he'd have, then Tyler and company proved that they did, at least in terms of music, have a point. Eminem's post-rehab comeback album *Relapse* was released in May of 2009 and became an instant favourite of the Odd Future crew. Tyler even borrows Eminem's 'Superman' flow for the first verse of 'Bitches Brewin''.

dark, bloody humour of his first three LPs. He has a perfume line now, and wears nail varnish; he writes love-sick pop songs for his girlfriend and waxes lyrical about the genius of Wes Anderson. On his 2017 album *Flower Boy*, Tyler revealed that he himself has been 'kissing white boys since 2004' and, in doing so, became one of the figures who helped young, queer MCs like Kevin Abstract and Princess Nokia be so open about their sexuality. It's a fact which would have stunned his fans a decade earlier.

Bastard is now a time capsule of a different era, a footnote in a discography filled with albums which greatly eclipse it in quality. What's interesting though, and testament to its maker's natural talent, is that despite all of the juvenile qualities which really should stand against it, *Bastard* holds up as a pretty great mixtape. It's not hard to see why it was the first to break Odd Future into a wider, international audience. Unlike the loose, kitchen-sink song-dumps of their sampler, *Bastard* tells a story: we're listening to a therapy session, between a doctor and a troubled teen who hates school, hates rap blogs, hates his absent father, and may also be the devil. The pitched-down vocals of Tyler playing his own therapist are so evocative that you can hear the mildew drip down the walls. It helps that Tyler is so captivating to listen to. Unlike the other OF members, his voice on *Bastard* doesn't age him. At seventeen, he already sounded as mature as he does today, producing words which sound like they're soaked in tar as they tumble from his lips; a lumbering drawl broken only by his p's and his f's, which he spits out like he's cursing us for listening.

Because of this, and despite the attention-seeking of his most puerile bars, *Bastard* often manages to sound genuinely sinister. 'I sold my soul to the devil for thirty percent off' is a silly bar, but when Tyler delivers it from the back of his throat, with dead eyes and a slack jaw, he makes it believable.

The utter hatred he musters for targets like rap blogs, a grievance so petty it would be tedious from the mouth of another artist, is so convincing that it becomes compelling. From the moment the opening track begins, Tyler does everything in his power to make the listener uncomfortable, and the fact he actually pulls it off is an achievement of sorts.

What is less obvious about *Bastard* is just how isolated the Odd Future sound was from almost anything else happening in rap in 2009. Like Cash Money in the late '90s, Odd Future was a closed-system enterprise. Most of its members lived within just a few miles of each other and, for four full years, not a single one of their twenty mixtapes featured anybody who wasn't at least affiliated with the group. Their entire sound was dictated by their three core producers: Left Brain, Matt Martians and Tyler. In LA in 2009, the airwaves were dominated by the rowdiness of Soulja Boy and Gucci Mane, but Odd Future existed in a different sonic universe, one informed by the infatuations of its creator.

There was a week, in 2003, when songs produced by The Neptunes (the Virginia Beach duo comprised of Chad Hugo and Pharrell Williams), made up 43 per cent of all new music played on US radio. As the guy who made 'Happy', Pharrell's cool is slightly tainted now but, as part of The Neptunes, he'd spent much of the previous decade achieving a degree of dominance only the likes of Quincy Jones had ever come close to. Hugo and Williams were middle-class boys (they met at a summer camp), but they integrated themselves quickly with street-storytellers like Noreaga and JAY-Z, whose beginnings were very different from their own. As they branched into bright, funky pop music, their sound muddied the waters between the favourites of rap purists like Snoop Dogg and chart smashes of Kelis and Nelly until, by the mid 2000s, they were one and the same.

Across the landscape from Beyoncé to Jeezy, hit singles were suddenly littered with teasing four-count intros, staccato chords, high-pitched melodies and chanted-hooks straight out of a summer camp singalong. The music of The Neptunes and Timbaland (that era's other dominant force) was fun; a huge cultural inversion which came in the wake of a decade of gangsta rap and macho rap-rock anthems. Pharrell even had a skate brand called the Ice Cream Team which Tyler adored, and whose logo – a big cartoon ice cream with a cherry for eyes – was clearly an influence on the early style of Odd Future. From the clothes to the songs, like Clipse's 'Grindin' and The Neptunes' 'Frontin'', it was an era filled with energy and bright, neon colours.

Tyler Okonma was eleven when he first heard 'Tape You' – a song by The Neptunes' rock spin-off N.E.R.D. – and became a Pharrell devotee instantaneously. So much of Tyler's later career, especially from *Flower Boy* onwards, is indebted to their whole era of bold, squelching synths and fizzing drums. The first few years of Odd Future were too but, to soundtrack their deranged raps, Tyler began his career hauling The Neptunes' sound through a hall of funhouse mirrors, creating beats which were bare, lolloping, and grimy as hell. When sunny chords do appear, they exist only to add mocking winks to the carnage. Listen to *Bastard*'s opening track, and the way those icy synths stab through the heart of that sombre, dirge-like piano. Other tracks like 'Blow', perhaps only by virtue of the fact they were made by true amateurs on old laptops, master a chaotic, punk energy, the kind Odd Future, even the non-rapping members, would launch at their live shows.

When Tyler first posted *Bastard* on the file-sharing site zShare, it was listened to by forty-six people. For the first few months of its existence, it mostly did the rounds on Hypebeast, the streetwear music forum where Tyler was an active, obnoxious poster. Over the next year though, Odd Future began to gain momentum. They were seized on by the indie-rap blogosphere; contenders to *Pitchfork* which sought to hype up the best projects in a moment when just about anyone, from Das Racist to Mac Miller, could release music online for free. Stoner-rapper Domo Genesis joined the collective, dropping *Rolling Papers*, a generic tape which was eaten alive by seventeen-year-olds discovering both Odd Future and marijuana for the first time. By the end of 2010, *Bastard* was being reviewed by burgeoning tastemakers like Anthony Fantano of YouTube channel *The Needle Drop*, a post-genre critic whose increasingly devout following introduced indie Internet kids to strange new rap. That was December 2010 and, two months later, Tyler dropped 'Yonkers'.

I remember the first time somebody at school told me to watch the 'Yonkers' music video. I didn't have a phone which could make notes so I remember writing 'Tiger The Creator' in the back of my notebook and typing it into the hand-me-down computer in the spare room. When it began to play, it immediately felt like something I shouldn't be watching. Even though this same man now spends most of his time talking about Italian lakes and his suitcase collection, 'Yonkers' *still* feels a little wrong. I'd never heard of the New York suburb, so the word was enticing. On screen, Tyler is a striking figure. He has that long face, which looks seventeen and forty at the same time. His voice sounds like an angry god but he's feminine too: lanky, moving his hands softly, wearing long socks which make him look like he should be wearing lederhosen.

The beat (which he made in eight minutes as a joke, to mock New York trends) sounds like a MIDI keyboard coughing up its final chord. Tyler's first words – 'I'm a fucking walking paradox . . . no I'm not' are everything which made Odd Future annoying and appealing in equal measure: an antagonistic pettiness which nobody over the age of twenty-one seems able to muster. He shouts out Bruno Mars and threatens to stab him. Then he disses Jesus. Days after it was released, Kanye West – only weeks removed from the high point of his career – tweeted that it was the video of the year. It's sinister, in a kind of outlandish way, and it made Tyler a star.

In the winter of 2010, Caius Pawson's Young Turks hosted Odd Future's first ever live show in the basement of The Drop pub in London's Stoke Newington (of all places). With ten of them onstage, OF live shows quickly descended into *Jackass*-style carnage. Within two years, there were queues around the block for every Odd Future show and, within six, their members were opening for Eminem on a stage at Wembley Stadium. Their rise was stratospheric and their influence among the teenagers of the generation cannot be overstated. In 2013, you could see skinny teenage boys in Birmingham trying to look like a bunch of skating teenagers from South Central LA. For a while everything Odd Future touched turned into commercial gold. Soon Lil Wayne was wearing Odd Future merchandise to the front row of NBA games. Billie Eilish, one of the biggest artists of the following decade, later said that Tyler 'inspired every part of everything about me'.

The success of Odd Future was really a triumph of self-promotion. Until 2011, the collective accrued a cult following without selling a single piece of music: every song they made was posted online for free. It was a strategy Tyler learned from the era he was raised in. In the late '90s, mixtapes were a way for MCs like 50 Cent, who had no contract or record connections, to spread their music around the neighbourhood. Some years later, rappers who already had distribution deals began using the digital versions of mixtapes to release music to their fans without getting caught up in corporate release strategies. By the normal metrics of the music industry, for example, Lil Wayne was in a fallow period in 2006 but, as any rap fan knows, Lil Wayne was actually on top of the world then, tearing up other rappers' beats on tapes like *Da Drought 3*, released for free online.

Odd Future had no presence in the rap game and no connections to the industry, full stop. They were, literally, children. But, just like the fake albums Tyler cut and stuck together in his front room as a kid, he treated each Odd Future mixtape like an official album release. They were packaged with artwork which looked closer to what a label might put together than the deliberately scrappy style of the Gangsta Grillz mixtapes. Another thing which distinguished Odd Future from the old guard is that they didn't post their tapes on DatPiff, but on the new social media sites like MySpace and Tumblr. Rather than being a one-way system, their fans could interact with them, and share the album to their pages. Internet virality was about participation rather than simple consumption. Now, we're used to – nay, *expect* – our artists to make themselves available online, but the Odd Future kids were using Tumblr to interact directly with their listeners years before Instagram and Twitter made that normal. If they could win enough teenagers over then Odd Future didn't *need* to make money from music, they could make it from socks and T-shirts instead. It was a strategy which worked so well, even those who had major label contracts began to look at them with envy.

In 2009, Lonny Breaux was an English literature graduate making his way around Hollywood studio sessions, penning a single for Brandy here, a tune for Bieber there. Tricky Stewart, the Illinois producer who wrote Rhianna's 'Umbrella' and Beyoncé's 'Single Ladies', took a liking to him and helped him get a solo deal on Def Jam Records. It should have been a breakthrough moment, but it soon became apparent that the contract was largely to ensure that he didn't take his talents elsewhere.

The money to make an album never materialised, and work on his debut stalled as quickly as it started. Lonny, it seemed, was destined to become another casualty of the music industry's relentless, grinding gears.

Born in Long Beach in 1987, Breaux moved with his mother and younger brother to New Orleans when he was five. His father, Calvin Cooksey, was a singer, but left the family early. The Breaux family were Pentecostal but, unlike Sam Cooke or Elvis, Lonny never performed in church. His real name was Christopher, but his grandfather, Lionel – who helped raise him when his father left – nicknamed him Lonny. Lionel was an addict of various kinds, and a big part of Lonny's childhood was spent sitting silently in NA and AA meetings by his side.

Lonny always had headphones strapped around his ears. Even as a boy, he had good taste and an old head. Some of his favourite songs were by Simon & Garfunkel and Roberta Flack. He split his own passions between music and poetry but, at twelve, he stopped imitating Langston Hughes and began trying to write like Stevie Wonder instead. He booked his first studio session when he was thirteen. Because Lonnie's dad had been a musician, his mother wasn't thrilled. 'You're going to follow that bum?' she asked. She wanted him to go to law school instead.

In 2005, it looked like Lonny wouldn't have a choice. When Hurricane Katrina hit, New Orleans turned to ruin. A 400-mile-wide storm ripped through the city and tens of thousands of homes were washed away or drowned in flood water. Lonny's DIY studio was destroyed but a sympathetic friend from LA offered him some discounted studio time as a gesture of solidarity. Lonny earned some money repairing the city – putting up drywall – and raised the funds. He moved to LA with $1,100 in his pocket. For the first four years he worked odd jobs until, one evening, he went to a listening party to pick up a backpack he'd left behind and found himself partying with a bunch of the producers in the room. They were testing out material: each of them plugging in their laptops and playing their shit to see what hit. When Lonny plugged in the aux cable, a couple of people with jobs in the right places liked what they heard, and invited him to the studio to write.

Soon, Lonny was spending almost every day in the studio. He could sing as well as write, and so began to act as a go-between for writers and producers. He viewed songwriting as a competitive sport, and tried to outclass the writers working in the studios either side of him. It worked. Within two years – by the time he was twenty-two – Breaux was already wealthy. He had a Beverly Hills apartment, a BMW and a couple of hundred thousand in the bank. He was also miserable. He got his heart broken, and was sucked into a crippling Def Jam deal. Writing for other musicians was supposed to be his gateway into the industry, but it felt like the gates had closed already. His situation was testament to the way capital and corporate machinations can stifle the very thing they're supposed to facilitate. Even as a teenager, paying for cheap studio time in New Orleans, he was able to write and release music. As an adult with a record deal, he could not.

It was Tyler who inspired his great escape. A mutual friend passed Lonny his number and one night, when he was at his lowest ebb, he decided to call him up. Lonny headed down to South Central LA and Tyler introduced him to the rest of Odd Future. Lonny was stunned by the way they were promoting their music. He had more money than all of them put together, but they were having fun, and their mixtapes were being heard. Lonny became more involved in Odd Future, singing some of the hooks of their songs (the first time the public had ever even heard his voice). Soon, he decided to follow their lead.

On October 2010, Lonny changed his name for the third time, to Frank Ocean (named after Sinatra, and *Ocean's Eleven* respectively). Five months later, he posted *nostalgia, ULTRA*, his debut mixtape on his Tumblr for free. There was no promotion. To Odd Future's growing fanbase, it was the next in a long line of mixtapes before it, but this one went further than them all. It created enough buzz within the industry to catch the ear of JAY-Z, who liked it so much that he burned the files onto a CD and started playing it in his car when he was driving with Beyoncé. When she heard it, she invited Frank to the studio the very next day.

Released in February 2011, in the wide-eyed early months of the '10s, *nostalgia, ULTRA* was also a project which set the mood for the shape of pop to come. It's easy to forget now but, in 2011, it was still considered fairly abhorrent for an independent artist – the type who'd post their music for free online – to enjoy a band like Coldplay, let alone rerecord one of their songs. Frank was, and remains, the ultimate post-genre, post-taste eclecticist, and he was ahead of his time. 'Strawberry Swing' (a song-length sample of the instrumental from Coldplay's song of the same name) plays straight into 'Novacane', a shuffling, tense R&B song about a dentist and part-time porn star who gets hooked on her own sedatives.

These contrasts, spread across the mixtape, are moments of cool meets uncool. Disparate moods are tied together by Frank's voice, a deceptively idiosyncratic delivery which is a picture of pure nonchalance. 'American Wedding' is *nostalgia, ULTRA*'s showstopper, a brazen remake of 'Hotel California' which lifts the instrumental and vocal melody of the original song, with lyrics which tell the tale of a shotgun marriage and its nasty demise. Even though the Eagles song is hardly hopeful, Ocean's version is a far grimmer tale. 'American Wedding' ends in a sudden rapped verse which underlines the intent of the entire mixtape. There is no easy classification for this; it's all mood and feeling, led not by a unifying taste or genre but the storytelling of its songwriter and his insouciant voice.

Frank funded *nostalgia, ULTRA* out of his own pocket, testing out demos made by his producer friends and trawling the Internet for instrumentals he could write songs to. He settled upon tracks by the Eagles, MGMT, Mr. Hudson and Coldplay. A month after posting the record, he took to Twitter and said 'i. did. this. not ISLAND DEF JAM. that's why you see no label logo on the artwork that I DID. guess its my fault for trusting my dumbass lawyer and signing my career over to a failing company. fuck Def Jam & any company that goes the length of signing a kid with dreams & talent w/no intention of following through. fuck em. Now back to my day. i want some oatmeal and toast.'

Frank had used the model Tyler had cooked up in his bedroom to circumvent his contract and capture the ear of not only OF teens but fans of Janelle Monáe and The-Dream too. Two months later, Def Jam offered to re-release the album's sample-free songs as an EP. For his next album, Frank asked for a million dollars upfront, and they said yes.* That album was teased by the single 'Thinkin Bout You' a hit song by even traditional radio standards, and one which turned *channel ORANGE* into

---

* Def Jam remained a punching bag for Frank Ocean. A few years after the release of his first studio album, he went on to pull an even grander stunt than the mixtape had been. At the peak of his fame, he released *Endless*, a visual album which – for years – could only be listened to with its accompanying visuals on Apple Music. It was nobody's definition of an 'album', that is, aside from in a contract, which Frank fulfilled by releasing it. He was a free agent. The same evening that he streamed *Endless*, he released *Blonde*, his second studio album proper on his own newly formed label, Boys Don't Cry. It was a sleight of hand which cost Def Jam a fortune.

a massive commercial success. Frank Ocean was on his way to becoming the generational songwriter he's recognised as today, a name which carries such weight that it would be easy to forget he was ever part of Odd Future, even though his music wouldn't have been made at all if he hadn't been.

Odd Future never really ended, it just evaporated. Some of its members remain friends to this day; others drifted. One of the greatest myths about the group is that they were all close in the first place. Some were sleep-on-the-sofa, ride-or-die kind of friends, others less so. As the only woman in the group, Syd Bennett began to feel increasingly isolated by the collective's reputation online. 'The gay community hated me for being part of Odd Future,' she told the *New York Times* in 2016. When touring in Australia, she separated from her then-girlfriend and felt totally isolated. One day she sat the guys down on the beach and told them she was leaving. It wasn't well received. 'They weren't happy about it,' she said. 'I was their get-out-of-jail-free card. It's easy to say they aren't homophobic because Syd is there.'

Syd wasn't the only queer member of Odd Future. On the 4th of July 2012, one week ahead of the release of *channel ORANGE*, Frank posted something to Tumblr which wasn't a mixtape, but was every bit as consequential as *nostalgia, ULTRA* had been. It was a short essay where he described the story of a romance which turned into a painful heartbreak. It also happened that his lover was a man. The outpouring of support for Frank was swift. Kanye West – who urged fellow rappers to 'stop the gay-bashing' back in 2005 – voiced his support. Tyler, the Creator did too, in a typical Tyler way: 'I was one of the first people he [came out to],' he told *Rolling Stone*. 'I kinda knew because he likes Pop Tarts without frosting on them, so I knew something was weird.'

Frank's note helped to bolster his image as a leader of a younger generation with an entirely different point of view, and its effect was intensified by his proximity to two things infamous for their latent homophobia: Odd Future, and rap. Right from its inception, beloved acts like Public Enemy and A Tribe Call Quest revelled in overt homophobia. The song 'Georgie Porgie' (from the otherwise magnificent *Low End Theory*) was a song so vitriolic in its hatred of gay men that Jive Records refused to release it. After Frank's note, things have never quite been the same. In 2021, ascendent Cleveland rapper DaBaby took to a festival stage and bizarrely pronounced 'if you didn't show up today with HIV, AIDS, or any of them deadly sexually transmitted diseases that'll make you die in two to three weeks, then put your cellphone lighter up.' His career essentially ended on the spot.

Odd Future only actually existed for around five years and you can count the number of truly great albums they released on a single hand.* Now the dust has settled however, its legacy is one almost nobody would have predicted: a launchpad for a generation of queer, Black artists whose independent beginnings meant that they could continue to create music freely, touching even the most machismo-obsessed corners of the industry. Frank Ocean, Tyler, the Creator and Syd Tha Kid's The Internet (who spawned their own acolytes in the shape of KAYTRANADA and Steve Lacy) all gained huge queer followings, and reshaped soul and funk into softer, more abstract forms.

In his book *Go Ahead in the Rain: Notes to A Tribe Called Quest*, poet Hanif Abdurraqib says that the only legitimate successor to Native Tongues (the New York collective of

* Domo Genesis & The Alchemist, *No Idols*; Tyler, the Creator, *Bastard*; MellowHype, *Yellowhite*; Frank Ocean, *nostalgia, ULTRA* – by my count.

progressive, spiritually minded rap artists like De La Soul, Tribe, Jungle Brothers and Queen Latifa) was Odd Future. What the group lacked in tight songs they made up for in raw, infectious energy. Look at their TV debut on *Late Night with Jimmy Fallon*, where Tyler and Hodgy Beats rap with the energy of an '80s punk group then jump on Jimmy Fallon's desk. So many TV debuts, understandably, feature a lot of shaky vocals or first-night nerves. Who else was making an entrance like *that*? 'I felt like they were invading Middle America's living room,' said XL Records founder Richard Russell, who happened to be watching from the sidelines. 'Tyler is a revolution'.* The masterful Mos Def, who happened to be on the show that day, goes wild for it, and joins in, grabbing the camera lens and screaming. Like Pusha T, Kanye West and Lil Wayne, Def was another icon of rap electrified by the Odd Future lightning bolt.

There can be no doubt about the man who made it happen. Like Mos Def or André 3000 before him, Tyler Okonma has the type of personality which, when exposed to fame, can't help but seep into the culture. Hip hop has never been completely welcome in the living rooms of white America, but many of the ideas Tyler carried from his childhood were an uneasy fit for rap too. He enthused about Iggy Pop in radio interviews and mocked the clichés which had come to define gangsta rap. He was arrested on charges of vandalism after a show in 2011, an incident many rappers would have used to flex their

* On his next appearance on the show in 2013, Tyler photo-bombed another talk show guest: future president Donald Trump. While Taco posed for a picture with him, Tyler jumped behind, pulling his top up and rubbing his nipples. It actually made Trump look pretty ridiculous, meaning a 22-year-old rapper achieved what the vast majority of the American media class and political establishment could not: he embarrassed him.

authenticity, but not Tyler: 'I don't know why rappers talk about jail like it's cool,' he said. 'I would go crazy.'

It was a strand of defiance Tyler had no choice but to develop as a kid. 'Seventh grade they used to fuck with me,' he told *Le Drone* in 2011. 'I wore black trucker hats and shiny little accessories, all black. Slipknot and Good Charlotte tees. They used to call me white boy. I hated that shit. Why can't I just be a fucking human? That shit irks me when people bring race into dumb shit.'* Indeed while Wiz Khalifa was burning through enough weed to power a small train, Tyler didn't even drink; the only thing he puffed onstage was his inhaler. He began his career dressed as a Thrasher-loving skater boy before transforming into a debonair aristocrat, with an ushanka hat to boot. His songs – from 'See You Again' to 'NEW MAGIC WAND' – eventually became undeniable too.

Like Native Tongues and the Soulquarians before them, this gang of obnoxious, amateurish teens spawned the careers of not one, not two, but three of a generation's leading voices in music, against all odds. Many of them started out poor and almost none had any kind of musical training. The impact they had is not simply unlikely, it's a borderline miracle. Frank Ocean and Tyler both made wonderful records, and their cultural weight is

---

* In 2011, three students at a college jazz programme in Toronto played a saxophone-led cover of 'Bastard' to their performance instructors and posted it online. They were one of the first jazz ensembles to distribute their music the way rappers did their mixtapes and, under the name BADBADNOTGOOD, they released two other free projects too: performing renditions of everything from Odd Future's viral tracks to Gucci Mane's 'Lemonade'. With a focus on video game scores and rap, this was post-bop jazz which caught the ear of a younger audience. Tyler loved it and soon joined them for a session. Cross-genre pollination happening in real time.

undeniable, but it was Odd Future's third-most notorious alum who would go on to make the most staggering, remarkable art.

Part 2 (Earl, Part 1)

Because hip hop emerged as an accompaniment to dance music, there's a distinction to be made between the start of hip hop and the start of *rap*. There were steady, rapped verses in blues songs like Joe Hill Louis' 'Gotta Let You Go' as early as the 1920s. What else was Muhammad Ali doing when he was limbering up to fight George Foreman and said 'You know I'm bad, just last week I murdered a rock / Injured a stone, hospitalized a brick / I'm so mean, I make medicine sick'? How about Langston Hughes, reciting his 'The Weary Blues' to the tempo of a jazz band in 1958? In the 1960s, Beat poet Amiri Baraka wanted to forge a clear distinction between poetry and Black poetry, and began to write in a style which ran closer to the repetition and syncopation of jazz. At the end of that decade, that idea captivated and inspired musicians like Gil Scott-Heron and The Last Poets: songwriters who were radicals not only musically, but politically too.

The Last Poets (a group with many iterations across the decades) were born out of a Harlem writers' workshop, and formed at Mount Morris Park (now Marcus Garvey Park) on the birthday of Malcolm X. The group's self-titled debut was released eleven months ahead of Marvin Gaye's *What's Going On* and it feels like that album's more radical twin. They were both state-of-the-nation indictments of Nixon's America, but where Gaye's album is wistful and luscious, the Poets' is all sharp edges: spoken, not sung, with a skittish, percussive backbone. Where Gaye laments the wounds of a nation, the Poets burn through it with an indignant fury, urging comrades not to fear revolution and set about destroying the romantic mythology of New York City.

The Last Poets received plenty of dues from rappers of the genre's first golden era; sampled by Digable Planets, Notorious B.I.G. and Brand Nubian alike. Their music sounded little like the hip hop which emerged from dance music at the end of the decade but the substance of their words isn't a million miles from the unapologetic politics of Public Enemy in the late 1980s.

The Last Poets' name was taken from the final stanza of 1969's 'Towards a Walk in the Sun' by South African poet Bra Willie. At the end of the '60s, Willie had come to believe that the planet's racial and economic tensions were about to explode, and leave something unrecognisable in its wake, something which would render art itself obsolete. 'When the moment hatches in time's womb there will be no art talk,' he wrote. 'The only poem you will hear will be the spearpoint pivoted in the punctured marrow of the villain . . . Therefore we are the last poets of the world.'

As a child Bra Willie (real name Keorapetse Kgositsile) was an avid reader of D.H. Lawrence, and dreamed of one day becoming a novelist himself. He was also intimately familiar with the jazz music of America. When he was young he was taken in by his Uncle Tholo, a teacher and music lover who had American records posted by jazz pianist Horace Silver, who he had befriended when Silver briefly toured the country. When he moved to Johannesburg as a teenager though, Kgositsile soon became involved in the serious business of journalism instead.* He joined the *New Age*, a Black communist

* Some biographies say that Kgositsile was born in Johannesburg, but he was actually born in the village of Dithakong. The discrepancy was not accidental: South Africa had laws about Black citizens moving around the country, and so his mother drilled the idea that he was born in Johannesburg into him from an early age. It might well have saved his life.

newspaper, for whom he penned lyrical poetry, seeking to inspire an armed uprising against the apartheid of the ruling National Party. When the *New Age* was shut down under anti-communist laws, the ANC recommended that its writers flee the country. Kgositsile agreed, heading for Pennsylvania. He didn't return for another twenty-nine years.

Kgositsile soon left rural Pennsylvania for New York City, and he headed straight for the jazz clubs of Brooklyn. Like Lou Reed, he was entranced by John Coltrane, Nina Simone and B.B. King, watching them intently through smoke-filled rooms. He came to realise that Black liberation was a struggle which existed far beyond South African apartheid. Watching the music of African Americans, he began to develop a theory of what he believed to be a uniquely Black aesthetic, one strongly centred around rhythms which moved the body, to which jazz and poetry were central. Kgositsile became a performer himself, delivering impassioned recitals of his poetry in downtown clubs. He released his most famous collection – *My Name Is Afrika* – at the start of 1971, the same year that he wrote the liner notes for Pharaoh Sanders' classic *Thembi*.

Kgositsile wasn't able to return to his home country for nearly three decades, when Nelson Mandela was freed and quickly came to power. When he did return, it was through sponsorship by the Congress of South African Writers, and he was hosted on a tour of the country he was born in. 'Hosts! In my own country,' he wrote in an essay about the ordeal. 'There are no memories here. The streets of Johannesburg cannot claim me. I cannot claim them either.' Still, South Africa's young artists did claim him, and Bra Willie became something of a legend among young Black activists, struggling with the remnants of apartheid and the different kind of conservatism brought about by the ANC. In 2006 he became South Africa's poet laureate.

In 1990, after years teaching in Kenya, Botswana and Zambia, Kgositsile returned to the US to teach at Michigan's Wayne State University. There he met Cheryl Harris, a civil rights professor who shared his deep love of jazz. In 1993 they married and, one year later, Harris gave birth to their only child, Thebe Neruda Kgositsile (pronounced 'I-beh', Setswana for 'shield'). For the next six years, the poet divided his time between the University of California – where he and Harris relocated – and South Africa's Fort Hare University. After their marriage fell apart though, Kgositsile left America for good in 2001. Thebe's middle name was a tribute to Kgositsile's friend and comrade, Pablo Neruda, the Chilean poet. Sterling D. Plumpp, another of Kgositsile's friends, wrote a prognostication for the newborn in 1996, in a piece titled 'Poet: For Thebe Neruda'. 'You were born with blues,' he wrote. 'With an ANC imprint on them. How you gon' do anything but rule?'

When the teenage fans of Odd Future, with socks hitched high around their calves and Supreme skateboards stuffed in their backpacks, began chanting 'Free Earl!' in 2010, they knew none of this. They didn't know that their idol – Earl Sweatshirt – was the son of a Poet Laureate, whose words had helped give birth to hip hop. They just wanted to see him rap, and it was easy to see why.

Thebe Kgositsile began writing rhymes when he was thirteen years old. He spent the entirety of his twelfth year listening to *Hip Hop Is Dead* on repeat. Rap had been sacred to him for a long time. His mother had banned him from listening to the likes of Dr Dre's *2001*, making it even more thrilling in the process. Thebe wrote his first bars in his father's university office in South Africa. While Keorapetse was teaching, Thebe sat and attempted to work out how to write a sixteen-bar verse. He was good at it – he'd listened to rap for his whole life – and soon he was making entire songs.

Less than a year in, he uploaded a track to MySpace under his first moniker, Sly Tendencies. He rhymed over *Madvillainy* beats and instrumentals made by his friend Loofy in his bedroom. Cheryl Harris had become a respected scholar of Critical Race Theory at UCLA (a niche field of academia which eventually became a bogeyman for the American right). At home, she raised Thebe on Nichiren Buddhism and jazz. She sent Thebe to a UCLA Lab School, an experimental institution which tested new theories about teaching and development on real Californian kids. At the Lab he met Sage Elsesser, a kid from a few years below. Elsesser would one day become a skateboarder and model, and eventually the deft and confessional rapper Navy Blue, but then he was just a kid who loved to skate.

When Elsesser was only twelve, his talent had already made him famous on the streets of West Hollywood. Through this he knew Tyler Okonma too. Thebe already admired *The Odd Future Tape Vol. 1* from afar and so, when Sage made their leader's acquaintance, he asked his friend to put them in touch. Elsesser, keen to impress his fifteen-year-old pal, obliged. When Tyler listened to the few loose Sly Tendencies songs, he knew that the kid was something special. As soon as he could, he invited Thebe round to the Trap.

In Odd Future, Thebe was put to immediate use. He changed his rap name to Earl Sweatshirt, chosen as part of a lifelong fascination with what he called 'old white people names'. Within a few weeks of meeting Thebe, Tyler gave him a feature on *Bastard,* and a verse on MellowHype's *Yellowhite* followed. Thebe's own mixtape, *Earl,* came quickly, dropping on the 31st of March 2010.

It took many blogs and forums almost a year to catch on to *Bastard* so *Earl* was truly the first Odd Future album to take off. What propelled the tape was the music video for its title track: a fish-eye nightmare where the OF gang drink a noxious blue drink which causes them to stagger around LA in a trance, their gums and nipples bleeding. It was part *Jackass*, part *Requiem for a Dream* and it rattled a few cages. Thebe's mixtape is goofy – self-effacing even – and went further than even *Bastard* had, and the entire twenty-four-minute project soon became an object of fascination online.

You can tell immediately that *Earl* is an Odd Future production. Right from its first grimy note, the tape is defined by the tinny drums and buzzing, squelchy synths which set it apart from all of those early Tyler and LeftBrain productions. Most of all though, it's packed full of that good, old-fashioned Odd Future sense of humour. Over ten songs, Thebe, Tyler, Vince Staples and Hodgy Beats take turns cycling giddily through the most appalling raps their adolescent minds could muster. Many of the laziest jokes are about as scintillating as being stuck on a train with a bunch of thirteen-year-olds, but even in this adolescent context, Thebe's precocious talent still manages to poke through the chaos. To actually shock takes a certain amount of inventiveness, and on songs like the title track Thebe doesn't *just* fire off a bunch of slurs, he also concocts tales of car-jackings and dates turned into nightmares, colouring them with violence which is cartoonish and bizarre. There's pure glee radiating off his pubescent voice, underscoring a repulsive comment in one moment with a sweet 'it's OF, buttercup' the next.

Thebe didn't rap like the other Odd Future members, not even Tyler. His words seem to tumble out his mouth in a flurry, hardly bothered by breathing. He spews vivid images and sharp references to everything from *Dawson's Creek* to *Psycho* with the effortlessness of someone who wrote them only two minutes earlier. Lil Wayne – who, for most of the 2000s, became the consensus pick for the most gifted rapper in a post-JAY-Z world – was only eight when he met Birdman and began rapping on his voicemail in New Orleans, but he could hardly put together a coherent verse until he was twenty. At fifteen Thebe was able to rap complex, knotty rhymes with a nonchalance so alluring that it made teenagers bragging about drawing swastikas worth sitting through.

Thebe's brilliance as an MC was a sentiment shared within Odd Future too. 'Tyler always treated him as sacred,' their manager Christian Clancy told the *New York Times*. 'They all did.' The first video on the Odd Future YouTube page, posted before any of Tyler's own music videos, was a clip entitled 'Earl Sweatshirt'. 'I've never seen nobody from my neighbourhood, from my community, do some shit like that,' Tyler raves in the video. In early press, Tyler liked to compare *Earl* to Nas' *Illmatic*, a claim which sounds pretty ridiculous when comparing those two albums directly, but as a forecast of the rapper to come, maybe less so.

When they finished working on *Earl*, Tyler and Thebe began plotting a joint mixtape together. If Odd Future had something to say beyond the novelty of provocation, then Thebe was the one saying it loudest, and he was central to Tyler's plan for world domination. He knew that his raps lent the group a degree of credibility they wouldn't have had otherwise. But it was a masterplan which wouldn't go very far. Just as the rap world was catching on to Odd Future, Earl Sweatshirt disappeared.

When Odd Future fans arrived at their show at LA's The Key Club in July 2010, they noticed one amendment to the flyer: Earl's name was crossed out in felt-tip, with a short explanation scrawled on the side. 'Will not be there, due to mom'. At the show, in between hurling themselves into the crowd, Hodgy Beats and Jasper started a chant: 'Free Earl!' Nobody in the crowd could have known what that meant, but those rappers inspired utter devotion from their fans, and the crowd shouted the chant back at them with furious agreement.

Soon 'Free Earl' was the next piece of Odd Future iconography. It was a slogan repeated on message boards, and printed on T-shirts mocked up like 'missing' posters. In an age where access to the private lives of artists was becoming the norm, here was a true, bona fide mystery for young fans to dig their teeth into. Rumours began to spread that Thebe's mom had listened to *Earl* and sent him off to a boot camp for unruly teenagers, a narrative which nicely suited Odd Future's cultivated image as punks who stuck their middle fingers up to totalitarian adults. Thebe, who had barely thirty minutes of music to his name, suddenly became a mythical figure, and 'Free Earl' morphed naturally into 'fuck Earl's mom'. Professor Harris started to find threatening notes at the door of her UCLA office. People found out where she lived and began driving by her house, shouting threats. Soon she was plunged into fear and distress, struggling to even get dressed in the morning.

The mystery of Earl Sweatshirt soon became a cottage industry in itself. In April 2011, *Complex* published a piece entitled 'We Found Earl Sweatshirt', which disclosed that Thebe was staying somewhere called the Coral Reef Academy in Samoa. It was a rehabilitation centre for teenage boys who'd fallen badly off the rails. The article itself, which led to a follow-up from the *New Yorker*, leaves a strange taste: here were prying pieces of investigative journalism by one of America's most respected weeklies, dedicating serious time to locating a sixteen-year-old boy. It was testament to the devotion he was able to inspire, but bizarre and invasive too, and it would shape Thebe's relationship with fame for years to come.

The truth wasn't quite as simple as Professor Harris having heard her son's music and sending him packing. To Odd Future's online following, Thebe was an exciting new rapper, but to Cheryl he was simply her son, and he was struggling. 'He was really very clearly going through a rough patch emotionally,' she later told the *New York Times*. Thebe had once been a star student but, not long after he began rapping, he became increasingly dependent on weed and started skipping classes. When he was caught cheating on exams, Cheryl decided to take definitive action, and Samoa was it.

In Samoa, Thebe had access to therapists daily. He secured a scuba diving licence, began learning piano and swam with whales. He didn't have weed or his phone, but he did have palm trees, and a ready-made family of boys like him. He read Manning Marable's biography of Malcolm X and Richard Fariña's counterculture fiction. But Thebe was a tough nut to crack. At the Coral Reef Academy, students' progress is marked with a sticker of a bus pinned to a map of the island; when that sticker arrives at the airport, they are free to leave, plain and simple. Thebe did everything he could to keep his sticker at the station.

'For that whole year . . . I was the worst. I became the one example that people give,' he told *GQ* in 2013. 'They always give new kids examples like "now if you want to leave here, you act like him. You don't want to be like him." After a year, I was the "you don't want to be like him . . ." I really learned how to be a real piece of shit.'

When he did eventually fly back to LA, seven months after he was sent away, things had changed, both for Thebe and everyone around him. In February 2012, he marked his return with (what else?) a new Tumblr account, where he posted a short song titled 'Home'. Within a month, he made his first appearance with Odd Future at the Hammerstein Ballroom in Manhattan, dressed in a Hawaiian shirt and a pink baseball cap. The rest of his friends had become stars in his absence, performing for two years straight, but there he was, making his live debut to a room of thousands.

Thebe's friends had assumed that Earl Sweatshirt would simply slot back into the Odd Future roster as soon as he returned. At first, that was true. Behind the scenes though, Thebe was already carving a trajectory distinct from the rest of the group. Witnessing the hype surrounding her son, Cheryl had realised, for the first time, that Thebe's talk of a rap career could actually become reality. While he was in Samoa, she arranged for Leila Steinberg, who had managed a teenage Tupac, to be his manager. While he was still at the Academy, Steinberg even began sending him writing exercises via email. When he returned home, she and his mother helped him sign a distribution deal with Columbia Records. The deal put him within Sony alongside the rest of Odd Future, but written into the contract was a guarantee that he could start his own imprint, Tan Cressida, too.

Before he could start, Cheryl made sure Thebe finished the business of being a teenager too. She moved them to Toronto so he could finish his senior year there, even if he spent it itching to begin his career; the only kid in class without a question mark at the end of everything. When he began touring with Odd Future though, Thebe began to resent the collective's following. At the end of 2015, *SPIN* asked him what he'd like people to understand about the history of the group. 'That it didn't start as a bunch of people who were friends who then miraculously discovered that they all had some sort of innate music ability,' he answered. 'We came together for a job, and we disbanded as a job.'

It would be a cliché to suggest that Thebe returned from Samoa a different person. He landed on that small island in the South Pacific when he was barely sixteen years old; at that age, he'd have been a different person if he'd taken a job at Subway. But the world knew Thebe for a character he played on *Earl*, and by the time he was eighteen, he was already tired of that himself. At the Coral Reef Academy, one of the duties assigned to him was performing community service at a support group for survivors of sexual abuse. There Thebe heard from survivors, seeing graphic images of the things he'd cracked jokes about just a few months earlier. *That* change was immediate. 'There was nothing you could do when you're looking at a . . . little girl that's been horribly abused,' he told *GQ*. Thebe was back, but that Earl, at least, was already gone.

Thebe was in America for only a few hours when work on his debut album began. On his second or third day in LA he visited Syd and Matt Martian's home in Marina Del Rey and together they made the instrumental for what would become the album's third single, 'Hive'. Thebe tended to work quickly. He'd chug coffee, smoke a ton of weed and sit over his notepad, writing and rewriting until he was happy, then recording his verse in a single take.

Once Thebe made it clear that he was willing to break away from the Odd Future ecosystem, Columbia's A&Rs began sending him suggestions for producers he might want to hit the studio with. One of those suggestions was Christian Rich – a duo of one-time investment bankers who had just produced Drake's 'Pound Cake'. Another was Tyler, the Creator's idols, The Neptunes. In 2012 one half of the duo – Chad Hugo – worked with Syd's group The Internet, and the duo stepped behind the boards to work with the group's prodigal son.

What's striking about 'Burgundy', the album track they produced, is that you wouldn't necessarily know it was them; their motifs are folded into Earl's universe, their stabbing piano softened into what feels like a sigh. This wasn't necessarily what Columbia had in mind when they hooked Thebe up with producers who made hits for JAY-Z and Nelly. Knowing where Thebe's career ended up, it's hilarious to know that this gloomy, sinister album could have ended up as a *Nothing Was the Same*-style pop crossover. Earl's first mixtape and the mythology of his vanishing had given him the kind of groundswell following which turns musicians into stars, and Columbia acted accordingly: sending him beats with John Legend choruses built in.

Over time, an album which looked like it might come together quickly ended up taking close to a year to make. Sometimes, he would call Vince Staples late at night in distress. 'Oh my god, I'm fucked,' Thebe remembered thinking. 'I'm gonna have to put out an album that I do not fuck with at all.' Thebe began smoking so much weed that he was high for days on end. When his grandmother passed away he got skinny. Very skinny. He began subsisting on only weed, Red Bull, cigarettes and Chick-Fil-A.

Despite featuring the work of half a dozen producers across the record, Thebe decided to go a different route, and ended up producing half of the album himself (credited anonymously as 'randomblackdude'). Rather than simply rapping over beats provided to him, Thebe was present for every session, and studied the processes of his producers closely. Just as Tyler was moving towards a brighter, jazz-funk-inspired palette, Thebe retained his friend's darker mode, and it was beats like those which he began coaxing out of his producers.

Released on the 20th of August 2013, *Doris* ended up cohering far better than it probably should have. It also feels strange, in retrospect, just how much it still feels like an Odd Future album. That's probably due to the strong and loud presence of Tyler, the Creator, whose additions to the album were recorded late in the day, just before the record was submitted. He produced both of the tracks he had guest verses on – 'Sasquatch' and 'Whoa' – and his fingers are all over them, in the ingenious onomatopoeic hook which comprises the beat of the latter, and the moment he threatens to kidnap some One Direction fans, of course.

While *Bastard* and *Goblin* were cartoon-scary though, *Doris* is often genuinely so. Defined by Thebe's drawling flow, there's an atmosphere of depressiveness which pervades the album. The opening song of Earl Sweatshirt's first mixtape had beat down on himself as a joke, but on *Doris* there's no real punchline. Like Tyler and Frank before him, he promoted the album live on *Jimmy Fallon* but, far from tearing up the set, Earl appeared with his eyes closed and hood up, firmly grasping the mic, barely moving a muscle. It was a performance which did justice to the *Doris* sound. With its heavy, lumbering drums and lyrics fixated on family, depression and the opinion of others, it is a cacophony, but one which exists almost entirely behind the eyes.

'Chum' was the album's first single: the first song he made with the brothers Christian Rich when they first connected. When it arrived in November of 2012, I remember it being startling. Then, Earl was mostly known then for his murderous, adult-baiting verses, but here he was direct, confessional and rhyming about his dad. 'It's probably been twelve years since my father left / Left me fatherless' he raps. 'I just used to say I hate him in dishonest jest / When honestly, I miss this n***a, like, when I was six / And every time I got the chance to say it, I would swallow it.'

The album's starkest song is its third single, 'Hive'. After the wooziness of 'Sunday', it arrives in the track-list like a predator emerging from the foliage. Where 'Sunday's beat was bashful, 'Hive's churns like a grindstone. Thebe sounds at least twice his age, and delivers every line as if he has sheer contempt for the beat he's rhyming over. But while he sounds like a heavyweight, he raps like a cruiser; there are so many internal rhymes in his verse that every sentence becomes a hook. The moment where he says 'in turn, these critics and interns / admittin' like he has a mouth full of molasses is as sticky as many of the decade's most infectious pop songs.*

While Thebe's first verse luxuriates on personal vices and inter-personal antipathies, his final bars serve as a stark change of tack. Delivered in tumbling fashion over the beat's eerie, disembodied moans, for the first time in his career Thebe offers a vision of Los Angeles through his eyes. The verse is imagistic and bizarre. 'From a city that's recession-hit / stress n****s could flex metal with peddle to rake pennies in,' he

---

* 'Hive' was also a breakout moment for Vince Staples, a Def Jam-signee who delivers an unbelievable verse in the song's second act. His voice is higher than Thebe's, and he cuts through 'Hive's heady beat like a scalpel. Vince's voice has always felt apt because his lyrics are direct to the same degree; there's hardly allegory or metaphor in his songs, he doesn't need them, he says the unsayable as plainly as day. Vince was taught how to enunciate and ad-lib by another rapper who has a guest verse on *Doris*: Mac Miller. Mac was one of the artists, alongside the likes of Chance the Rapper and Action Bronson, who headed up a wave of colourful, proudly independent young rappers in the first half of the 2010s. His debut album, *Blue Slide Park*, became the first independently released album to earn a Billboard number one since 1995. Because of his exile to Samoa, Thebe was largely absent for the years Mac was coming to prominence and, when Thebe first heard him rhyme, he wasn't impressed. That was, until he met him. When they first hung out, Thebe realised that, like him, Mac had ambitions to not only rap better, but produce his own work too. Miller ran his own rap camps called The Sanctuary: freestyle sessions inspired by The Alchemist's set-up where young MCs could come over to write together and fight over beats. Miller eventually overcame the shortcomings of his early work and on albums like *Faces* and *Swimming* – released just before his death from an accidental overdose when he was only twenty-six – he really came into his own.

raps. Thebe's version of his city is as treacherous as his depictions of his mind; there's lead in the water, newspapers treat murder like a scoreboard, and even his own music is just a part of an ugly tapestry: 'Provider of the backdrop music / for the crack rock user and the mascot, Earl,' he raps. Thebe had grown out of the ghoulish horror stories of his debut mixtape but somehow this world, the real world, is uglier still.

The thing which makes Thebe succeed as an MC, even though his flow is often so languid and droll, is his explosive use of language. In those teenage years, while he was striving to write with as much complexity as he possibly could, Thebe had one main lyricist of inspiration: MF DOOM. Thebe and Tyler were both big fans of DOOM; it was one of the first things they bonded over when they met.* In Tyler, DOOM's lyrical influence is less apparent, but in the lines of Earl – forever the more studious of the two – the Long Island legend looms large.

Daniel Dumile (to use his birth name) was an all-time great lyricist, and his strongest talent was the ability to knot words together like he was weaving wicker; finding polysyllabic rhymes which somehow still formed coherent, potent images. Dumile was nearly thirty by the time he settled on that style with 1999's *Operation: Doomsday*, but Thebe learned his tricks early. Just listen to 'Whoa'. After a four-count stutter, Thebe steps into the verse emphasising the assonant rhymes at either

---

* One of the most fun photographs from the Odd Future era is of Tyler and Thebe, baby-faced, sat staring up at MF DOOM, mouths agog. Another video shows them front row at the same show, rapping every word to *Madvillainy*'s 'Curls'. When they met backstage, Tyler was sure to give him his props, and Dumile replied: 'I'm not as wild as you n****s! I'm trying to keep up!' Later that year, Earl would appear alongside DOOM on Captain Murphy's 'Between Villains'. For a boy who was visibly teary eyed to meet him, it must have been a crazy moment.

end of each bar firmly. His flow creates its own rhythm in this way, sounding like a marble rolling across the decks of a listing ship. There are plenty of moments on the record where Earl's lyrics are worth tuning into but on 'Whoa' what he's actually saying hardly matters; he creates an entire counter-melody by finding an opposite for every syllable. It's woozy and intoxicating, and he hardly needs to break a sweat to do it.

The attributes which define the best songs on *Doris* – the confessional quality of 'Chum', 'Hive's depictions of the city as a psychedelic purgatory – would become the defining traits of Earl Sweatshirt's music. Even on his most commercially successful and accessible album though, Thebe was making choices which demonstrated not only a reticence about his burgeoning fame but a willingness to reject it artistically. He had a Columbia deal many musicians would kill for. He was being handed the kind of resources which can turn a young MC into a hip hop star. Hell, when The Neptunes were working on 'Burgundy', Pharrell was literally making 'Blurred Lines' in the studio next door. In the end though, Thebe's show-stopping guest appearance on Frank Ocean's 'Super Rich Kids' from the blockbuster *channel ORANGE* is likely the closest glimpse we'll get into a world where Thebe chose celebrity.

Thebe followed *Doris* with a prolific string of features on records like Freddie Gibbs and Madlib's classic LP *Piñata*, and those songs solidified him as a special presence on the mic. As they would throughout his career, legends like Yasiin Bey (Mos Def) started to call him the young rapper they loved the most. In 2015, Kendrick Lamar, one month after being showered in a lifetime's worth of accolades for *To Pimp a Butterfly*, said that Earl was his favourite MC.

But while Kendrick's missives to Black America were winning plaudits, Thebe expressed reticence in return. 'I just don't do it in the same way as Kendrick,' he told *Grantland* in 2015. 'Kendrick is so explicit in the way that [he] writes. He's the opposite of mystery. Everything is fully spelled out . . . It's sophisticated but it doesn't take a lot to understand what he's talking about.' At the end of 2015, instead of *To Pimp a Butterfly*, Thebe took to Twitter to name *Days with Dr. Yen Lo* – the newest album from Brownsville rapper and New York firefighter Ka – his favourite record of the year.

At the time, Ka was part of a wave of older, underground rappers like Uncommon Nasa, Billy Woods and Roc Marciano who felt somewhat without a lane of their own. Albums like *The Night's Gambit* were lyrical masterworks: cryptic, patience-testing and defined by existential themes. Amid the young, show-stopping rosters of Top Dawg Entertainment or A$AP Mob, their mysterious and imagistic rhymes felt like total anomalies. In 2015, for a 21-year-old rapper like Thebe to praise an album like *Dr. Yen Lo* so proudly felt very left-field indeed. It wouldn't for long. A new wave was coming, and Earl Sweatshirt was about to get very mysterious too.

Part 3 (I Don't Go To Sleep, I Tread Water 'Til I Sink)

Thebe came up with the title of his next record while he was touring his first. *I Don't Like Shit, I Don't Go Outside.* It was supposed to be funny; he was very much outside, travelling Europe and touring relentlessly. Before long, it became his reality.

Thebe spent the duration of his first solo tour eating less and drinking more. After losing his grandmother he took to filling the waiting hours on tour with weed and emotionless sex, which quickly became part of his writing process. After long nights getting wasted, Thebe would sit down, head spinning, and begin writing verses for the record. 'A lot of shit was written right in the moment, if I'd just stayed up an entire night and it's like, eight in the morning,' he told *CRACK* in 2015. 'That's when you just be having bars. Because you're tired, so you're kind of discombobulated and you're not as quick to throw up the defences that you subconsciously throw up during the day.'

As the tour stretched into Eastern Europe, where all they seemed to serve was pork (which Thebe doesn't eat), he almost stopped eating entirely. In two years he lost nearly three stone and, at his lowest, weighed only eight stone in total. In July 2014, he cancelled the tour's final leg with concerns for his health. Not going outside was actually the directive the doctors gave him and Thebe obeyed, embarking on a hermitic period of recovery. After three weeks of straight sleeping he left the house to skateboard and immediately tore his meniscus. It made his leg atrophy, and he was confined to his bed again. It was there, dosed up on Vicodin, where he made the rest of the album.

Early in the process Thebe had attempted to recruit Flying Lotus to produce the record but, after hearing some of Thebe's own production, FlyLo suggested that he should produce it himself. The album is short, less than thirty minutes long, but it couldn't be longer: an aberrant black hole of a record, weighted down by thumping drums, swirling samples and bars delivered with utter contempt. 'I spent the day drinkin' and missin' my grandmother' he raps on 'Huey'. 'I'm toastin' myself, and a toast to all my n****s / ain't no time limit, I'm toasted as hell / And I gotta jot it quick 'cause I can't focus so well.'

If *I Don't Like Shit . . .* sounds like a woozy blur then that's because it was written in one. There is no better title for the record. If it wasn't called that, that's how I'd caption it in my brain. 'When I run, don't chase me' he raps on 'Faucet'. 'I don't know whose house to call home lately / I hope my phone break, let it ring.' Even the way his voice sounds on the album was the result of enforced quiet. 'In the apartment I live in, the room that I do music in is right above where little girls sleep, so I can't be like, slamming that shit,' he told *CRACK*. 'That's the true test of something that's good to me. If you're doing something that's not very loud, but it's fire as fuck.' Indeed, the beat for tracks like 'Grief' trudge rather than knock, ominous samples lingering like a waking thought, and Thebe feels trapped among the density. Given its brevity, *I Don't Like Shit . . .* is striking for the black stain listening to it tends to leave upon your day. The music feels heavy, literally heavy, like you're being trawled backwards through a mental fog.

A year later, Thebe delivered a guest verse on another record which existed in the same psychic quagmire. After a streak of feature verses in 2014, Earl had been relatively inactive for a couple of years, making his return on 'Really Doe' even more striking. The song, from Danny Brown's fourth album, has a line-up for the ages: Danny himself, Ab-Soul and Kendrick Lamar, and yet Thebe somehow wipes the floor with them all. He was an artist who had been a teenager for his entire career to that point but he was twenty-one when he recorded this verse, and hearing him as a man is striking. He deploys his new weaponry to menacing effect, delivering a bitterly antisocial verse as the song's stinger. 'I'm the type of n***a it ain't never been an honour to judge' he growls. 'I just broke up with my b***h cause we ain't argue enough.'

The song 'Really Doe' appeared on *Atrocity Exhibition*, which feels like *I Don't Like Shit . . .* on a different narcotic. Its creator, Danny, was on ecstasy when he made it, but the album contains nothing like the glorious mind-orgasm depicted in Kanye's 'Blood on the Leaves'. For Danny, the drug is nothing more than medication, taken not in the hallways of a Parisian hotel but alone in a room which turns into a pit. 'I'm sweating like I'm in a rave' he raps, 'Been in this room for three days / Think I'm hearing voices / Paranoid and think I'm seeing ghost-es.'

Atrocity Exhibition's first song, 'Downward Spiral', is named after the 1994 Nine Inch Nails record of the same name, and Danny aspired to make rap's version of that dark stain of a record. Released on Warp Records, it's fair to say that *Atrocity Exhibition* isn't like any other hip hop album I've ever heard. Across fifteen songs, it veers between unvarnished mania and sheer, clattering chaos. On 'Ain't It Funny', a squealing horn sample jump-starts an entire, spasming circus carnival and Danny somehow finds a pocket in it, with a voice which sounds like the yelp Tom emits when Jerry steps on his tail. Its subject matter veers between trauma (on the second track he tells the story of a childhood friend killed in a neighbourhood liquor store) and the means he chose to deal with it. Like the album's cover, it feels like the sound of civility slipping, leaving Brown floating amid the cold waters of depression.

Danny recorded most of the album in London with producer Paul White. He gave everything to the record, spending $70,000 on samples alone (leaving a debt which, in 2023, he said he was still paying off). For a young MC chasing a hit, sampling may come down to chopping up a beloved chorus to help turn your song into a hit, but Brown and White thought differently, seeking to find the most bizarre, discombobulating samples and isolating them from their original context completely. Just listen to the tribal rhythms of 'Dance in the Water' or the creepy mariachi of 'Lost'; you know they come from different eras and cultures but it's impossible to know which, or where. On a record like *Atrocity Exhibition*, that makes for a pretty heady psychic stew.

Both *I Don't Like Shit . . .* and *Atrocity Exhibition* are psychedelic music, just not as we tend to know it. They seek to capture their creators' mental states in song: Thebe stoned on Vicodin in bed, Danny tripping on MDMA with the phone lines cut. Hip hop has engaged explicitly in psychedelia for almost as long as it's existed. In 1989, the Beastie Boys sampled a bunch of Beatles songs on 'The Sounds of Science'. In the '90s, songs like Gravediggaz' 'Defective Trip', Digable Planets' 'Time & Space (A New Refutation Of)' and OutKast's magnificent 'Synthesizer' all dealt in the consciousness-broadening effects of psychotropic drugs. After a couple of decades at the periphery, the 2010s saw a new generation of rappers engage in psychedelic culture ravenously. There was A$AP Rocky's 'L$D' and Chance the Rapper's *Acid Rap*. Kanye West and Kid Cudi made a tiny opus about it with *Kids See Ghosts* and, perhaps most obviously, there's Travis Scott, who hit the peak of commercial success creating paeans to the psychedelic on 2018's *Astroworld* and 2023's *UTOPIA*; both records doused in woozy synths and clipped voices, rambling philosophical. In 2023, Lil Yachty turned heads with *Let's Start Here*, where he took a break from rapping over *Finding Nemo* samples to pull off a genuinely impressive Pink Floyd impersonation.

Sixties psychedelia is one of the most successful countercultural ideas in modern history. The imagery of flower power and Ken Kesey's Acid Tests are as active and prevalent today as they ever have been. But time has also worn away at the shine of that specific, Californian moment. The hippy wave of San Francisco Bay morphed into the rabid individualism of Silicon Valley, and the CIA's role in the foundation of the movement has brought its entire substance into question. The aesthetic of '60s psychedelic acts like The Zombies and the Grateful Dead are as popular as ever but, when listening to the music of a Kevin Parker or a Travis Scott, it's hard to shake the feeling that they're not really making *psychedelic* music at all. The style and the sound of that small yet colossal moment in

American culture sought to emulate the effects of psychoactive substances on the consciousness and the body, but these new artists espouse aesthetic choices, first and foremost: an emulation of an emulation.

From Woodstock to paganism, psychedelia has also long carried connotations of the pastoral: of rolling fields and flower chains and open skies. In films like Ari Aster's *Midsommar* (where a grieving millennial is turned into a May Queen through micro-dosing), or albums like Grumbling Fur's *Glynnaestra* or Richard Dawson's 2017 freak-folk epic *Peasant*, it's a connection which persists. Danny Brown loves that type of music (his favourite album is Love's *Forever Changes*). *Atrocity Exhibition* certainly contains many of the tenets of music as played by The Flaming Lips, from the back-tracked vocals to the swirling synths. What he and Earl Sweatshirt were engaging in though was of a different breed: psychedelia of the city. If psychedelic rock was born from psychoactive trips taken in Bay Area mountains, these doom-laden records are instead inspired by the mind-altering, body-numbing effects of urban spaces.

This distinctly twenty-first-century music is born of a type of lifestyle a great many of us are intimately familiar with. In 1980, less than 40 per cent of the world's population lived in cities. Now, more than half do. In the mid 2010s, Earl and Danny began to subsume all the things that kind of living entails: the psychic stress of close confinement, the strain of seeing more people in a day than we were evolved to interact with in a lifetime, and then the anxious retreat: an acute isolation only possible in an age when we're forever surrounded by people. Sure, the wooziness and mania of these albums are fuelled by weed and ecstasy, but they're as much about falling low as getting high. As we now know for sure: depression and trauma are their own kind of out-of-body experience. They warp the mind. Anyone who's lived in a busy city can also attest to the discombobulating stress of noise pollution or the pungent stench of black mould.

In Danny Brown's music the derelict buildings of post-industrial Detroit are the stage his tragic tales unfold against. On *XXX*'s 'Scrap or Die' he twists the chorus of Jeezy's 'Trap or Die' into a story about breaking into houses and stripping them of scrap metal to sell for cash. 'Rolling Stone' is a trip but, across the course of the song, Danny doesn't move beyond the white glare of his phone: late nights on the Internet forging surreal networks of the lonely.

City psychedelia isn't exactly new. Just look at *High Rise*, by J.G. Ballard (whose novella *The Atrocity Exhibition* inspired the Joy Division song which gave Danny's album its name). In music there's plenty of the strangeness of urban living in the ghosts which stalk Burial's *Untrue* and in Chris Cunningham's music videos for Aphex Twin. In the depressed economies of the '70s, while bands like Led Zeppelin were evoking the mystical aspects of psychedelic rock, Joy Division captured the numbing head-buzz of working-class life in a de-industrialising city with the cold mechanism of Synare drums and the dead-eyed, shamanistic delivery of Ian Curtis.

Despite being born out of housing projects and long focussing on trap houses and hood politics, city psychedelia was new to rap. The likes of Mobb Deep and Tupac had long been rhyming about the stress and paranoia induced by gang-banging, but Earl Sweatshirt and Danny Brown matched form with function. These were two men who had made it, by every metric society holds dear: they had women and parties and burgeoning fame, but none of it was making them especially happy. Their albums – broadcasts from the brink – ran, literally, counter to the culture.

After *I Don't Like Shit . . .*, it felt like Earl Sweatshirt had disappeared again. Given the sound of that record there was already the notion that he was developing an increasingly antagonistic relationship with his fans. Then, for a couple of years, he seemed to abandon the mic entirely. It was so much a thing that, by the time Vince Staples released his album *FM!* in late 2018, there was an interlude called 'New Earl Sweatshirt' which got a ride out of teasing fans with just a few short bars from a man who was, for the second time, missing in action.

In truth, Thebe was still active, just in places we didn't expect to find him. After producing most of *I Don't Like Shit . . .* himself, he began to dive deeper into beat-making. LA producer Knxwledge was properly introduced to the craft of sampling and Thebe became inspired. He began to spend more time at his mom's house and, while there, he'd sift through her stacks of vinyl, finding Ethiopian jazz and gospel records and finding ways to cut them up. In 2017 Haitian-American MC Mach Hommy released *Dump Gawd: Hommy Edition* on BandCamp, and it featured three new beats from Thebe; each of them looping and sample-based, turning fragments of songs into stuttering ghosts.

Thebe had produced for friends like Mac Miller before, but it's fair to say that Hommy was not the kind of artist people associated with Earl Sweatshirt. Hommy was born in Newark but had spent half of his childhood in Port-au-Prince. His music is unashamedly demanding: defined by knotty imagery and allusions to Haiti's bloody colonial past. Their collaboration was the first sign that Thebe was edging towards a different scene, but few people noticed because that album cost $1,000.

Hommy dropped *Dump Gawd* on BandCamp, a music distribution site which played a pivotal role in the outsized popularity of underground rap in the late 2010s. BandCamp was launched in 2007 as a means for artists to sell their music online directly, skirting the major label–industrial complex, the site taking only a 15 per cent cut. It first began to look like a viable option for artists in the summer of 2010, when songwriter Amanda Palmer left her label and began selling her records direct to fans on the platform instead.

Just like MySpace and Tumblr, BandCamp was another way for artists to reach their audience directly in the Internet age, and the success of acts like Car Seat Headrest made it a new vanguard for cult and underground music, bolstered by musicians making music too weird to secure them a major label deal or uninterested in acquiring one. Mach Hommy used the platform to take an even stronger approach; using the ability for artists to set their own price to his advantage and targeting a few hyper-obsessive fans who might actually pay $1,000 for an album rather than getting pennies off the masses. In an era where enormous corporations pay artists fractions of a penny for streams of their songs, Hommy found a way to capitalise on his mystique and put food on the table.

Thebe was a fiend for BandCamp, SoundCloud and other direct-to-audience sites. They were petri dishes for exciting, bold new ideas from the fringes and the young. As his image as an Odd Future alum began to fade, he became notorious instead for being an artist with an eye on every corner of rap. He had his opinions, but he embraced music far beyond the style of his own. He said that the goth-punk madness of Playboi Carti, for example, reminded him of the 'manic discovery at the dawn of hip hop'.

Just as he was leaving the likes of The Neptunes and Frank Ocean behind him, Thebe took to scouring SoundCloud and BandCamp, looking for new music which excited him. One of the albums he stumbled upon was by a young MC bold enough to call himself simply one word: MIKE.

When Michael Bonema received a BandCamp purchase email with the name 'Thebe Neruda Kgositsile' in the subject line, he freaked out. It was only a few months earlier that he and his friend Adé Hakim (a young producer who then went by 6press) had spotted Thebe browsing a Supreme store in Soho, New York, and introduced themselves as fans ('my first impression of Thebe was that he didn't trust anybody,' Hakim had said). When Thebe, by sheer coincidence, bought Michael's EP *longest day, shortest night* from BandCamp soon after, Bonema – then only seventeen – seized the moment and emailed him right back. Thebe was already impressed by the music and so arranged for them to meet at the New York offices of XL Recordings when he was next in the city. When they did, they became fast friends.

Michael was born in New Jersey but discovered rap in England. His family had moved to London's Hackney when he was five and, when he heard his sister blasting grime on Channel U, he soon became hooked on Skepta, Chipmunk and N-Dubz.* Just as he became accustomed to the idea of being raised a Brit however, things took a drastic change of course; one summer, when Bonema was twelve, his mum returned to Nigeria for work and ended up stuck there, caught in a bureaucratic web. Michael and his sister moved in with their

* There isn't much of a place for UK rap in this chapter but the 2010s were as transformative for British hip hop as they were to the rest of the world. After decades of MCs like Roots Manuva being badly underserved outside of the British Isles, UK rappers finally broke America in the last decade. Old hands like Skepta made records with Pharrell and appeared with major stars like Kanye West. Perpetual cultural magpie Drake eventually caught on to grime and drill too, bringing MCs like Tottenham's Headie One to an international platform. Stormzy and Dave and Central Cee reaped the rewards, but for me it's the magnificent Little Simz – who released two masterpiece albums in *GREY Area* and *Sometimes I Might Be Introvert* – who really expanded people's conception of what my nation's rap can be.

dad, this time in Philadelphia, and Mike had to learn to be an American again.

In 2014, Bonema moved in with his auntie in the Bronx and it was there, isolated from his new neighbours and tumbling into an adolescent depression, that he landed upon the style which he put into his bars. Growing to a towering height and heavy build, Mike was a sensitive giant, carefully attuned to the world around him and the working of his mind. Like Thebe, while other rappers were flashy with their flows, MIKE's songs break every rule in the book: burying his voice in the mix, and rapping in long, run-on sentences. In his lyrics, he often ruminates on a surrealness Devonté Hynes felt too: of living day to day in a city with a legacy of apartheid built into its foundations, enshrined in the very names of its streets. 'I hated Penn station / then I figured that they hated me first.'

Like Tyler Okonma, soon after MIKE first started posting raps online he decided to start a collective. The first member he drafted was Adé Hakim, a producer whose beats he first encountered on SoundCloud. When they discovered that they lived only ten minutes apart, MIKE formed a group out of himself and five other teenagers – Jodi.10k, King Carter, Darryl Johnson and Mason – from across the boroughs of the city. They called themselves sLUms. Like Odd Future, here was a new wave of teenage rappers and producers with their own singular sound. Instead of being into the sound of The Neptunes or Eminem, they were into Earl Sweatshirt. Where OF used MySpace and Tumblr, sLUms used SoundCloud and BandCamp. Where Frank and Tyler converged on Syd's Trap, MIKE put together 'the cabin'.

The city itself was sLUms' muse. As they converged from across the different boroughs, they spent the long subway rides staring out the window, funnelling the strange little happenings of New York streets into the bars they laid down when they arrived. City psychedelia. Even their name was inspired by urban living: 'You know how slums are like a bunch of little houses?' MIKE explained to *NYU Local* in 2017. 'It's a bunch of people in their own cribs with something different to offer.' Their constellation of producers and MCs widened to include the likes of MAVI and Thebe's school friend Sage Elsesser, the skateboarding prodigy who introduced him to Tyler. Thebe become an honorary member of sLUms. Just as he had done with Odd Future, with Mac Miller and Vince Staples, with Christian Rich and with The Alchemist, Thebe had found himself a new camp, and was invigorated by those teenage MCs.

Thebe, despite only being five years older himself, quickly became a mentor to MIKE. The fact somebody of Earl's fame would spare his time wasn't lost on him. 'Nobody out here's putting money in our pockets other than people really supporting us, and he's one of them,' he told *WECB* in 2017. 'He was once in a similar predicament as a young Black boy in America.' When Bonema had nothing left in his bank account, Thebe brought him lunch at a Sri Lankan restaurant. The attention of Thebe's co-sign soon turned MIKE into a star in his city, but their chance encounter changed Earl Sweatshirt's music too.

After the sheer depressiveness of *I Don't Like Shit, I Don't Go Outside*, and a wait of three years, I don't think I was the only Earl Sweatshirt fan hoping that his next album would be an about-face: an album filled with the kind of nasty, screw-faced verses he'd delivered at the end of 'Really Doe'. That wasn't what we got.

When 'Nowhere2go' was released on the 8th of November 2018, it transpired that Thebe had plunged even further down the hole his second album had opened up. Its beat crackles and pops but it doesn't seem to actually ever start. There are smatterings of bright guitar strings but they refuse to break into a rhythm, cut into tiny sonic ribbons instead. As Thebe raps, his verses are stalked by unsettling, disembodied voices which suffocate his words, the low-end swallowed whole by dusty, ambient bass. At the time, it felt like his grand return was an unearthed demo from a cult MC who'd vanished in the '90s. There were no quotable bars. Some of the words were barely even audible. Then, after only two minutes, it's over. Was this really what we'd been waiting for?

To be honest, I don't believe *anyone* who claims they understood *Some Rap Songs* immediately, because few albums had ever sounded like this one. At less than twenty-five minutes in length, with songs which sometimes last barely a minute, Thebe and his collaborators had attempted to capture the sound of a waking dream. It could have been even weirder: Gio Escobar of New York avant-garde collective Standing on the Corner, who mixed the album, pushed for the entire thing to be released as a single song, in the vein of Thebe's 2015 single 'Solace'. There are flashes of more traditional tunes, but those snatches are so brief that they sound like you've caught them flicking between radio stations. Any recognisable instruments are looped into delirium. Here is a hip hop album – the genre most centred on language – where sometimes you can hardly hear what the rapper is saying. At the start of 'Azucar' Thebe's mic even glitches, so it sounds like he's rapping the song's first words through a blanket. The only overriding sonic trait across the entire length of the album is the lingering hiss of white noise.

Some Rap Songs is not immediate music, so it's no wonder many didn't like it upon first hearing it. It's an LP which arrives in a wash of garbled sound, and it seems to take the mind some time to sift through the fog. Once heard, even the writing bucks expectations. Thebe had mastered the intricate, polysyllabic pen game of MCs like DOOM by the time he was nineteen, and here he raps more simply, the complexity of his writing delivered through metaphor and cultural allusions instead. As a result the album, as short as some EPs, feels as dense as many albums twice its length. It continues to deal in its predecessors' topical fixations – depression, isolation and grief – and yet, across a short runtime, it tells a story of reconciliation too. It has a reputation as a bleak record, but 'Azucar' and 'Veins' are among the first truly hopeful songs Thebe had ever written.

As you keep listening to *Some Rap Songs*, a magic trick begins to occur. All that heaviness seems to scatter like a dissipating mist. Each song, once part of the deluge of sound, becomes distinct, and the little rhythms woven into the loops become apparent. Sometimes I even feel myself bobbing my head in time to grooves which I once didn't know were there.

Before he was born, Thebe's father had worked to consolidate a distinct African American aesthetic, and these are rhythms which Thebe considered to be uniquely Black too. 'It's for a specific chemical equation,' he told *Pitchfork* in 2018. The song 'December 24' even begins with a quote from 1970's *The Dialect of the Black American*: 'it is surely time that the speech of the Black culture of America be recognized as a genuine dialect of English,' the clip goes. It was an assertion which echoed his father's life work.

Despite the long silence which preceded it, work on *Some Rap Songs* began quite quickly after *I Don't Like Shit . . .*'s release. 'December 24' was the first finished song which would make it on to the record: a Denmark Vessey production and the first track where Thebe felt like he'd hit upon the sound he'd been searching for. Thebe had begun a lifelong practice of playing demos and unreleased tracks at his shows, and when he played 'December 24', it floated around in fan circles for two years, nicknamed 'Bad Acid'.

A lot of people didn't realise it at first, because his new collaborators were still so obscure, but *Some Rap Songs* is certainly made in sLUms' image. MIKE and Adé Hakim also liked to add lashings of hiss and crackle to their beats, inspired by a love of King Krule's habit of doing the same. Shortly after meeting him, Hakim emailed Thebe the wonky groove which became 'Nowhere2go'. Sage Elsesser was a constant presence too, lacing him with the beats for 'The Bends', 'Azucar' and 'The Mint' (the latter of which he rapped on too). sLUms had a sound conceived in New York but much of *Some Rap Songs* was actually recorded in LA, in Thebe's home studio. It was a bare little room littered only with recording equipment and a picture of Ol' Dirty Bastard, pinned to the wall.

Early on, Thebe decided to privilege brevity. 'It's really dense,' he told *Okayplayer* in 2018. 'It can be overwhelming and have an air of exclusivity to it, a pompousness that I feel is only balanced out by me being like . . . I know what I'm doing to you. So I'mma act like your time is valuable.' It was a deliberate choice. He would replace dense rhymes with a density of meaning, and switch aggressive flows for a nonchalance which was, in effect, far more intense.

The album begins in a moment of sheer panic; a discontentment matched by the strangeness of the beat. 'Why did nobody tell me I was bleeding?' Thebe slurs. 'Why did nobody tell me I was sinking? / Why did nobody tell me I could leave.' With the disembodied coos of a Cincinnati soul group beneath him, this is more absurdism, more psychedelia: the sound of someone looking down at their life from above. It's a state of paralysis which persists throughout the record, portrayed on 'Eclipse' as a force that infects the body: 'say goodbye to my openness, total eclipse / of my shine that I've grown to miss when holding shit in / open my lids, my eyes said my soul is amiss.' Almost every word Thebe utters on *Some Rap Songs* is excruciatingly intimate; the kind of music which feels like it was made as a personal exorcism as much as a piece of entertainment for the listener.

A great many of rap's most beloved producers – like 9th Wonder, for example – work their samples into their beats so delicately that they can feel like they were recorded for the album anew. That's not how Thebe and his collaborators go about it. On songs like the gorgeous 'Ontheway!', Gio Escobar and Thebe arrange an old soul sample so it jolts on among lashings of sound, the seams still showing. In 2018, Thebe told Craig Jenkins that, while he was working on the album's sound, he was thinking of J Dilla, a producer whose style he'd loved ever since he found a CD of *Like Water for Chocolate* in his mum's study. 'When you're doing the Dilla thing . . . it makes people glitch,' he said. 'People that can't comprehend it, they flip the fuck out and then they have to box that shit. It's a wavy line, not a linear, staccato thing.'

Many of the album's beats revolve around single samples, looped until the song fizzles out. No chorus, no bridge: no interruptions. The effect is hypnotic and, when paired with a rapper's voice, gives the impression of a moment frozen in time. 'It's infinitum. It's the snake eating its tail,' Thebe told Jenkins. 'To write something complete to a loop, I feel like it takes a lot, and you have to be potent for that shit to matter. If you ain't got shit to say, n****s really are not gonna want to hear you on a loop.' Thebe came to that philosophy himself but, for some of his collaborators, faith in the loop came from deeper roots. For Gio Escobar, it was his time playing the organ in a church. 'Repetition is aligned with the church and the Bible,' he told *Interview* magazine in 2019. 'Every time you read the words in the Bible, you get something different. And the more you do it, the more the truth reveals itself.'

One part of the denseness of Thebe's design is that the samples he chose throughout the making of the instrumentals are often as referential as his words are. The record is laced with family history. The soul music of North America woven in with South African jazz. It's a compositional detail which charts a process of reconciliation with his family history which develops as *Some Rap Songs* plays on. Thebe began his career wrestling with his father's absence and writing a song of loathing directed at his mother, but here his lyrics are intimate: 'Mama said she used to see my father in me,' he raps on 'Azucar', 'I was not offended.' Three tracks later, Thebe enacts a kind of sonic reunion, cutting together the audio of his father reciting his poem 'Anguish Longer Than Sorrow' with the sound of his mother giving a keynote address. Speaking over a throbbing drone which sounds more like ambient noise than hip hop, Thebe creates a dialogue between both of his estranged parents.

Sampling has always been, in part, about showing off your life's influences in song, but this is something else. It's a piece of sound design as poignant as any lyric. Thebe planned to keep the appearance of his parents on his record a surprise; to simply send the album to his father as a conciliatory gesture when it was done. It would be the first time Keorapetse heard any Earl Sweatshirt music.

Tragically, he didn't quite make it. On the 3rd of January 2018, a few months before the record was done, Bra Willie died suddenly. He was seventy-nine years old.

In the wake of Keorapetse's passing, Thebe took a week-long trip to South Africa which turned into months. He experienced first-hand the strange status of being the son of an icon. His private loss played out to the tune of a day of national mourning. President Zuma announced that Keorapetse would receive an official state funeral and the national flag was lowered to half-mast.

When Thebe returned to America, he largely kept *Some Rap Songs* as it was, but added two songs as an epilogue. 'Tryna catch some rays, death and hops a sour taste,' he rapped on 'Peanut'. 'Bless my pops, we sent him off and not an hour late.' That brief song of mourning is followed by 'Riot!', which closes the record with a moment of joy in the shape of a fairly untouched sample of South African trumpeter Hugh Masekela's song of the same name. Masekela was a friend of Keorapetse's – they were sent into exile together in the 1960s – and a man Thebe called 'uncle'. He died two weeks after his father did.*

Some Rap Songs is one of the few 'experimental' rap albums which actually lives up to that claim. There are very few records quite like it. The whole thing has the atmosphere of delirium, of a series of dreams: an intrusive thought one moment, a fond memory the next. What's so remarkable about it is that it wasn't made by studying a mentor or an idol; quite the opposite. It was inspired by a bunch of teenagers who had been inspired by himself. The snake ate its tail, in a delicious way.

Experiments don't equate to pretentiousness either. The most surprising thing about *Some Rap Songs* is that, despite its weirdness, it was an effort to achieve the opposite. When Thebe was making the record he returned to the roots of his love for rap: watching *2 Raw for the Streets* battles and listening to old radio freestyles. It's why he gave the album

* Throughout his career, Thebe's work would, predictably, be compared to his father's. For journalists looking to create a narrative hook it was, after all, a fairly easy point to make. Thebe pushed back against it. He claimed that it diminished his father's work. 'I think what kind of churns my stomach about it is . . . this man, when he was twenty-one years old, got exiled,' he told NPR. 'When I was twenty-one, I was at SXSW, you know what I'm saying? Different lifestyles, bro.'

that title. What at first appears to be irony actually expresses a sincere attempt to get to the core of hip hop's most distinct qualities: its diaristic tendencies, its ability to act as a sonic confession booth. In interviews he even made a distinction between himself and his rap name, referring to Earl Sweatshirt varyingly as a 'thing' and an 'operation'. He felt like only this unaffected approach could get him to where he wanted to be. 'They say in all the creative writing books,' he told *Pitchfork*, 'keep it primitive: that's a space where you can stay excited.'

For underground hip hop fans, there was an increasing amount to be excited about. From 2018 onwards something fascinating began to happen among the artists Thebe had begun to surround himself with. Just as El-P's label Def Jux had become the nexus of alternative rap in the early noughties – uniting the likes of Company Flow, Cannibal Ox and Aesop Rock – so too did a new generation of underground MCs begin to knit together in the Internet age. Rappers like Earl Sweatshirt, MIKE, Vince Staples, Mach-Hommy, Quelle Chris, Navy Blue, Wiki, Moor Mother, Danny Brown, Open Mike Eagle, Freddie Gibbs, AKAI SOLO, Noname, Pink Siifu, Boldy James, Roc Marciano, Larry June, Billy Woods, Elucid, JPEGMAFIA, R.A.P. Ferreira, Action Bronson, MAVI, $ilkmoney, Zeelooperz, B. Cool-Aid, Denzel Curry – many of whom already had distinct careers – began to come together like a backpacker *Avengers*. They began producing tapes for one another, making entire records together, and blessing each other's songs with miraculous verses. All of these artists, dipping their toes in the pool of each other's work, began to feel like one gigantic, magnificent supergroup.

A great many things connected these artists. Online they were discussed by the same places: from rap review channels like *Dead End Hip Hop* to the HipHopHeads Reddit page. Collaboration was key, and many of them coalesced around the same phenomenal producers, from The Alchemist to Daringer and Preservation. There was something else which united them though. Across all of their dozens of different cadences and flows and genres of rap, a great many of these artists seemed to be tapping into the same thing Danny Brown had on *Atrocity Exhibition* and Thebe had on *Some Rap Songs*: absurdity. Sometimes it was found in their beats, sometimes their bars, but it was there nonetheless: a renewed commitment to the surreal; an attempt to portray a reality which is stranger than fiction in song.[*]/[†]

Take for example Moor Mother; an assistant professor at the University of Southern California by day and the woman behind a raft of discordant hip hop and jazz records by night. Her particular surrealism is to locate absurdities of America's colonial past, sometimes time-travelling through an entire history within

---

* This kind of reaction against a zeitgeist has occurred plenty of times in hip hop before. In the late 1990s, artists like now-disgraced entrepreneur Puffy signed artists who he directed away from the unvarnished street reportage delivered by KRS-One and NWA, and began dressing like millionaires instead. It was a reaction, perhaps, to the heaviness which had overcome the scene in the wake of Tupac and Biggie Smalls' deaths. The likes of Busta Rhymes and Jadakiss began donning slick leather suits, and lavishness ruled the day. While the hits stacked up though, so did the counter-reaction. In 1998, DMX released *It's Dark and Hell Is Hot* – a nasty, skeletal album which was almost apocalyptic in its violence. Maybe people really were sick of the shiny suits, because it shot to the top of the Billboard Charts.

† It was a stylistic evolution which extended beyond music onto screens, from surreal horror films like Jordan Peele's *Get Out* to Boots Riley's *Sorry to Bother You*, and especially the waking fairytale of the TV show *Atlanta* which was created, tellingly, by another rapper: Donald Glover (or Childish Gambino as a Wu-Tang Generator named him).

a single song. Then there's JPEGMAFIA, the Flatbush-born army veteran who spent much of his military tour listening to Janelle Monáe and James Blake in the desert and making beats in the barracks. When he settled in Baltimore, he fell in love with the city's rich, raucous, punk and rap scenes and his music ended up as a dizzying amalgam of both. There's no real putting his sound into words: his is truly the kind of genre-rupturing, brain-mangling music which would have bamboozled pretty much any music fan fifteen years earlier.

JPEGMAFIA's breed of psychedelia is based mostly around the lines of the Internet; his saturated, splintering production feels like having your cheek mashed into a phone screen and being hauled through webspace, face first. His music is hilarious, energetic, but purposefully demanding. On his earlier records he used the titles of his songs as a litmus test to deter the kind of listeners he didn't want hearing them: naming tracks 'Black Ben Carson' and 'I Cannot Fucking Wait Til Morrissey Dies' in the knowledge that they would discourage people who would be offended by those words, but not the real-world violence which informed them. His music makes even the freakiest moments of '90s rap sound small fry. It's pretty amazing.

Like the beginnings of hip hop itself, some of the surrealness was baked into these twisted, hypnotic beats but, other times, it came in the form of the pen. After becoming infatuated by the knotty rhymes of a rapper like Ka, Billy Woods was the next MC who inspired Thebe's increasingly esoteric bars. An older MC, Woods was used to getting his accolades a little later than due. He had been around in the first wave of New York underground rap in the early 2000s, but success didn't come to him until nearly two decades later, thanks in no small part to the co-signs of beloved names like Earl Sweatshirt and The Alchemist. His relative obscurity was hiding a revelation. Woods was not just a great MC: he's one of my generation's great lyricists, full stop.

*

Like Thebe, Billy Woods was born to an exile. His father, a Marxist political agitator from the African state of Rhodesia, fled to America when a war of independence broke out across the nation. An internal settlement was signed in March 1978, and rule by the country's white minority was concluded. Woods' family returned to the newly named Republic of Zimbabwe in 1980. His father joined the new nation's first government and, with that level of status, Woods was raised far wealthier than many of the nation's adolescents.* Nonetheless, he was still only a touching distance from extreme poverty: from rural townships where the clothes children wore were the only ones they owned.

When Billy's father died, his family returned to Washington D.C. and remained in America for good. Woods was raised by two academics (his mother was a Jamaican feminist intellectual) and the shelves of his childhood home were stacked with books. Woods became an avid fan of literature, adoring James Baldwin and Cormac McCarthy alike. But, despite the greats who lined the shelves, it was Public Enemy who won his heart.

At an early age, Woods was given a stark lesson in the fluidity of nationhood, wealth and identity. He didn't find returning to Zimbabwe to be the biggest culture shock though; that was coming back to America. 'White Rhodesians had been openly racist to me in a way I rarely experienced in the US,' he told *The Guardian* in 2023. 'I remember being with some white friends, going back to their house to get a soda and them warning me their father didn't like "kaffirs". But it didn't have any real effect on my self-esteem, because our country had a

* It also makes Billy the only rapper who comes to mind who has met Robert Mugabe face to face (unless there's something Big Sean isn't telling us). When Thebe's father was in exile from South Africa, a young Woods met him too.

black president, our house was bigger than theirs, my dad had a better job than his . . . I didn't feel like a second-class citizen in Zimbabwe, because I wasn't. There wasn't the power behind that racism that there is here. The ways American apartheid was enforced were more subtle and unspoken and indirect, but based on the powerlessness of being that minority. The power imbalance in everything made it totally different. People would do shit to you, and it was left up to you to figure out.'

This insidiousness became a defining trait of Woods' music. In his songs colonialism and race often linger like ghouls, but his writing also tends to make cosmic jokes about daily life in a society where power imbalances are a fact of living. He veers between everyday inanities and evocative, impossible images which are as surreal and psychedelic as the way *Some Rap Songs* sounds. On his 2023 record *Maps*, to take just one example, this is how he describes his insomnia: 'Suck me deep, heart beat in my jugular / Snow-capped peaks, rugged / Hindu kush, a Sikh surrounded by thuggers / Chasing dragons on aluminum sheets / It's flying carpets out this motherfucker / I don't sleep, I hover outside myself, watching my body survive.'

If that moment finds him simply lying in bed, things get even sketchier as he moves around the world. On that album's lead single, 'FaceTime', Woods staggers downstairs to a hotel lobby late one evening to find himself in the middle of a party of European teenagers turning up after a Playboi Carti gig. Woods doesn't retreat to his room though, instead he stumbles about his business, stoned out of his mind in a nightgown as they rap along to Carti's lyrics. It feels heightened, like it might have happened but not quite to that ridiculous an extent. There's something funny about it too; all these rich, young white kids going crazy for rap, when they might be inclined to steer clear of somebody who looked like many a rapper on the street. These ironies are everywhere in his music, as in his classic 2017 track 'Police Came to My Show', where a pair of cops show up to his show in disguise, scaring all his fans from buying the merch.

These are funny songs, but make no mistake – Woods' music is always cut through with an underlying weariness towards a world which seems to make a mockery of any concept of natural justice. 'It could be nuclear winter with an earthquake / The worst people'll wiggle out the rubble' he raps on *Maps*' 'Soft Landing'. If you chose any Billy Woods song, or any Armand Hammer song (the duo he formed with another outstandingly gifted MC, Elucid) you will find moments as compelling as these.

For me, Woods sealed his fate as one of the all-time greats on *Hiding Places*, his 2019 album-length collaboration with Kenny Segal, a producer whose high school was just a few miles from Woods' as kids. Like the famous red-brick ruin photographed on the album's cover, *Hiding Places* feels like a stroll through the rooms of a haunted mansion. The beats twitch and creak, and Woods' words turn street violence, personal grievances and scenes of drug addiction into bizarre, fantastical dreams. On 'A Day in a Week in a Year' there's a sense, not of a higher power at work, but the lack of one: a world where fate doesn't reside within the hands of the living but sheer, dumb luck. It's a feeling I think we all occasionally feel, creeping into our most paranoid moments, and one he captures with a vignette of himself stood in an arcade, dropping cents into a machine. 'Dollar movie theater, dingy foyer, little kid, not a penny to my name,' he raps, over a beat which sounds like it's sighing. 'Fuckin' with the joystick / pretendin' I was really playin'.'

The following song, 'Bedtime', is, by contrast, pure surrealist fiction. Woods imagines a series of darkly fantastical worlds: one in which all of history's murdered women come back to life, and another where all of the children of earth wake up to find that all the adults have suddenly disappeared. Woods' music weaves deftly between the expressly everyday – a boy in an arcade playing with a joystick – to the purely surreal, almost as if the line between the two isn't especially distinct. As Frida Khalo said: 'they thought I was a surrealist, but I wasn't. I never painted dreams. I painted my own reality.' Even *Hiding Places*' cover plays a part. It's a photograph of a red-brick mansion found in the Brush Park district of Danny Brown's Detroit, so dilapidated that it looks like something conjured from the imagination of the Brothers Grimm, but it's real. Urban decay, turned into a fairy tale. City psychedelia.*

What Woods does so brilliantly – like many of these artists from MIKE to Moor Mother and Earl Sweatshirt – is to use the absurd to reflect the real. The insidiousness of racism in the West – so insidious that some pundits can stand before TV cameras and deny its existence – is surreal in a way that outright bigotry is too explicit to allow room for. Here's sLUms affiliate AKAI SOLO on gentrification, a process of exclusion which isn't explicitly racist in character, but usually ends up displacing minority groups from their homes nonetheless: 'You always feel like you're on acid when you're walking down a block,' he told *Okayplayer* in 2021. 'It's just so strange. You have this side-by-side, split vision when you walk through places that you

* In much of classic rock, lyrical masters were recognised and eulogised in every music publication in the land. It's a tragedy that the likes of Woods and Thebe have yet to receive the same treatment. Woods doesn't have the influence or the stature of the five artists at the heart of this book, but his discography could compete with any of them. From 2012's *History Will Absolve Me* to 2023's Armand Hammer album *We Buy Diabetic Test Strips,* he had one of – if not *the* – most remarkable runs of LPs this century, releasing *sixteen* albums which were not only good, but pretty phenomenal.

grew up in that've been hit with the influx of gentrification. It's one thing to leave a place and then come back to it and just be confronted with that, but to watch it happen around you is another type of a slow push with the knife in the side."*

The presence of artists who reflect this reality serve as a reminder of what a miracle hip hop has always been from its inception. So much of the art people consume daily is made by the same people, to an almost stunning degree. Now more so than ever you have to be rich to be an artist. *EastEnders* is written by middle-class people. *The Sun* is written by middle-class people. Often those people come from the same towns, sometimes they even come from the same schools. But culture is universal, art is universal; we just need the means to hear it.

Places like Syd's Trap or sLUms' Cabin have popped up through the history of hip hop. OutKast started out in Rico Wade's basement. Lil Wayne and Juvenile began in poverty, recording in a kitchen in the Magnolia projects in New Orleans. Hip hop itself began in the recreation room of a block party, raising money so the DJ's sister could afford new clothes for school. Rap music has always been Black music, but the part which gets talked about less is that it's often Black and working class. Where else in the art world but in hip hop can you so easily hear from the likes of Billy Woods or Juvenile or MIKE or Danny Brown?

---

* Unsurprisingly, plenty of songs in recent years have dealt with gentrification. There's JPEGMAFIA's 'I'll Never Forgive Hipsters for What They Did To Brooklyn' and 'Once They Build a Starbucks It's Ova'. In 2023, Danny Brown turned the very word into a pun on 'Jenn's Terrific Vacation', where he raps 'On the corner just built a Starbucks / I was just looking for a come up / right there used to be a crack house / now it's an organic garden'. On 2023's 'Free the Ruler' Thebe put it more simply: 'how you 'gon allocate me my own fuckin' land?'

MCs like Billy Woods can take hours to understand. JPEGMAFIA and Moor Mother make music which is abrasive, confrontational and tough. *Some Rap Songs* sounds like it was recorded in a stupor. So why listen? I am not Black but I am working class and, to be honest, I've always found this music more reassuring than I have difficult. This music is made by artists who see the world as I've always understood it to be. Life *is* absurd, especially when you're poor. You turn your radiators off in the winter and watch the black mould grow while a man in a gold carriage is paraded through the streets. You hear of little Black boys like Aderrien Murry, a kid who called the police because his mother was being abused, and ended up being shot by the cops himself. You watch as the wealthiest men on earth sit in front of the rocket ships they paid to have made for them and thank, with a straight face, the workers they exploited to get them there. All the world really does is make you wonder why *more* music isn't as odd as this, when normality is often so flagrantly absurd.

Part 4 (Earl, Part 2)

Thebe was struck with grief in the wake of his father's passing. Although *Some Rap Songs,* released only months after Keorapetse's death, was interpreted by the press to be a response to his loss, his next EP, *Feet of Clay*, was actually the first project made in the midst of mourning. He left Columbia records and joined Warner, itching to make what he described as 'riskier' music. *Feet of Clay* – an even slighter, fifteen-minute project – was named after an end-times prophecy from the Book of Daniel. Across its seven tracks, Thebe's bars reflected not only the depths of his grief but also a growing cynicism about the world he was waking back up to. 'We at the feet of clay right now,' Kgositsile told *Apple Music*. 'We posted up live from burning Rome.' These seven short songs are the absolute antithesis of pop. The mix is messy, his words cracking and occasionally lost in naked, creaking loops. From the ghostly warbles which stretch out across 'EL TORO COMBO MEAL' to the drawling, dusty echoes of '74', it feels close in mood to Basinski's *The Disintegration Loops*. I don't listen to it often.

Thebe produced his fourth album, *Sick!*, fairly quickly afterwards. It was a step in a different direction. For half a decade, Thebe's music worked like an optical illusion does: listen long enough and, eventually, the obscure became apparent. *Sick!* doesn't make you work so hard. The drums make a return and so does the bounce. The beat of a song like 'Titanic' even ramps up, the percussion pressed and squeezed until it bursts into a bona fide groove. Some of the 2018-era muddiness remains, but it sits side by side with drill and trap beats, the type which the uninitiated never would never have expected Thebe to touch.

Still refusing to waste his listeners' time, *Sick!* runs at only twenty-four minutes, but boasts the most eclectic production roster to date. It features an old friend in The Alchemist, but acts as a showcase for the likes of Samiyam, Navy Blue and Black Noi$e too (the latter's debut album was the first to be released on Thebe's Tan Cressida imprint). The album feels like tuning in to a radio station curated by a devotee of modern rap, from Alchemist's luscious, crate-digging horns to the synthetic textures of 'Lobby': two different modes of hip hop, with Thebe making himself at home on both.

The years between *Feet of Clay* and *Sick!* had been far kinder to Thebe than those before them. The family healing which underwrote 'Playing Possum' continued in the wake of his father's death. Through his father, Thebe has six siblings he hardly knew, but Keorapetse's death brought them together. At the end of 2019, Thebe and his mom interviewed each other onstage at the Museum of Contemporary Art in LA; as much a public declaration of reconciliation as a conversation, and one which arrived almost ten years from the date that his adolescent fans decided that she was a villain. Thebe began to eat better, and his auntie – a practitioner of Eastern medicine and acupuncture who he christened Professor X – worked on his chakras. In 2019, he read a *Pitchfork* tweet which said 'just imagine the music this n***a would make if he would drink some water.' Thebe laughed. 'Facts, bro.'

Shortly after his father passed, Thebe became one himself. 'God is a comedian,' he told *The Guardian* in 2023. After his father died, he sat with his brother and told him how he would be a good dad, how it wouldn't even be that hard, 'and then God was like: "go ahead – have a child, bro . . ."' A while after he was born, Thebe mentioned his son on Twitter, and almost immediately issued a retraction: 'y'all already makin too much hullaballoo about the situation and y'all makin' me nervous.'

When he set about making *Sick!*, Thebe had planned to shape it around *The People Could Fly*, a 1985 collection of Black American folk stories his mom read to him as a child. Then COVID-19 arrived, and he decided to change the record's focus. 'Once the lockdowns hit, people couldn't fly anymore,' he told *Pitchfork*. 'People were sick. The people were angry and isolated and relentless. I leaned into the chaos because it was apparent that it wasn't going anywhere. These songs are what happened when I would come up for air.'

For the first time since his verse on 'Really Doe' in 2016, Thebe's voice was mixed in a way which didn't sound like he was rhyming from a swamp. As he put it on 'Old Friend', 'know I came from out the thicket smilin''. The songs were mixed by Young Guru, an industry legend who has engineered albums for everyone from Ludacris to Pete Rock, so not the kind of man who you'd recruit to continue the more evasive sound of the sLUms MCs. This time, Thebe's voice was crystal clear, and for an artist whose very voice had always been so closely tied to his mind-state, it was a choice made at a moment of sharper mental clarity. *Sick!* also marked new developments in the evolution of Thebe's flow. Where he once chased complexity and pointed assonance, he continued to move even further from that mode, downplaying his verbosity until some bars last only a single word.

Despite his already long career, Thebe is far younger than many of the notoriously verbose MCs like Ka and Billy Woods who he admired, and so he has also remained tapped into young, underground rap, watching how the Internet spawned careers with the fascination of a fan. Across the decade, it has been a joy to observe the many flows and infections which emerged in distinct ways across the cities of America. In Philly, where MIKE first landed in the US, MCs like Ot7Quanny don't rap in a hurry; they take their time, choosing when to deliver a punchline with the thump of a right hook. In the Bay Area, SOB X RBE skate across the surface of their beats, pressing on where most rappers would pause for breath. In LA, Drakeo the Ruler pioneered a distinctly West Coast flow, bouncing up and down his register and delivering constants with a jolt.

Plenty of people assumed that these MCs were rappers Earl Sweatshirt was not only distinct from, but a kind of corrective to. In reality though, Thebe followed these regional scenes as closely as he did the imagistic poetry of Billy Woods and Mach-Hommy, and his own flows began to reflect it, as on the lurching, rhythmic flow her delivers on the phenomenal 2023 loosie 'Making the Band': a skittish banger produced by EvilGiane, the progenitor of sample-drill.

Sick! isn't a perfect album – it's too scatter-brained for that – but what it does is something almost as rare: it has not one, but *two* perfect songs. The first of them is named 'Tabula Rasa'.

*

Released in December 2021 as the album's second single, 'Tabula Rasa' was surely designed to capture the attention of underground rap nerds like me. It was the third and best coming together of Earl Sweatshirt, Billy Woods and Elucid, a posse cut for people who enjoy Joseph Conrad and RZA in equal measure. The beat was made by producers Theravada, Rob Chambers and Thebe himself. There's a contemplative, twinkling piano to set it off, and a sample of a Philly soul legend: half a word repeated in snatches. The beat is smattered with the sounds of the outside world: lips smacking, bottles clinking. It feels like a living space, one designed to induce reflection.

When he recruited Elucid and Billy Woods for the song, Thebe outlined the track's philosophy to them. Tabula rasa is a Latin phrase which refers, symbolically, to the clearing of the mind. It's a melding of 'tabula', a wax-coated tablet, and the process by which it was wiped clean by heating and melting it, called 'rasa'. In other words, a blank page, literally. In therapists' offices, tabula rasa refers to both the origin of trauma and the remedy for it: the idea that the form every human is born in – blank, unshaped by experience – is also a state to be induced, enabling strategies for healing. It was with this in mind that each of these three masterful MCs stood behind the mic and approached their verses on the track: picking apart the roots of their lives and developing strategies for the future.

Ever generous, Thebe's verse lands last on his own song. Instead, Elucid begins, and begins pensively, investigating the make-up of his mind. Then Woods enters and offers his version of the same, detailing a blistering journey through his life in New York City and his childhood in Zimbabwe, with allusions to the kind of political icons his father would have brushed shoulders with, in the most gleeful way. 'Kofi Annan in the booth, Soyinka in the stu' / Sese Seko Mobutu if the DJ play something smooth.' Like all good rap lyricism, their verses are as much about performance as they are poetry. It is not made to be read on the page, and doing so hides little beautiful details, like the way Woods repeats 'I don't dance, but maybe tonight . . . maybe tonight'; bottling enough pensive promise that you can almost hear the dance floor clearing.

My favourite moment arrives at the end of Woods' verse, where the overview of his life comes to a screeching halt and he finds himself in his apartment late at night, cooking in silence while his partner sleeps in the room next door. 'Live for the living / I made chicken late night in my boxers, burning up the kitchen,' he raps. 'She passed out right when I was done fixing / I watch reruns in the dark, fingers and lips glistening.' From the allusion to drug use to the description of his grease-coated hands, it's imagery so vivid that you can smell the oil bubbling. It's not necessarily a flattering image, but this music isn't about flattery, it's about finding beauty in the ordinary.

Thebe's own verse arrives after a pause for breath. He drifts in sloppily, riding all over the loop like his psyche is unspooling. In his words, he's doing exactly that. For an artist who had spent five years rapping from the midst of a crisis, for the first time in a long time he sounds resilient and unbothered. In the video for the song, directed by Joseph Mault, each rapper takes their turn in the spotlight, moving around a house until it settles on Thebe in a hooded sweatshirt, Boldy James and The Alchemist beside him bobbing their heads. Joy isn't promised, but for five masters of their craft, maybe joy isn't much more complicated than that.

It says a lot about the potency of the scenes which Thebe had been embroiled in throughout his career that one decade on from *Doris* almost every rapper his career had intersected with released a new album, and all of them were sublime. Tyler dropped *The Estate Sale*, an addendum to his 2021 album which features 'HEAVEN TO ME', a song on which he reminisces about his days catching the city bus with Jasper in the early days of Odd Future. (There's also, incredibly, a bisexual love song featuring a self-proclaimed thug.) MIKE dropped *Burning Desire*, easily his most refined record to date and one where he began to inject sLUms' hazy production with flashes of reggae and electro-funk. Billy Woods released two projects: *Maps* with Kenny Segal and an Armand Hammer record with Elucid, a socially adventurous LP which pulled their sound in a percussive, tribal direction.

At forty-three, Danny Brown dropped *Quaranta*, an album which replaced the mania of *Atrocity Exhibition* with slow, gasping songs of regret and redemption. Danny also tapped into his manic side on a team-up with JPEGMAFIA with whom he released *Scaring the Hoes*; both of their frantic energies combined into a stunning exercise in pure organised chaos, which also happens to sample 'Milkshake' by Kelis. In August of that year, Earl Sweatshirt joined the fun.

Voir Dire was a project surrounded by mythology before it was even announced. Its title is a legal term meaning 'speaking the truth', a phrase Thebe had always known through his mother. It was a climax of sorts to the first decade of his career, one spotted with friends old and new. It was also the fulfilment of a promise Thebe made to Uncle Al when he first started hanging out at his studio in 2012: a full-length collaboration. If The Alchemist was to be believed, it was a promise which had been fulfilled years earlier.

In May 2021, the producer tweeted: '[Earl and I] hid an entire album on YouTube under a fake name . . . Fake album cover, song titles, the whole nine. Nobody found it yet.' Of course, that tweet set about a worldwide scavenger hunt on the rap Discord servers and Reddit pages but, even with thousands of backpacker sleuths scouring through every obscure, no-name rap song YouTube had to offer, the album was never found. Then, on August 2023, *Voir Dire* arrived in its place.

By sheer coincidence, as I was wrapping up work on this chapter, Thebe announced a series of tenth-anniversary shows for *Doris*. The first, in LA, doubled as an Odd Future reunion. Syd and Frank aside, the whole gang showed up. Tyler arrived onstage for his 'Whoa' verse and, when he was done rapping, he and Thebe hugged. The Alchemist even brought cake. By the time of the London leg, a victory lap for an album Thebe never fully embraced had become something else: a launch party for *Voir Dire*.

We still can't be completely sure whether the album we have today was the one supposedly posted in secret to YouTube two years earlier, or whether Alc had made the whole thing up. Regardless, the album is a beautiful one, unified by the sound Alchemist had brought to full-lengths with Conway the Machine, Action Bronson and Freddie Gibbs alike. His beats, simple and languorous, deliver sexiness from a simpler time, filled with flips of Turkish funk and obscure '80s gospel. It was a welcome, brighter backdrop for Thebe, an elegant canvas upon which his increasingly relaxed flow fit like a glove.

Thebe Neruda Kgositsile has a reputation as one of the most maudlin men in rap but, as author Ismail Muhammad wrote, a different way to approach his music is 'as a map of complex joy'. Ever since he returned from that island, being mobbed by teenage fans who knew him for raps about rape, Thebe seemed to become uninterested in the easy or unearned. The same applies to happiness. In his music, people are blank pages. He isn't a nihilist; he doesn't believe that misery is promised, but he thinks the same of bliss. His music is filled with moments of strife and moments of salvation in equal measure, and he makes clear that neither is possible without the other. In a song like 'Sirius Blac', it is the very acceptance of that fact which paves the way to better days.

From the swirling void of *I Don't Like Shit . . .* to the head trip of *Some Rap Songs*, the sonic trickiness of Earl Sweatshirt's music is an extension of his refusal to look away from life as he finds it. 'People don't deal with that level of clarity at a societal level,' he told *CLASH* in 2020. 'That can be construed as psychedelic, or abstract, when in fact it's the exact opposite. There's a lot of things that I'm saying at high speed. It's very dense. They're stacked on one another so it can be very overwhelming. But I think you need a good tour guide through a crazy place.'

In August 2023, as I stood at the bar of Camden's KOKO waiting for the *Doris* anniversary show to begin, I couldn't help but notice a man my age leaning against the bar, ranting about the explanation he'd given his girlfriend for why he had to miss date night, just this once. 'I said you don't understand, babe,' he slurred. 'This is *my* Beyoncé. This is *my* Taylor Swift.' Thebe stands in unique stead, because he has made some of the most challenging music in this book and yet, because of his affiliation with artists who have become generational stars, he is also probably the most famous and adored too.

When the first single from *Voir Dire* dropped two days before that Camden show (the MIKE-featuring 'Sentry'), another of his era's great rappers – ScHoolboy Q – took to Twitter and asked a question people had been asking for a decade at least. 'BraH' he wrote. 'How do Earl be doing tHis sHit so easy . . .?' The truth is, Thebe made it look easy from the start.

APPLE MUSIC

SPOTIFY

5. SOPHIE

It was a drizzly night in Glasgow, April 2005. Eight hundred Scots sloped their way up the long incline of Scott Street and filed into The Art School: a brutalist, dungeon-like club which sits innocuously alongside the terraced houses, and host, for one night only, to one of Manchester's finest cultural exports. Light of the North, destroyers of ears: Autechre (Or-Tec-A, in the original Manc). Tickets cost fifteen quid apiece. The ravers crammed into the brick-clad basement and gathered beneath a looming metal rig. They were about to witness the stuff of folklore.

In a career full of highs, that particular Autechre performance would prove to be one of Sean Booth and Rob Brown's finest hours. It was positive affirmation of their reputation as mad professors: capable of creating sounds the likes of which nobody had previously encountered and delivering them in propulsive, hypnotic barrages which were 'songs' only in the sense that they happened to be comprised of sound. Among funnelling smoke and pulsing lights, Booth and Brown operated like surgeons on banks of sequencers and samplers. Nord Modulars and MPC1000s and Bitstream MIDI controllers. Alien names for alien noises. They were playing skittish, bastardised versions of an album they'd release just three days later – the notoriously tricky *Untilted* – a record which *The Independent* called, damningly, 'a clutter of clicks and bleeps'.

In Glasgow though, Autechre took those modulated noises and wrestled them into more coherent shapes: twitchy, spasmodic grooves forged out of repetition and pure, calculated energy. They made the danceable out of architecture, the kind of music which hypnotises and noodles at deep cavities of the brain, commandeering limbs as if by surgical intervention.

In the age of YouTube livestreams and TikTok, much live music is available in the home the second it debuts online, but in 2005, music like that became legendary from word of mouth alone. *Autechre Live at [Glasgow] 2005-04-15* (as the bootleg soundboard recordings lovingly came to be known) became mythic for ravers in the know, and spread like wildfire on music forums and the kind of MP3 blogs frequented by Daniel Lopatin.

Among the thousands who downloaded the bootlegs of that legendary show, among the hundreds who were irreversibly changed by it, was another twenty-first century icon in gestation. Like Autechre, she would go on to use the boundless tools of sonic synthesis to reinvent the way electronic music worked, remaining avant-garde while sauntering far closer to the mainstream than Booth and Brown ever have.

SOPHIE was nineteen, surfing late at night in her university dorm room, when she first downloaded those soundboard rips. She already had an encyclopaedic knowledge of '90s electronica, but what she heard when she clicked 'play' on those MP3s was new to even her. It wasn't the kicks and acid lines which dazzled her, nor the way they had transformed their trickiest work into something you could actually dance to. No, what astounded SOPHIE was the *sounds* themselves. Developed and hammered out of pure, unmodulated sine-waves, Booth and Brown's drums sounded like they were being stamped into sheet iron. The bass lines felt like they were made out of a steel as light as air. She didn't know music was capable of those things.

'It's almost like you're sticking your hand into a goopy material,' she told *CRACK*, thirteen years later. 'It's a very human thing . . . responding to materials and emotions through sound.' If the very best music moves you, then what Autechre produced in Glasgow struck at a molecular level, rattling the brain and sending your insides reeling. In that moment, as the hairs on her neck bristled, SOPHIE decided that creating sounds like those, sounds so vivid you could wrap your hands around them, was going to become the work of her life.

It was an impossible task, choosing five artists to represent an entire decade. There is no country music in this book, and little indie rock either. Where is Lana Del Rey? Where is Metro Boomin or Roc Marciano or Beyoncé Knowles? The five artists I did select are pioneers, no doubt; they're magnificent artists with thrilling and original ideas, but that is true of several others who – in another universe – could have been chosen to tell the story of a book like this. Not SOPHIE though. She was always there. She *had to be there*, right from the start.

Few musicians are capable of embodying exactly what we writers want them to. They are human, after all. Their careers and their work are messy and shoot in half a dozen different, often contradictory, directions at once. Sometimes they release music which is lazy or derivative, and mess the whole thing up. But SOPHIE makes my job easy. Here is an artist whose modus operandi was pure, relentless creativity. Her every move was an act of sheer, wilful imagination because she was interested in nothing else. For millions of listeners around the world, her name is synonymous with the future because it's all she was interested in. She was a perfectionist, not in the sense that she was bothered if a mic glitched or somebody tripped onstage, but because she wanted to give her audience something they'd never seen before, every single night. Not doing so bothered her. She protected the details of her life and history, not out of shyness or even out of privacy, but because she didn't understand why it mattered. She knew that an artist's life could only distract from the music, and nothing mattered more than that. I think there's a good chance she would have hated a book like this. But SOPHIE deserves to be written into the history books. In less than a decade of work, she earned it; not because of her tragic passing, but long before it. This is how she did it.

SOPHIE was born in September 1986. By the time she was ten, she was already a musician. Her dad was a raver, taking his children to see pulsing, mind-warping dance music several years before it was probably responsible. Nineties electronic music is a hell of a thing to thrust upon a malleable young brain, and SOPHIE's dad did everything he could to ensure it stayed stuck. As he drove them from place to place, he'd crank Orbital and Moby cassettes so loud in the car that the glove box would rattle. In the midst of Britpop-mania, he would disparage the music which was, once again, being brought back to the centre of the zeitgeist. Why obsess over decades-old rock 'n' roll, he asked. Jungle, garage, trip hop, trance . . . didn't people know that they were in the middle of a new revolution? Listen kids, *this* is the real sound of the future.

This music imprinted on all his children, but it worked on SOPHIE most of all. When she was little she began stealing those cassettes from her father's car, arriving home from school, climbing the stairs and locking herself in her bedroom with a Walkman and the keyboard she'd been bought for her birthday. From an early age, she spoke with a sense of calm authority about a great many things, a thoughtfulness which set her apart from the boisterousness which defines many a teenage year. One day, her father took her to visit a friend who was clearing out the gear from his studio, and she picked up some accessories to add to her den.

The music SOPHIE made in those early years was already bizarre, melding all the inputs her dad had pushed her way while sucking up the oddities of her world. When she noticed her mum's friend's shrill voice on the phone, she asked her mum to call her up so she could sample it in a song. By the time puberty hit, she had already decided she wanted to be an electronic producer, and threatened to drop out of school to make it happen. One day her half-sister (not truly understanding what SOPHIE was doing up there in her bedroom) asked her to DJ at her wedding in Lanzarote. SOPHIE was a songwriter, not a selector, but she didn't say no; instead she learned how to DJ quickly from tutorials online, and played the gig without a word.

SOPHIE studied fine art and sculpture – not music – at university, but spent most of those years as they're meant to be spent: DJing and clubbing. She was a regular at queer club nights like Homoelectric, and started her own under the name Pasquo and Getwax with friends. In 2008, she moved to Berlin to study art further, learning some broken German and joining the band Motherland with Sabine Gottfried, Matthew Lutz-Kinoy and Marcella Dvsi. Lutz-Kinoy started performing one-man musicals, and asked SOPHIE if she could provide the soundtrack. She immediately began thinking of how she could make music as physical as his choreography. 'It would be nice to think that you could build in all the excitement of a live performance to the recorded tracks,' she told *BOMB* in 2012, 'the music would be so vivid it could almost emanate the colours, materials and movements of a performance.'

SOPHIE's technicolour scores earned her a reputation among arts and dance circles, from New York to Amsterdam. In October 2010, she released the first piece of music under her own name, a remix of 'A Certain Person', a single by New York new wave outfit Light Asylum. She moved to London, and SOPHIE began. Originally, she intended the project to be a series of live, analogue performances. She was booked by James Cooper, a university friend and the co-founder of Revive-HER Records, to play the upstairs room at London's XOYO in 2010. That set landed with bemusement upon a crowd of ravers, but the gig was seen by Andrew Thompson – founder of the Scottish electronica label Huntleys + Palmers. He loved what he saw. Thompson commissioned SOPHIE to remix an Auntie Flo track, and soon released SOPHIE's debut singles in February 2013: the sparkling house cut 'Nothing More to Say', and it's B-side 'Eeehhh'.

By the early 2010s, at twenty-four years old, SOPHIE was already beginning to become enmeshed in London and Glasgow's electronica scenes, far more so than her reputation for mysteriousness would suggest. Her inclinations though were already drifting from the micro-house which defined nights like those. She recognised much of it as the sounds of her childhood, and that was already decades old. She'd taken the words of her father seriously. They were electronic musicians. They were supposed to be writing the *future.*

Perhaps because she'd had access to those tools far sooner than most kids could dream of, by her mid-twenties SOPHIE was already familiar with, and bored by, the way traditional synthesisers and sequencers worked. She shared her father's resentments about the infatuation with songs made by rock bands and recognised that many of the tools of electronic music were written to imitate a form of songwriting which those very machines had made redundant.

'Polyphony was required in the times of orchestras and even three or four-piece rock bands of the last century because different shaped instruments would produce different sounds and timbres,' she told *Radio Wave* in 2014. 'With synthesis you can produce the full frequency range with one instrument, so there's no reason to think about music polyphonically . . . It should just sound like one morphing, elastic, full-frequency spectrum composition.' What is the point, she asked in *Elektronauts*, in 'a computer pretending to be a band from the '70s'?

After downloading the bootleg MP3s of *Autechre Live at [Glasgow]* from her university bedroom, SOPHIE began to trawl electronica forums to find out how they did it; how Booth and Brown had made sounds which seemed less inclined to play by the rules of the past. It was on those forums that she first read the name of the device which would become her most beloved collaborator: the Elektron Monomachine.

Launched to market only a couple of years earlier, the Monomachine is a sequencer and synthesiser, first designed by its Swedish inventor for a university computer-class assignment. Autechre were very early adopters, which made SOPHIE one too. Unlike the tools she was so critical of, the Monomachine is an instrument which allows its owner to involve themselves far earlier in the process of sound creation than almost all other synthesisers do; producing single-frequency sine-waves which can be modulated and manipulated in a million potential combinations. Melodies can be transformed into percussion, or vice versa. The rules are off the table when it's all just born in the box.

This work is usually prebuilt into most synthesisers in the form of presets, but starting at this primordial stage, you can essentially create a brand-new instrument every single time you use it . . . if you're inventive enough. Many of the artists in this book – from Blood Orange to The Alchemist – work like collagists. SOPHIE though was trained as a sculptor, and she approached music like a sculptor would: making her materials from scratch and moving them to her computer to craft the finished piece.

When SOPHIE finally got her hands on an Elektron Monomachine, she studied how to modulate its sine-waves with one intention: to make sounds as muscular and tactile as Booth and Brown had inflicted upon that Glaswegian night. 'This means considering the physical properties of materials and how those inform the acoustic properties,' she told *Billboard* in 2014. 'Why does a bubble have an ascending pitch when popped . . . why does metal clang when struck and what is this clanging sound in terms of pitch and timbre over time? How do I synthesize this?'

With this experiment in mind, SOPHIE began to assemble – completely from scratch – a living library of playable synths which mimicked the sounds made by real-world objects without ever sampling them. She created timbres which mimicked the whipping of corrugated iron or the quiver of an elastic band and, because they existed in the Monomachine, each of those synths could be played as easily as the keys of a grand piano.

The influence of the Monomachine (which SOPHIE nicknamed her 'little black box') on her sound cannot be overstated. Over the years, she didn't simply become competent at the Monomachine; she became a master of it. If her chosen instrument was a Stratocaster or a harp, SOPHIE would be known, first and foremost, as a virtuosic player. She once met people from Elektron personally, and even *they* didn't know how she was doing what she was doing. All of this masterful sound design is all the more impressive if you actually *see* a Monomachine: it's a box. There's no simple, intuitive interface; there are just rows of grey plastic buttons which you need to learn intuitively before you can begin to get a single thing out of it. 'These are synths that I've never heard anybody design before,' Canadian artist Backxwash said years later, 'not even people who have been in the game for so long.'

In London in 2012, SOPHIE worked from the basement of a converted Camden chapel which she affectionally dubbed 'the crypt'. While she was working, she would often venture out to watch classical concerts, just to witness the act of sound creation unfold before her very eyes. As she watched composers like Thomas Adès conduct their pieces, she observed the relationship classical has with the underpinning of dance music: a low sub-bass undulating away, while the string sections played a melody in unison. When she returned to the crypt, she began thinking about those orchestras, and how the Monomachine could apply those principles unburdened by the bounds of reality. What if there were 2,000 violins playing at the same time? If there was a piano the size of a mountain, what would one of its strings sound like in a song?

SOPHIE began to write the songs which would become her first singles as early as 2010, but it took time to find a home for them. That changed in 2012 when James Cooper offered SOPHIE as a taxi service to a friend. Scottish DJ Jack 'Jackmaster' Revill had signed up to open a night at XOYO in London and close a set in Bristol that same night. He need to get there fast. The only person Cooper knew with a car was SOPHIE, and so he asked her to drive him.

SOPHIE chain-smoked for the entirety of the drive. On the car stereo, she played her own demos for the first hour of the journey, and Bach for the second. Revill was intrigued to say the least. He had recently launched the Glaswegian indie label Numbers, already becoming home to bright, maximalist future-bass by the likes of Hudson Mohawke and Rustie. As soon as he could, Revill quickly signed SOPHIE too. Soon, she sent him a song she thought could work as her first single. 'When she sent us "BIPP",' Calum Morton, co-founder of Numbers told *DJ Mag*, 'I smiled for about a month.'

What SOPHIE had sent them had its inception in the music of Booth and Brown, but didn't sound like Autechre at all. Absent were the ominous, knotty mazes of *Untilted*, or even the uneasy modernist collages of *Exai*, the album they had released that same year. No, instead it sounded like the Spice Girls, squeezed through a tube of toothpaste.

Few pieces of music embody their cover to quite the extent that 'BIPP' does. It's a simple image: a 3D rendering of a plastic waterslide, clad in undulating stripes of pink and blue. The song feels exactly like a trip down that slide would: legs in the air, bouncing over every curve. It begins with a revving synth which sounds like the engine of a miniature car. The drums are so gloopy that they stick around in the mix for a few seconds every time they hit, bubbles of percussion popping all around. This is dance music in carbonated form. A female vocalist sings in a sweet girlish tone straight out of the pink aisle in a toy shop. 'I can make you feel better, if you let me!' she coos, 'I can make you feel better, if you want me to . . . You know you want to!' It's a Kylie chorus or a Britney chorus, only doused in sugar and high on helium. Those vocals stack on top of each other impossibly, becoming as dense as a church choir, until it all ends, like a waterslide would, with a pop, and a splash.

'BIPP' was released with B-side 'ELLE' on the 7th of June 2013. Numbers let the single sit there for fourteen more months before she produced another, in August 2014. 'BIPP' was sweet, but it had nothing on 'LEMONADE'. The chorus couldn't be more garish if it tried: another excitable voice repeating the song's title out in a cheerleader chant. 'Lemonade, luh, luh, lemonade!' The synths fizzle like bubbles streaming up a cold glass of pop. It feels like a hyperactive pop song left to simmer in the sun, boiled down into a thick, sticky syrup. Released with B-side 'HARD', all four songs came adorned with their own synthetic waterslide, each feeling like little treats unto themselves; complete with hooks as sticky as any you'd find on any pop chart, but delivered as unapologetically as a bucket of slime to the face. Like a great many people, I'd never heard anything like them.

SOPHIE's singles couldn't have been further from the mood of serious British electronica in the years they were released. Many permutations of electronic music had been born in queer club nights and had been accelerated in the debauched fields of rural England. For some time though, so-called dance music had become enveloped in a decidedly heady state of mind. The British press had concocted a moral panic around rave culture and, by the early 2000s, had largely won its war against the youth. Music began to sound far gloomier as a result. I love Autechre, but their most noodling, mid-noughties records can sometimes feel like you're being lectured in Morse code. This 'intelligent dance music' was better suited for listening to with headphones on than in crowded fields.

In 2005, London producer Burial began releasing ominous, murky EPs which felt designed for this kind of solitary, late-night consumption. His debut album and 2007's *Untrue* left long shadows, in no small part due to their sheer brilliance. Around them, cultural theorists coined concepts like 'hauntology', a term for music filled with the ghosts of alternative futures, erased by the total victory of capitalism. A new generation of Englishmen worked in Burial's shadow: albums like Actress' *Splazsh*, Andy Stott's *Luxury Problems* and Forest Swords' *Engravings* all being made in a post-*Untrue* universe haunted by rhythmic slippages, shuddering loops and ghostly samples. These records were beautiful, yes, but depressive too, lit in various tones of black, white and grey.

Against this dour backdrop, SOPHIE felt like somebody wearing a feather boa to a wake. 'BIPP', 'ELLE', 'LEMONADE' and 'HARD' are songs of dazzling intensity. They're hyperactive and, importantly, more than a little silly. Artists of the Burial school filled their mixes with sonic weight, their tracks smothered in glitches and crackles, and underscored by subterranean drones. SOPHIE's sound, on the other hand, is pristine. There is no fog on 'BIPP'. The synths SOPHIE eked out of the Monomachine's sine-waves sound like plastic shooting through a void. Every track is nimble and bright, minimalist components bouncing off each other and leaving no debris behind. Rather than amassing volume, her songs blast through high-pitched ecstasy, and tend to be over in three minutes flat.

It's almost an unspoken rule of electronic music that one should blur the line between man and machine. The programmed drums of Kraftwerk's *Autobahn* replicate the motorik drumming of Krautrock bands, and were often adorned with violin and flute. A song like Four Tet's gorgeous 'Morning Side' takes a performance from a Bollywood star and uses her voice to propel the listener toward bliss. Jon Hopkins' *Immunity* begins with the sound of him turning the key to his studio; Jlin's *Black Origami* is alive with the percussive weight of industry.

SOPHIE, on the other hand, found this to be a strange affectation. 'You have the possibility, with electronic music, to generate any texture and any sound, so why would any musician want to limit themselves?' she told *Arte Tracks* in 2018. 'When you imagine things in your head . . . you hear the idea pure. It's almost like gaining access to someone's imagination, and you don't have to bring it down to earth.' As such, SOPHIE crafted her songs with no sonic signposts to the world which exists around them. Songs like 'BIPP' and 'HARD' sound like raves being hosted in a vacuum.

The design of the Elektron Monomachine lends itself to this kind of writing. It's a brilliant but limited piece of equipment, allowing only six monophonic lines to be worked on at once. If you're writing songs on it, there's absolutely no room for any extraneous details. Even still, keeping the world out of your music is no easy feat, and SOPHIE made a great deal of trying to keep out what other artists force in. During the making of her early singles, SOPHIE listened to little other music aside from her own, and tried to keep the spaces where she worked immaculate and clutter-free, manufacturing a cleanliness she hoped would work its way into her songs.

This effect is more uncanny the more you pay attention to it. It's a sound we don't hear often. The human mistakes which leak into every song, no matter how hard producers may try to avoid them, are completely absent from a track like 'BIPP'. The tuning of a guitar, the shuffle of an audience, the breath of an MC: SOPHIE eradicated all signs of human touch completely. It's a style which is an affectation in itself (take a look at even the AI art of the 2020s and it's *full* of strange, nonsensical mistakes), but this was the environment of SOPHIE's choosing: a furious, concentrated rush towards an idea of how the future could sound. 'I'm more interested in plastic taking on the physical appearance of metal or liquids than I am those materials themselves,' she told *Radio Wave* in 2014. 'Synthetic reconstructions of the material world.'

The sense of proud artificiality is heightened by the types of songs which the hooks and melodies of 'LEMONADE' and 'BIPP' seem to reference: the gaudy, propulsive Eurodance which filled package holiday club nights throughout the 2000s. As far as chintz goes, 'LEMONADE' goes beyond even the most garish Kylie dance-pop. Singer Nabihah Iqbal delivers its hook with the kind of numb, wide-eyed incessantness I'd only ever heard in tunes like the Romanian hit 'Dragostea Din Tei' (a song which – entirely against my will – basically defined my childhood years). If you asked a stranger (or worse, a music critic) in 2013 which songs were the most completely vacuous then, chances are, tunes like those would be the first to spring to mind. For music whose production style already revelled in its own synthetic-ness, there was no better cultural reference point. SOPHIE found herself asking questions not dissimilar to the ones Daniel Lopatin confronted on *R Plus Seven*: what is so wrong about popular music? How are the sounds produced by guitar strings more 'real' than those generated on a Mac?

When they were released, SOPHIE's singles created one thing above all else: discourse, and lots of it. It was 2014, before bedroom-born stars like Billie Eilish and Lil Yachty had even begun to take hold. We were still at the very inception of what Daniel Lopatin called the implosion of the mainstream and the underground, both in effect and sensibility, and SOPHIE's music was utterly confounding because of it. 'BIPP' was released on a Scottish indie label and straight to sites like SoundCloud: the proving grounds of the underground and avant-garde. As such, music critics and many fans alike quickly came to one obvious explanation: SOPHIE was taking the piss.

This impression was, to be fair, not something which SOPHIE did anything to dispel. I can tell you because I was there. In those early days, we music nerds knew absolutely *nothing* about SOPHIE, even when we tried to find out. For more than two full years, we had only those brilliant, slightly unnerving singles, and that all-caps name. We had no photographs, no biography, no gender: just six songs, a little over twenty minutes in length. It was a mystery she maintained even at her live shows. When she performed at LA's legendary Boiler Room in September 2014, she hired rapper and drag queen Ben Woozy to pretend to DJ, while she stood offstage in a suit, pretending to be her own security. When she called in to BBC Radio 1 to give her first on-air interview, she used a voice-changer to turn her voice into a pitched-up squeak. 'Sorry,' she said, 'I've got a cough.' When the bemused DJ asked her what genre she'd like 'BIPP' to be called, she said simply, 'It's dance-pop music, just like everything else.'

SOPHIE clearly enjoyed getting a ride out of bewildered journalists, but the idea that she was acting purely out of shyness is a misconception. When she arrived on the London club scene, she made no attempt to hide herself. The first thing she did in the city was print her name out on a stack of bright-pink business cards and hand them out at to artists at every show she played. 'Hi. I'm SOPHIE,' it read. 'I'm a pop producer. Would you like to work with me?'

Instead, her mysteriousness was an extension of the approach she took when mixing her songs: she wanted to remove them of all context and let the compositions speak for themselves. It was a strategy inspired by the type of listening she'd come to enjoy most: walking to her local corner shop in Camden and hearing the songs they played on some obscure radio station. Even when she loved a song, she had no idea what they were or who made them, and it was something she wanted to manufacture for herself.

Therefore, the narrative cooked up by the music press persisted. Some relished the supposed satire, finding great joy in the apparent mockery of the likes of LMFAO and Nicki Minaj. On the other hand, others seethed at the snobbery. 'If you can make intriguing, futuristic pop music, why not just do that?' Alexis Petridis wrote in *The Guardian*. 'The uncharitable answer is that [s]he thinks it's a bit below [her], that [s]he's less interested in making pop music or celebrating it in all its neon-bright, two-fingers-to-good-taste glory than in sneering.'

In reality, SOPHIE wasn't just uncynical about pop music, she was a complete devotee. As a child, her mother had offset the harsher edges of her father's EDM with lashings of disco.

SOPHIE was raised on the hits of The Pet Shop Boys and Depeche Mode. She said that she first fell in love to the Spice Girls' '2 Become 1'. Like Tyler Okonma, she was fascinated by The Neptunes-era of early-2000s pop, especially their masterpiece, 'Grindin''. She geeked out over disco with her younger brother Ben and, just before arriving at university, became obsessed with Tim Lawrence's book *Love Saves the Day: A History of American Dance Music Culture, 1970–1979*, deeply inspired by the wave of radically joyous music which ripped through Boston, Chicago, Miami and LA in the wake of the Vietnam War, and the polymorphous sexuality which surrounded it. Her favourite artist from the era was Leroy Burgess, a Harlem-born polymath who founded the band Logg, a funk and electro-pop outfit who made blissed-out twists on post-disco soul.

'Mainstream music is much more appealing because it lives in the lives of so many more people,' she told *CRACK* in 2018. 'It's not exclusive, it's not elitist, and those are the standards I want to maintain.' SOPHIE made the first singles of her career with the expressed intention of making music which delivered the pleasures of Leroy Burgess and Pharrell Williams as directly as possible. 'It would be extremely exciting if music could take you on the same sort of high-thrill three-minute ride as a theme-park rollercoaster,' she told *BOMB*, just months before 'BIPP'/'ELLE' were released. 'It spins you upside down, dips you in water, flashes strobe lights at you, takes you on a slow incline to the peak, and then drops you vertically down a smoky tunnel, then stops with a jerk, and your hair is all messed up, and some people feel sick, and others are laughing. Then you buy a key ring.'

Unlike Daniel Lopatin, when SOPHIE was young music consumed her life so completely that she had little time for cinema. There was only really one film which she ever expressed admiration for publicly: 1971's *Willy Wonka & the Chocolate Factory*.

It makes sense that, out of all of cinema's protagonists, SOPHIE would relate to Wonka the most. After all, she approached her singles not like a musician, but a chocolatier. In the beginning she released only two songs per year, but those singles, each barely three minutes in length, felt satiating because each were built around such distinct sonic flavours, like each was a little foil-wrapped sweetie. She wanted to delight her listeners with the sounds she'd spent years crafting from scratch on the Monomachine and she treated her synths like a gourmet chef presents a fine ingredient: sparingly.

'With sound design there are certain ways in which you can create sounds to produce an instinctive reaction,' she told *BOMB*. 'It's like in horror films; special effects can be used to produce a knee-jerk reaction, like jumping out of your seat.' She wanted each of her songs to literally excite the body, and deliver what she called 'exothermic body reactions', like Autechre had once done for her. Unlike Booth and Brown, she wanted to delight as many people as possible as she did it. Pop music as confectionery.

Because this approach suited the single format so well, SOPHIE's debut album wasn't an album at all, but a compilation. On the 27th of November 2015, Numbers released *PRODUCT*, which contained 'BIPP', 'ELLE', 'LEMONADE', 'HARD', and four new tracks. Even arranged together in this way, each song retains the sensation of being a distinct universe unto itself. 'MSMSMSM' is sour, filled with the clangs of steel and the twangs of springs. There's a slight G-funk bounce to it; you could almost hear Clipse doing wonders with its final thirty seconds. Then there's 'VYZEE': an outrageously fun dance-pop bop lavished with throat wheezes and fat, squelching blobs of percussion with squelch through the mix like dollops of mayonnaise. 'You've got to twist your body, twirl it all around!' singer Raffy giggles. 'Make it pop and sizzle! / Now squish it on the ground!' The one true eye-opener of the collection was the final song – 'JUST LIKE WE NEVER SAID GOODBYE'; the first SOPHIE song which – aside from the girlish pitch of the vocals – sounds like a more conventional pop epic. With some additional niceties, it could even be a Sia song: gorgeous surging synths rising to uplift the sentiment of the lyrics, and not the other way around.

Despite SOPHIE's belief in the populism of pop music, it goes without saying that none of the songs on *PRODUCT* became hits, or even appeared on a top 40 chart. As testament to the still-evident divide between mainstream and underground, these dance pop songs remained decidedly niche concerns, enjoyed by the same devotees of eccentric electronica who might have followed Autechre in their prime. There are several reasons for this, but chief among them is a pretty simple explanation: for all the fun and bounce of *PRODUCT*, it can be pretty fucking scary when it wants to be. SOPHIE used many tricks to jolt reactions out of her listeners, and she knew that pure sweetness doesn't work in isolation. It's this fact which separates her music from the most vacuous pop music. Even at her cutest, there's usually something deranged at play too.

It's a quality present in *PRODUCT*'s more uneasy songs (the groaning ripples of 'ELLE'; the caffeinated head-squeeze of 'L.O.V.E.') but it's there in the middle of bangers like 'BIPP' too. Things are pretty intense on that song. Even as the chorus coos 'I can make you feel better', there's a sinister sub-bass rumbling beneath, a twist on the Eskibeat Wiley used to evoke the grime which gave his genre its name. Throughout *PRODUCT* in fact, synths fire off like sonic cannons; drums hit like fists to the wall. SOPHIE was a child of the '90s, and she loved that a song as nasty and rowdy as The Prodigy's 'Firestarter' had made it to UK number one. She channelled that violent energy into her own music. If another word for 'pop' is 'explode', then a song like 'HARD' is the reason why. After all, roller coasters aren't fun because you giggle, they're fun because part of you knows you might plummet to your death.

The harsher edges of SOPHIE's sound aren't the only reason these songs cause unease and pleasure in equal measure. There's also the effect of the uncanny valley. After all, much of the music we listen to is full of the kind of signifiers SOPHIE deliberately abstained from; signposts to so-called 'authenticity' which tend to come in the form of allusions to the past. When she broke out, Lady Gaga liked to dress up like a cyborg, but her songs operated just like the arena rock hits of the early '80s had: with squiggling synths in place of guitars and arena-sized kicks in place of a bass drum. In the Earl Sweatshirt chapter I referenced the way rappers like Travis Scott use the aesthetic of psychedelia to confer depth upon the emotionally vacant.

Even when it's not as explicit though, vast swathes of modern pop production tend to be littered with little sonic signifiers to sounds whose sounds infer authenticity, from a tastefully placed slide guitar to the old-fashioned strumming of an acoustic. The songs of *PRODUCT*, on the other hand, are remarkable because they feel completely untethered from any specific time or place. SOPHIE is a British artist and yet she's so rarely mentioned alongside names of great British musicians perhaps because there's nothing in her songs – not a vocal intonation, not a sonic reference point, not a nod to specific styles or sensibilities – which could tie a song like 'VYZEE' to the musical lineage of the UK. It's hard to even think of any other artists for whom this is the case for to such an extent.

Of course, SOPHIE is not unique in the tools she used to make her music. Most of her songs were made in the way the majority of modern songs across all genres are: on a laptop, using Ableton Live. The difference is that most songs tend to make great efforts to hide that fact, and SOPHIE didn't. That can feel more than a little unsettling. After all, so many of the products and services which are now part of our daily lives – from Amazon to Uber or our favourite coffee brand – hide their various crimes and human rights abuses through the frictionless way they're presented to us, and this music prods at the reality behind that digital disguise.

As discourse around her music pressed on, SOPHIE doubled down on her love for the proudly synthetic. The vinyl version of *PRODUCT*, for example, wasn't released in a cardboard sleeve but rather a fleshy rubber one which she described simply as a 'skin-safe, odourless and tasteless platinum silicon product'. On her website her music was explicitly framed as an accessory to the merchandise, not the other way around. If you brought one of her jet-black, double-pronged dildos, for example, then you got *PRODUCT*'s WAV files for free.

In 2014, SOPHIE worked with London producer A.G. Cook and performance artist Hayden Dunham to write 'Hey QT', a single promoted as the debut single from a new (and fundamentally fictional) pop star named QT. The song acted as an ad campaign for an energy drink which (for a while at least) didn't even exist. These ideas of absolute consumerism detached from any semblance of material reality may seem a little obvious now, but QT was conceived five years before people began spending hundreds of thousands of dollars on digital images of cartoon monkeys. It was, in fact, remarkably prescient.

'People want to be sold something but they don't want to feel like they're being sold something,' SOPHIE told the *Travel Almanac* in 2015. 'They need a selling point to a musical product, but they don't want to acknowledge that they're being sold anything . . . They want to feel it's "real". Of course, in most cases it's not real, it's a fabrication or exaggeration of the truth or an alter-ego being performed by someone. A pretence, or a posture. But people are fine with that.'

SOPHIE's early music *was* countercultural then, just not in the plainly satirical sense people projected onto it in those early days. Most of the most beloved and radical countercultural music, from jazz to hip hop, are reactions *against* inclinations prevalent in the culture of the day, but SOPHIE's music wasn't. Instead, the sounds she created and the imagery she paired them with are things which we're all excruciatingly familiar with: the open-eyed glee of advertising, the unrelenting pulse of dance-pop, the promise and the artifice of the products we buy. What was radical was a refusal to mask the artificiality central to her art. In a society comprised of spectacles, we're used to a little more sugaring of the pill.*

For 'Hey QT', SOPHIE came together with two collaborators who helped to shape her early career. The face of QT was Hayden Dunham, a Texan performance artist who was by SOPHIE's side for the making of a great many of *PRODUCT*'s singles.

When they first met, in New York in 2011, Hayden and SOPHIE were fascinated with each other. They were wearing the same outfit, but inverted: Hayden in all cream, SOPHIE in all black. Hayden was a sculptor, just like SOPHIE. In the years before, she had been working on large-scale sculptures constructed from transformational materials: the ones which explode or melt or evaporate, and cannot easily be contained. As someone fascinated by materials to the extent that SOPHIE was, this appealed to her greatly. The day after they met, they both happened to be flying to Texas at almost the same time, by sheer coincidence. Soon after, they began dating.

'During those early years she had a super-soft interior, but a uniform exterior,' Hayden told me over video-call. 'She

* In a startlingly apt moment, in 2015 Kim Kardashian was accused of plagiarising QT in adverts for her own drink, Hype Energy, right down to the cropped bob and wide, doll-like eyes. That same year, 'LEMONADE' appeared in a McDonald's ad.

wore the same outfit every single day, and I think there was a comfort in it. It allowed the really soft things to come through.' Throughout their six-year relationship, Hayden and SOPHIE communicated through their respective mediums, first and foremost. 'We loved to play this game of making new materials,' she said. 'We would try to combine two things which rarely exist side by side into one; I would create it physically, and she would make it in a wave form. A lot of our love and our work started from this place of curiosity about what was possible here on earth, how to "shake it up and make it fizz".'

Sugary liquids had always played an improbably large part in SOPHIE's life. Her father was a businessman who helped to revolutionise the British orange juice industry, and drinks were a way Hayden expressed affection too. 'If we woke up and she was feeling heavy, I would make something with spring water and a mineral composition which would be uplifting,' she told me. 'This was just part of our life.' It was from a love of those elixirs that the idea of a song revolving around energy drinks was born, and they decided to name it after a term of endearment Hayden, a typical Texan, had a habit of greeting people with: 'hey cutie'.

Around that time, SOPHIE met another kindred spirit who completely changed the way she went about her work. It so happened that another Londoner was coming to the idea of blurring the lines of pop and the avant-garde at the same exact time. While SOPHIE was toiling in the crypt, across the city, A.G. Cook – a musical-computing graduate and son of renowned architect Sir Peter Cook – was beginning to produce his own home-spun pop songs just like hers. In 2013, Cook began putting together a network of like-minded artists who – just like Tyler Okonma before him – he began treating as if they were already stadium-filling pop stars. They called themselves PC Music.

Even more explicitly than in SOPHIE's songs, PC Music was utterly devoted to the sticky-sweet choruses of '00s ringtone-ready electro-pop. It was startling, because it was a complete inversion of how things were supposed to work. This was a time when major-label acts Mumford & Sons were affecting grassroots, indie credentials, but there was PC Music, making music in their bedrooms but acting as if they were Destiny's Child. One of Cook's friends Hannah Amond (who called herself Hannah Diamond) was a fashion student, and a gifted one. She helped to craft and polish the look of the group, taking 'signees' like Danny L Harle, Easyfun and Planet 1999 and presenting them in a way which treated the sheen of *X Factor* finalists and JD Sports adverts with a fetishistic admiration.

Cook first encountered SOPHIE on SoundCloud in 2012. He was browsing and pressed play on a thirty-second demo of 'BIPP', and another unreleased song named 'OOH'. He was stunned. 'I couldn't believe that there was someone out there, let alone someone in London, with such a strong vision and almost no regard for the walls between pop and experimental art,' he later wrote. He emailed her msmsmsm.com address and she responded straight away. SOPHIE already knew of Cook too, from an early track he'd produced called 'Party on My Own' which, improbably, had become a drinking anthem for her and her friends. Shortly after, they met over FaceTime while SOPHIE was staying at Hayden's parents' house in Texas, and QT was born.

SOPHIE was fascinated by PC Music. She was intrigued by the way Cook used a rotating cast of friends as vocalists for his songs: a disregard for the import of authorship far more common in major-label songwriting than independent music. 'Everything felt like the property of the scene and no one person,' Caroline Polachek told me. 'I've never witnessed anything else like that.'

SOPHIE was a collaborative person. She had been in a band, she had begun club nights and scored performance pieces. Rarely though had her collaborators found their way into her solo work. From her childhood bedroom to her student house, songwriting had been something she worked on alone. Dunham and Cook changed that, overnight. Cook later said that he was the first person she ever let touch her laptop. The three of them quickly formed a unit, first performing together in the March of 2013 at SXSW, in Hayden's home state. They went to a local Walmart and spent all their money on inflatables and paddling pools, and it was from this that the idea for the waterslides which would appear on the covers of 'BIPP' and 'LEMONADE' were born.

It wasn't only artists of the SoundCloud world who took an interest in SOPHIE's work either. Madonna did too. Just as Arca had been quickly swept up by the likes of Björk and Kanye West, SOPHIE too was sucked from the fringes of the underground and placed at the centre of pop culture with remarkable speed. SOPHIE was invited to work on Madonna's thirteenth album *Rebel Heart* in 2014* and, true to her professed populism, soon began spreading her talents across a spectrum of music, from Danish superstar MØ to Norfolk-born indie duo Let's Eat Grandma. The magnificent 'Hot Pink' (which she produced with her childhood friend, Faris Badwan of The Horrors) is bristling, pummelling music which would have fit nobody's idea of 'indie' just five years earlier. SOPHIE's most enduring collaboration, though, was with an artist who was, at that very moment, front and centre of some of the most ubiquitous pop songs on the planet.

---

* The song which SOPHIE produced with Diplo – 'Bitch I'm Madonna' – is pretty awful, but it *is* the only Madonna song which features a drop which sounds like someone yanking at a roll of Sellotape, and that's not nothing.

*

By 2015 Charlotte Aitchison wasn't quite a household name, but her voice had hardly left the radio in years. It was a run she began in 2012 when she was twenty years old, performing as Charli xcx (a name which began as her MySpace handle) and delivered a guest verse on Icona Pop's 'I Love It'. A Hot 100 hit, 'I Love It' is a boisterous, gleeful pop song, one so ubiquitous during my first year of university that I can't hear it without tasting blue WKD. Charli followed the success of that single with Iggy Azalea's 'Fancy', a US number one every bit as grating as 'I Love It' was brilliant. Then, in 2014, her own single 'Boom Clap' earned her a place on the UK Top Ten.

Because of those huge songs, in 2014 Charli was perceived as a very different artist to the one she is today. Her songs had the stomp of club music but the guitar-driven pulse of rock songs, and Charli was no lover of rock music. 'Club electronic music is what makes me feel most alive,' she told *Rolling Stone* in 2024,. 'My nightmare is going to see a pop show or, like, a band.' Like all the artists in this book, Charli was a teenager as MP3 and online culture was becoming de rigueur. She discovered Justice's thumping 2007 album *Cross* on MySpace when she was fifteen, dragging her down a rabbit hole of obnoxious, messy club music by the likes of Ed Banger and French-American singer/rapper Uffie. 'I fell in love with music, production and partying, all at once, from my computer screen', she told Resident Advisor. 'Chopping vocals, using them not only as an instrument but as rhythm and part of the percussion. It made me want to live in that world.'

It goes without saying that 'Boom Clap' wasn't quite scratching that itch; in fact very few of the dozens of producers Atlantic Records sat her down with seemed able to tap into the exact energy Aitchison had felt squinting at her computer in Hertfordshire as a teenager. That changed when she met SOPHIE at a writing camp in Sweden. 'It was a total sham,' Charli told Resident Advisor. 'We basically just made songs that would never get pitched or go anywhere. We just partied all the time.' Nevertheless, SOPHIE was the first artist Charli had met who seemed able to give her what she had been craving for so long. 'When I met SOPHIE, it was like: wow, you get it, and you get me, and you also make me feel something,' she told *Vogue* in 2019. 'There are very few artists who make me feel something up my core and make me wanna cry. Justice and Uffie made me feel something when I was fourteen, and I didn't really have that feeling again until I met SOPHIE. I felt this rush of: fuck, this is the coolest shit I have ever heard.'

Perhaps because she was a pop star with club music embedded in the very roots of her musical identity, Charli became one of the very first major-label artists to invest in the technicolour intensity of both SOPHIE and PC Music completely. She hired A.G. as the creative director for her next album, and in February 2016 she and SOPHIE released *Vroom Vroom,* a joint EP which took the clean, punchy production of her albums *True Romance* and *Sucker*, and replaced it with thumping, ultra-violent synths. As A.G Cook wrote in 2021, 'Charli was the first artist whose voice and presence could actually sit over a full-blown SOPHIE instrumental intact.' It wasn't for nothing that Charli's voice alone soon became a dance music staple. 'Specifically for queer DJs and queer spaces', trance DJ Doss told Resident Advisor. 'Charli has been a staple for years – edits, remixes, straight-up tracks, they've always been played.'

Over time, Charli's music became a living embodiment of the weirder edges SOPHIE brought to pop. Like George Michael or Britney Spears before her, by the time of 2024's phenomenal *BRAT* (a record littered with PC Music alums like

Cook and Easyfun), Charli had become the kind of artist which entire cultures form around. From *Vroom Vroom* onwards, Aitchison turned down the kind of career a hit like 'Fancy' could have afforded her and committed to garish, maximalist pop songs with one foot in club music instead. Albums like 2019's *Charli* were an apotheosis of the stylistic and cultural transformations which had been provoked by SOPHIE and PC Music: a genre-hopping toy box of an album with hair-flicking noughties throwbacks like '1999' squeezed alongside Laurel Canyon excursions like 'Warm' and utterly demented bangers like 'Click' and 'Shake It', nasty, raunchy goliaths which lurch between robotic breathiness and pummelling, metallic bass. Neither *Charli* nor *BRAT* were actually made with SOPHIE, but they couldn't have existed without her.

The willingness of young artists like Charli to commit to a sound as ostentatious and wonky as SOPHIE's did a great deal to freak up the mainstream in the late 2010s. Electronic music at the start of the decade was dominated by EDM and hard dubsteb, and it was an ugly, machismo-driven scene. The enormous drops of Knife Party, the sneering hooks of LMFAO; they were great, sonic penises thrusting out across spring-break beach parties. The music of SOPHIE and A.G. Cook felt like a breath of fresh air in comparison. SOPHIE's songs feature female vocals exclusively, just as PC Music's did, their music filled with the sexual bravado of women instead. Charli xcx and collaborators like Troye Sivan and Clairo quickly amassed huge queer followings, the unhinged sounds of SOPHIE's waveform manipulations reinventing the liberating ecstasy of disco for the digital age.

SOPHIE's sound was so radical that it turned heads in spaces far beyond her own. While figures from the pop world looked to her to make their music more outlandish, some indie artists began to feel nervous about the anachronisms of their sound. Caroline Polachek told me about her experience of discovering SOPHIE's music, and the way she made her question her own trajectory. 'I first heard SOPHIE on NTS Radio while I was doing a photoshoot for a project called Mona Lisa,' she told me. 'It was a very conceptual, historically tinged project; suddenly "LEMONADE" comes on and I didn't know how to feel. I had no social context for it, no visual context for it. I actually felt very threatened, because there was I making the visuals for this very classical project and it really hurt me that it was so contemporary that I didn't even understand what was happening.

'In 2015 my publisher said "do you want to try a session with this producer called SOPHIE?" I said "oh my god, SOPHIE from 'LEMONADE'?" So we got into the studio. I was emotional because, the day prior, my father-in-law had brain surgery and the feelings were very raw. Then SOPHIE appeared. She was this very beautiful, Bowie-esque person who arrived with nothing but her laptop and her Monomachine. I kind of had a total emotional breakdown. There was nothing I could sing that day which matched the tone of what she was doing, and I could feel us both really trying to accommodate each other. She was like "let's try again tomorrow". You could tell we hadn't struck gold but we were very intrigued by each other.

'The next time we met was at SXSW in 2016,' she continued. 'I'd just done a session with Danny L Harle, making a song called "Ashes of Love". SOPHIE asked to be on the guest list for my Chairlift show and I was like . . . "SOPHIE wants to hear my indie band play . . .?" She brought the whole crew – a big mob of PC Music affiliates – and I was really intimidated because they were all there just watching us and our guitars. But we spent the rest of the night – SOPHIE, Hayden, Danny L Harle – running around for Charli's *Vroom Vroom* launch. It was a very much a playback show, with SOPHIE there in black leather behind the DJ booth, and it was the first time I really saw and understood that format. It was very new and contemporary, I remember feeling embarrassed to be playing in a band.'

Caroline and Charli xcx were among the first artists to catch on to SOPHIE's music, but they were far from the last. In 2019 a new wave of musicians (who were teenagers themselves when SOPHIE released 'BIPP') sieved through the brash and propulsive elements of *PRODUCT* and *PC Music Vol. 1* and applied their approaches to a wild array of genres. The likes of 100 gecs, underscores and Dorian Electra created great, kinetic wrecks of sound out of everything from ska to crunk, propelled by kinetic BPMs and built around structures which can (if you squint hard enough) be recognised as pop songs. This post-genre genre was a sound born of the streaming age, a manic menagerie given its name, aptly, by a famous Spotify playlist: 'hyper-pop'.

The heavy pulse of SOPHIE's production also lent itself, naturally, to rap. SOPHIE has produced ominous, twitchy beats for US rapper and ballerina Le1f and grime MC GAIKA; but her finest rap venture was with Thebe Kgositsile's old friend, Vince Staples.

Like Charli xcx, after releasing his debut album *Summertime '06* in 2015, Vince began moving towards sounds few ever expected to hear from him: twitchy house, UK garage and squonking, maximalist trap. Against all the odds it was the woman behind 'LEMONADE' who helped him find what he was looking for.

Staples and SOPHIE met on tour in Australia in the winter of 2016. Both were support acts for Flume. Flume is a big deal in Australia, and Staples and SOPHIE were still warming up, so their hotel rooms tended to be stifling and small. Both of them were early risers and so, when they headed down to the hotel pools to get some air, they often found the other there already, working away in the sun. As things tended to with SOPHIE, conversations soon turned to music. SOPHIE would bring her Monomachine and her laptop down by the water, working on sketches for a potential new album, and it was there that she devised the beat for what would become Vince's single 'Yeah Right'.

SOPHIE was very particular about how Vince used her beats. When he first attempted to rhyme over the instrumental in the vein of *Summertime '06* – sharp and introspective – SOPHIE quickly shut that down. 'Don't tell stories,' Vince remembered her saying. 'I don't care what you're talking about. Attention, is what's important.' In other words: 'Don't let the verse be deep or heartfelt, 'cause she stopping the computer and walking outside until you get bacc [*sic*] on some gangsta shit.' The end result – track seven on Staples' miniature masterpiece *Big Fish Theory* – was gangsta shit indeed. The feature verse on the song is Kendrick Lamar, and the idea of three generational talents sharing the space of a single song felt too good to be true. Somehow 'Yeah Right' managed to exceed expectations.

'Yeah Right' begins, as almost no rap songs do, with a bright, whipping synth. Despite the brashness, there's a lot of space in the mix, and Vince matches that patience with a villainous flow, repeating the song's title in a sneer, like a sprinter pacing the start line. Then the starting gun explodes. All of that tension is shattered by a squeezed, high-pitched vocal being whipped side to side in the mix, and suddenly everything is warfare. The hi-hats sound like scattered bullets; the bass is the kind which shakes the dust off bricks and Vince – an MC whose vitriol is expressed with carefully pronounced consonants rather than guttural rage – slots effortlessly among the beat's sharp edges, asking questions as if he has the listener's hands cuffed to the table.

It's not until Kendrick utters his first breath though that things really start to explode. After proving everything on *To Pimp a Butterfly*, K.Dot seemed to grow increasingly unconcerned about demonstrating his linguistic prowess and began playing around with his voice instead. On his 2021 tracks with cousin Baby Keem, Lamar delivers bonkers flows where he pitches his words into cartoonish, frenzied rhythms; what he's saying becoming less compelling than the freakish way in which he's saying it. Well, the first appearance of *that* Kendrick Lamar is on 'Yeah Right'. It's one of those rap songs where the MC seems to go to war with his own beat. His flow and SOPHIE's thumping, elastic sound compete for space in the mix. By the time a walloping beat drops and Kendrick is spitting 'I don't fair fight but I bear fight / looking for my next roll-kill for the headlight,' his voice might as well be an automatic weapon. It's one of the most adrenaline-inducing rap songs I've ever heard.

Staples spoke about SOPHIE's other contribution to the album, 'SAMO', in a 2021 interview with *Rolling Stone*. 'I was working on *Big Fish Theory* at EastWest and she came to the studio when she was in town. She was with Jimmy Edgar, and they'd just gone to Disneyland. She popped up at the studio randomly in Mickey Mouse ears and a leather jacket on. It was 100 degrees outside. That's the type of shit she does. Jimmy played "745", and SOPHIE grabbed a water bottle and left. She was there for, like, three minutes. Later on I said "are you still here?" She was like, "Yeah." I said "I need something else for the album." She was like, "I have one." That was the "SAMO" track . . . She didn't care who you were: this was the beat she had for you, and that's what you were going to use, or not.'

Even as her influence began to feel ubiquitous, SOPHIE didn't drop her proper debut album until six years into her career. *OIL*

OF EVERY PEARL'S UN-INSIDES was released on the 15th of June 2018 through Transgressive Records and MSMSMSM, SOPHIE'S own label. What fans heard when they hit play on that new body of work was something different entirely. If early singles like 'BIPP' were the delivery of a single, brilliantly executed idea, then *OIL* was a showcase of everything she'd become capable of. Dipping between industrial music and ballads, between ambient suites and hyper-pop, it was evidence that SOPHIE was as explorative as she was exacting.

Despite the breadth of its styles, *OIL* still feels as cohesive as the songs of *PRODUCT* were. Sometimes, two tracks even feel like alternative views of the same idea. When the menacing sludge of 'Pretending' gives birth to the bright, ecstatic pop of 'Immaterial', it's as if SOPHIE had taken the ominous drones which underpin dance-pop classics like 'Poker Face' and stripped them for parts. Elsewhere songs articulate the same, ecstatic feelings in a variety of ways. The fourth track, 'Is It Cold in the Water?', feels like a poetic articulation of bliss, while the second track – 'Ponyboy' – captures that same passion, only expressed through kinky, debauched sex instead.

'Ponyboy' is the closest *OIL* gets to the pop confectionery of *PRODUCT*. In spirit, it feels like the child of *The Teaches of Peaches*, transfused with a mastery of an instrument SOPHIE had be honing for a decade. Synths slash like daggers; the percussion seems to be forged out of someone's last, asphyxiated breath. As ever, SOPHIE conceived of the timbre of those sounds before any other aspect of the song, its metallic creaks inspired by J.G. Ballard's *Crash*. Like all of her songs, 'Ponyboy' thrills with pure contradiction: it's a song about sexual submission performed with the swagger of a dominatrix. 'Crack down your whip / Make the pony bite the bit' a demonic voice croaks. It's filth.

While it's possible to imagine a world where 'Ponyboy' appeared on *PRODUCT*, the rest of *OIL* sounds like a proper evolution of that sound. SOPHIE advertised the broadening of her arsenal upfront by releasing one of the album's most divergent songs – 'It's Okay to Cry' – as its lead single. I can still remember the storm that song caused online the day it was released, in October 2017. Before it, SOPHIE had remained as protective about her image as she had been in the time of 'LEMONADE'. I think I assumed she was like Daft Punk: an act whose face would never be part of her work. But then the music video for 'It's Okay to Cry' came out, and there she was: not just present, but stood in full view of the spotlight, lips painted red, two carrot-orange curls framing her face. As she sings and moves and smiles, images of distant galaxies cascade around her. It's extra and more than a little cheeky, but the joy feels sincere. 'The intention has always been to be how I want to be,' she told *Interview* magazine in 2017. 'I'm just going with my instincts, and this is what I feel like doing. I don't see any difference.'

Her visage wasn't the only thing which felt new; the sound of the song was unlike anything SOPHIE had ever made too. For the first time she sings on one of her tracks, forging a huge power ballad complete with twinkling synths and drums which burst like fireworks. 'I can see the truth through all the lies' she sings, with a breathy intonation. 'And even after all this time / Just know you've got nothing to hide / It's okay to cry.' When the single was released, I remember that I didn't quite trust it. I was so used to SOPHIE's music maintaining that state of explicit artificiality that I felt suspicious about the intent of a song which seemed to want to make your hairs stand on end instead. Now though, I recognise it for what it is; a type of tune we all know well: the sincere and heartfelt hits of the pre-postmodern era, songs like Ben E. King's 'Stand By

Me' or The Ronettes' 'Be My Baby'; songs whose sincerity we never feel compelled to question at all.

On the day the song debuted, *Interview* magazine released a feature with SOPHIE in which she revealed, for the first time, that she was trans. In a piece A.G. Cook posted to his website in February 2021, he remembered the moment that she first explained that to him too. 'SOPHIE and I had a lunch date that she uncharacteristically scheduled,' he wrote. 'She had an aversion to the whole notion of "coming out" to describe a process that is more about actualisation than transformation, but there was an honest pride in that particular moment. She talked about hormones, gender and her own experiences with a new lightness that I hadn't seen before. It was an emotional realisation for me, that what I had always interpreted as confidence and androgyny had been just a small window into a much more multi-layered dysphoria, one that she was now openly reorganising. This was immediately followed by SOPHIE taking me for a drive and playing me demos of what would end up being the first four tracks of [*OIL OF EVERY PEARL'S UN-INSIDES*]; strong, impactful pieces of music in any context, let alone when presented with such symmetry.'

In this light, 'It's Okay to Cry's emotional nakedness feels more complicated than a great many power ballads: more like a plea for self-love, and mutual support. 'I've always dreamt of creating some sort of community atmosphere, which is queer, fluid, diverse, genderless and dynamic . . .' SOPHIE told *VICE* in 2018. 'It's Okay to Cry' was a decisive step towards building a community around her music, and a profound statement for an artist whose music many people once mistook for mockery.

Releasing albums didn't come naturally to SOPHIE. She was somebody who balked at almost every convention and, in music, there's nothing more conventional than the LP. SOPHIE tended to view even her released songs as moments in an ongoing evolution. (Even her very first singles – 'Nothing More to Say' and 'Eeehhh' – were presented in both 'dub' and 'vox' versions.) Despite her limited discography, SOPHIE was incredibly prolific, sometimes writing twenty songs a day, but many of them we simply haven't heard because, by the time she articulated one idea she became excited by the next, and quickly moved on. The music which did make it out into the world tended to be born of collaboration, be it her songs with Vince Staples or *Vroom Vroom*. *OIL OF EVERY PEARL'S UN-INSIDES* is seen as a solo album, but it too is an extended collaboration, with a Canadian songwriter named Cecile Believe.

SOPHIE tried to woo Caila Thompson-Hannant into collaborating with her from the first day they met. Believe had released her first EP, *HELLO*, as Mozart's Sister on Merok, the British label which was the first home of The Klaxons and Crystal Castles. Merok carried a degree of prestige in the British indie scene SOPHIE first emerged into, and so she checked *HELLO* out, and fell in love immediately. At the same SXSW where she, Hayden and A.G. Cook had performed with Walmart inflatables, SOPHIE made sure to catch the Mozart's Sister show.

'She was wearing this jacket,' Believe told me, 'a jean jacket which had the word "Vancouver" in sequins on the back. That's where I was born, so I was like "who is this red-headed vision with a Vancouver sequin jacket who knows who I am?"' she laughed. They exchanged emails, and SOPHIE sent Believe a remix of one of the songs from the EP, just as a gift.

Believe lived in Montreal, and when SOPHIE played a set in the city the following year, she told her to come to the show. The next night SOPHIE suggested that they write together. Believe was apprehensive. She had first moved to Montreal as a teenager and had become enmeshed in its now-storied indie scene, bumping shoulders with the likes of Grimes, Mac

DeMarco and Arcade Fire. Like a great many artists in the DIY underground, Believe was used to playing with bands, cutting tracks right there in the room. SOPHIE came from a different world: a pop world, where people meet each other for the first time and sit down to write a song.

When Believe eventually arrived at the makeshift studio SOPHIE had set up in an apartment block in the city, it was the first time Believe had collaborated with another person and their computer. Believe found it exhilarating, and SOPHIE did too. Believe could do it all; she was a classically trained singer who, in Montreal, had fronted indie and punk bands too. She could, in other words, slot into whatever SOPHIE threw at her. The crazier her performances got, the happier SOPHIE seemed. 'I was becoming frustrated with other producers because they'd try to settle me down,' she told me, 'SOPHIE loved that I would just go wild!'

Believe was in LA to rehearse with her band Tops in 2016 when SOPHIE invited her to her apartment for another session. It was winter, and SOPHIE had just returned from her tour with Flume and Vince Staples. 'Ponyboy' was almost finished; 'It's Okay to Cry' was too, but that was it. Over the next bountiful fortnight, almost the entirety of *OIL OF EVERY PEARL'S UN-INSIDES* was made. 'We spent Christmas and New Year together,' Believe told me. 'My granny just died and I'd had a break-up, so we made ourselves this little bubble. LA over the holidays is so quiet and bizarre, so she rented this really beautiful little back-house in the Hills, and we spent two weeks together.'

One of the early breakthroughs of those sessions was the song which would become the album's fourth track, 'Is It Cold in the Water?' It was a song grown out of an instrumental SOPHIE had written some time earlier in the south of Italy, when she had almost no equipment to hand. She had expected it to remain an instrumental but, in that lonely Californian Christmas at the end of 2016, she asked Believe to try and add vocals. They began recording after driving the winding roads of the Santa Monica Mountains, listening to Joni Mitchell's *Blue* on the car stereo as the sun began to set. When they returned, they tried to channel that music into the song.

SOPHIE played Believe the instrumental and she remembered being shocked by the sheer prowess of her new friend. 'Oh you're like Michael Nyman or something,' she remembered thinking, 'Michael Nyman isn't even good enough, you're like Tchaikovsky!' Believe began singing melodies off the top of her head, channelling Joni and just a little Liz Phair. SOPHIE took those spontaneous moments, chopped them up, and pieced them back together again, creating a floating, disembodied melody for Believe to sing anew.

I still haven't heard another song quite like 'Is It Cold in the Water?' Unlike the familiarity of 'It's Okay to Cry', this is a formless, cascading tune which persists through sheer intensity alone. The gorgeous, spasming synths which open the song proceed unchangingly throughout, charting a singular path. Believe sings in a way which sounds like an ache at first – 'I'm freezing / I'm burning / I've left my home' – until, forty-eight seconds in, she opens up her throat and coos the most gorgeous, gleaming vocal line, asking the question posed by the song. The word 'cold' lasts forever, extended into a soaring arc. As Believe repeats that time and time again, those throbbing synths grow in power and scale, turning a question into a rhetorical plea. The only thing it really reminds me of is Joy Division's 'Transmission', another song which, without broadcasting it, continues to grow in fierceness across its runtime until it feels like your skull is going to crack. It's enchanting, and a large part of that power resides in the mystery of that titular question. It sounds like somebody waiting to be rescued.

Beyond containing music of such incredible power, *OIL OF EVERY PEARL'S UN-INSIDES* is an LP which rejects binaries in every conceivable direction. I can't think of any other record which contains both huge, industrial electro-pop like 'Not Okay' right next to a wordless, hissing epic like 'Pretending', which wouldn't be out of place on a Tim Hecker album.

It feels reasonable to speculate that SOPHIE's natural and fundamental disdain for the tired binaries of old was implicit in her trans-ness. After all, false boundaries are projected on to trans people from the moment they're born, and that experience must make you incredibly suspicious of them. It certainly seemed to for SOPHIE. 'The trans condition is a beautiful mystery,' ANOHNI, of the magnificent ANOHNI and the Johnsons, once told *The Guardian*. 'What an incredible impulse, that compels a five-year-old child to tell its parents it isn't what they think it is. Given just a tiny bit of oxygen, those children can flourish and be such a gift. They give other people licence to explore themselves more deeply, allowing the colours in their own psyche to flourish.' It is perhaps for this reason that trans and queer artists have always played such an outsized role in the development of all culture, from house to hyper-pop. It also explains why, conversely, those styles of music have so often been treated as inherently trivial by a heteronormative society at large.

Perceptions of gender are so closely tied to certain types of songwriting that, across the history of music criticism, even the masculinity of straight men who make softer, more subtle music has been called into question by the music press. In a 2023 conversation with James Blake, Brian Eno remembered how – after the release of his 1978 ambient record *Music for Airports* – his name became a pejorative byword. 'Eno-esque meant pathetic, wimpy and indecisive,' he said. Blake agreed. 'Masculinity is tied to how aggressive your music is or how loud or abrasive your music is,' he said, 'as if masculinity is, by nature, aggressive and brash.'

One of the brilliant things about SOPHIE's music is the way it so proudly subverts those preconceptions. Her music is tender and playful, but it's also furious and industrial, with bass tough enough to pop an eardrum. SOPHIE had an uncanny ability to keep her songs accessible and entertaining even in her most dissonant moments, which is likely why her weirder, harsher edges were able to transition into the sounds of more popular artists while so many others remained niche concerns. This was an intent she was pretty unequivocal about: 'for queer people, and for anyone making music that's deemed to be somehow alternative or inaccessible,' she told *DJ Mag* in 2019, 'they shouldn't be made to feel like their identities are not mainstream, or be marginalised through genre and categories. I think it's really important to break down those binaries, and not feel that because you are making "weird" music you are a "weird" person. To create those bridges is possible. It's one of the most important things for artists to do.'

The other duality which SOPHIE had been fascinated by since she began writing 'BIPP' in 2010 was the difference between the synthetic and the real. After years of prodding, *OIL OF EVERY PEARL'S UN-INSIDES* contains her most definitive statement on the subject: a little tune called 'Faceshopping'.

At its core, 'Faceshopping' is a pop song. It's catchy as all hell and, if you squint through the metallic madness, it races along like early-'80s synth-pop: Gary Numan's 'Cars', melded with the rowdy choruses of Toni Basil or 'Boom Clap'. It's still demented though, and not really in the business of subtlety. It takes the pressure-cooker synths Giorgio Moroder ran through 'I Feel Love' and cranks them so tightly that they sound like a hydraulic lift. I imagine this is the kind of music my dad has in mind when he moans about 'the music of today'. I once showed it to a flatmate, an accomplished pianist, and he told me that he didn't think it qualifies as music at all.

As ever, this was a provocation SOPHIE levelled with intent. The song's music video, for example, positively bristles with the artificial: all the things which should never appear in a piece of high art. The font of the Coca-Cola logo. Beads of sweat on skin, so pristine it can only be untrue. Hairdryers, rows and rows of lip gloss, and, flashing between the fleeting images of each of them, a giant, rubber rendering of SOPHIE's head.

As these images flash across the screen, a thick, crunchy sub-bass throbs until an enormous drop erupts. The synths don't sound like synths, they sound like bow saws ripping through sheet metal. The drum track doesn't feature drums at all, but a voice, twisted into a growl. In the video, SOPHIE's CGI face twists in half around the point of her nose and then collapses entirely. The song's lyrics, essentially inaudible, flash on screen, movie-trailer style: 'artificial bloom / hydroponic skin / chemical release / synthesise the real.' A chorus of little voices cheers each sentence on, all while SOPHIE's face, utterly expressionless, is thrown about like a rag doll: rippling like a whoopee cushion, then splitting into slices which fall away from each other like a sushi roll. At the end of the chorus, Cecile Believe sings a pleasant little melody '*na-nah na-nah nah-nah na-nah-na*', like this is just a Spice Girls song, like this isn't fucking insane.*

* In 2024, I spoke to Aaron Chan, one of the directors who helped stitch the manic patchwork of the 'Faceshopping' video together. Chan is a self-taught editor from Canada who, in 2014, was living in London, cutting music videos for grime artists like D Double E and Dizzee Rascal. One day he was asked to cut together some promotional footage for a grime-heavy showcase called Just Jam at the Barbican, where SOPHIE was due to perform alongside the likes of Jme and Big Narstie (the event which would eventually be called off by the police, due to spurious 'safety concerns'). All of them nodded Chan's edits through, except for one. When she saw Chan's edit, SOPHIE asked for his number, and called him.

Despite all its manic energy, 'Faceshopping' stands as one of the few pieces of music which succeeds in articulating the absurd head-rush of life in the information age. In its video

---

She was kind, and friendly, but exacting about what she wanted instead: images of pigs, cut together with endoscopy footage. Aaron laughed and obliged.

Like a great many people she chose to work with, Chan was soon folded into SOPHIE's life. He became the go-to video editor for her live shows, which meant spending many nights together on the road, bonding over Thai take-out and Williamsburg Pizza. He would stay at the pool house SOPHIE shared with Hayden Dunham in LA and, as they drove around various food spots in the city, she'd play him unreleased music in the car. Hearing him describe his work on 'Faceshopping' was a great insight into the way she worked: excitable, reactive and fast. Chan became adept at listening to her rapidly produced ideas – pigs! tentacles! – and translating them into coherent art. At one point, in a 'Faceshopping' text thread, SOPHIE asked for the 3D rendering of her face to turn into '*South Park*-style animation', an utterly abstract request which Chan had eventually interpreted as the little waddling character which her face morphs into at one point in the video.

It seems that it was this skill, the ability to keep up with the pace of her references (which tended to be objects or colours, rather than other artists' work) which drew SOPHIE to Aaron. 'How I managed to interpret SOPHIE's ideas felt like an organic workflow,' he told me. 'In the moment, you don't really realise you might make something significant . . . My work was really just trying to make the silliest things possible and make her laugh. The goal was always to give her the best version of anything, the truest form of expression, since her music inspired that in me.' It makes sense that SOPHIE admired this quality, because it's one which she aspired to herself. She wanted to become so masterful with instruments like the Monomachine that she could become a tool to her collaborators herself, translating the ideas of anybody she found herself in the studio with into music in an instant.

and its lyrics, symbols are entirely detached from the meaning of what they represent and everything – in this floating mass of spectacle – can be twisted in any direction you please. It's a trick best articulated in the clever linguistic jigsaw which comprises the song's chorus – 'my face is the front of shop / my face is the real shop front', and then the absurd, 'my shop is the face I front'. Product and person. In a time when data is the planet's most valuable resource, they're one and the same.

'Faceshopping' doesn't dare be so simplistic though. In its most ingenious twist, it pushes against that idea too. Two minutes and twenty-three seconds in, something extraordinary happens. After a complete sensory onslaught, the carnage pauses, and a silence opens up. Cecile Believe reappears on the track but the aggressiveness in her voice is gone. Instead, she sings beautifully and clearly instead. 'So you must be the one that I've seen in my dreams,' she moans. 'Touch me / set my spirit free.' The mix twinkles with glitter, and synths swell, creating a glorious, sparkling wash of sound. It is, amid a gluttony of synthetic pleasures, a beautiful return to feeling.

Songs like 'LEMONADE' and 'Hey QT' framed SOPHIE as a postmodern artist: the Jeff Koons of pop, making songs which acknowledge their own artifice rather than distancing themselves from it. But a moment like this is one step beyond. Sure, 'Faceshopping' still acknowledges a framework of artificiality and consumerism, but, in moments like its bridge, or on entire songs like 'Is It Cold in the Water?', SOPHIE began to weave in moments of sincere emotion too, perhaps urging the same from the listener as she did it, yanking us out of our own rapacious lives.

This combination of the postmodern and the sincere culminates in the album's most outwardly joyous song: 'Immaterial'. Read that title in the track-list and it might sound like classic SOPHIE, a tongue-in-cheek remake of 'Material Girl', surely.

But that's not what the song is. Instead, 'Immaterial' is a glittering, pounding electro-pop song whose only connection to Madonna is the way it makes you want dance around your bedroom like a teenager again. Vocals lash around the mix like they're whipping around in the wind. There are handclaps (yes, handclaps!), as crisp and clear as daylight. Believe's vocals fizz with infectious energy. When the synths finally arrive, they sound like they're being played by a piano the size of a mountain. It's euphoric.

Like 'Faceshopping', 'Immaterial' is far from straightforward. It reminds of all of those motivational hits from the first half of the 2010s: the like of 'Roar' and 'Fight Song' and 'Titanium'. Those songs produced a great deal of noise about abstract feelings. 'Immaterial' does this too, but the sensation SOPHIE seeks to capture isn't world-beating invincibility but metaphysical complexity. That word, 'immaterial', points to a world beyond easy, objective truths and the jubilation of its delivery suggests such a world isn't a cause for panic at all, but for optimism instead. What if all the stymying, suffocating labels of gender and genre could be rendered redundant? What if we could be whoever we chose to be? Just small souls in a massive universe, at once more informed and more clueless than ever before: immaterial boys, and immaterial girls.

SOPHIE's debut ends with a track which comprises a quarter of the album's entire runtime. It would be easy to speculate on the meaning of a song with a title like 'Whole New World/Pretend World' but, in all honestly, I've always just interpreted it as one massive flex. SOPHIE had grown so far beyond the brief thrills of her early singles, and in one song here she is, laying out all the many things her music had become in one wild, ten-minute epic. It's easily her most dense song, a maelstrom of super saws and warped, battered vocals cut through with only a glimpse of lyrics and *Sonic*-dings among the chaos. If, on a song like 'Immaterial', SOPHIE had produced her version of a perfect pop song, then its sequel feels like an urgent reminder that her interests shoot as fervently in the opposite direction: a window to the future, left wide open.

OIL OF EVERY PEARL'S UN-INSIDES was nominated for Best Dance/Electronic Album at the sixty-first Grammy Awards. On the day, SOPHIE walked the red carpet with the likes of Miley Cyrus and BTS. In September of 2018, she began touring a live show with Cecile Believe where she appeared, for the first time, front of stage: sealed inside tight latex, wheeling around her instruments on a trolley so that there was as little as possible between the audience and herself. SOPHIE treated her live shows like studio sessions, mixing and tweaking songs in real time. She continued to collaborate furiously too, cutting tracks with Jimmy Edgar, Arca, Basside, LIZ, Flume, Kim Petras and Shygirl, and forming a new duo named Analemma with Juliana Huxtable. She performed at Unsound, the Polish festival of experimental music, for which she released a collaboration with Jlin.

'SOPHIE was in the middle of an intensely creative period,' her friend Faris Badwan told *VICE* in 2021. 'She was fascinated by technology; new forms of expression, new means of playing instruments, further ways of calibrating her body. Every time I saw her she would show or play me something incredible, exploring genuinely innovative ideas for lighting, stage sets, and sound.' For a decade or more SOPHIE had rhapsodised about the 1977 dystopian novel *The Passion of New Eve*, a book which had such an effect on her when she read it as a teenager that she'd long hoped to turn it into an opera. She planned to develop a schedule not dissimilar to the director Guillermo Del Toro: releasing one 'pop' album, followed by a challenging, experimental work. Sometimes she was making entire albums worth of music, week upon week.

In the summer of 2020, in the midst of the COVID-19 pandemic, SOPHIE participated in an online fundraiser for roving LA club night HEAV3N, debuting twenty minutes of new music which offered an indication of new directions for her sound. The music was softer and more expansive, with hints of the shifting bass of New York drill and piercing, bright appreciated synths: a warmer, more delicate return to house.

SOPHIE wasn't interested simply in the act of creation either. Just as she maintained exacting control over her music, she wanted artists to act like CEOs of their careers too, maximising the amount of revenue they were able to keep for themselves. With this in mind, she had begun to develop ideas for a next-generation streaming platform which would give listeners access to not only her entire catalogue, but to her songs' stems, snippets and revisions too. These plans were extensions of her impatience with the past: why were so-called technologists wasting their time on albums, a format which had last been radical eighty-something years ago?

When the COVID-19 pandemic began, SOPHIE returned to her childhood home in Northampton. As somebody whose relationship with music had always been played out in the living world, she struggled with the restrictiveness of the lockdowns. She had been dating the Greek singer Evita Manji and so, in late 2020, she moved out to Greece to be with her, and set up a new home studio in Athens. She was energised and excited.

Shortly before midnight on the 29th of January 2021, SOPHIE climbed onto the roof of their apartment building to take a picture of a full moon, but she slipped and fell three storeys to the ground. When she was recovered by the paramedics, she was rushed to the Attikon University Hospital in a bad way. She died at around 4 a.m. the next day.

When I woke up on the 30th of January and opened *Pitchfork* to see the headline announcing SOPHIE's death, it felt like there must have been a mistake. She had dropped an unreleased *PRODUCT* song called 'UNISIL' just two days earlier. She was an active, thrilling presence in the life of music obsessives like me. She was one of the names who, at the start of each year, you were waiting to hear new music from soon. Exactly one month earlier, on New Year's Eve 2020, the news of the death of another legendary artist – MF DOOM – had also broken suddenly. To myself and millions of others, SOPHIE and Daniel Dumile were two artists who represent all the things which make music such an integral part of life. Their art was thrilling and mind-expanding and new. They felt, in a word, like the future. In the depths of that bleak pandemic month, with both of them gone, it felt like the future had died with them. I put on my headphones, laced up my running shoes and ran slow laps around the wet concrete of the deserted football stadium I used to live beside. As I ran, I listened to every song SOPHIE had ever released. I didn't know what else to do.

Upon the news of her death, tributes to SOPHIE poured in from across the spectrum of music: from Rihanna to Christine and the Queens, from Sam Smith to Nile Rodgers, from Arca, Flying Lotus and Grimes. 'Behind the visual aesthetic was real technical ability,' Faris Badwan wrote. 'She knew exactly how different textures were created, how many layers you need to synthesise a snare drum that hits harder than anything else, how to make a sound like rending sheet metal. It was challenging but accessible, the hardest trick to pull off.' SOPHIE received tweets of adoration from the younger artists whose music she had inspired too. 'It's impossible to overstate the influence SOPHIE had on me and countless others,' Laura Les of 100 gecs wrote 'We're still going to be catching up to her for years to come.'

Sometimes this was literally true. In 2017, SOPHIE had released a 258-file pack of the percussion, glitches and snares she had conjured with the Monomachine, which several artists, such as Polaris Prize-winning musician Backxwash, said they were still weaving into their music years later. In 2023, Caroline Polachek released the song 'I Believe', which she dedicated to SOPHIE, who she described as 'like no other person I've ever met'. In 2022, the International Astronomical Union named the exo-planet Sophiexeon in her honour.

'SOPHIE was a very, very unique person,' Vince Staples told *Rolling Stone* in 2021. 'When SOPHIE walks in a room, you know SOPHIE's there. Doesn't matter who else is in the room. She was very bright, very fun, even though she doesn't talk at all. When she does talk, it's probably going to be some wild shit. I've seen SOPHIE around a dozen sessions, around different kinds of people, different genres, different races, different backgrounds, and she was never afraid. I never saw her once afraid to be who she was, to wear what she wanted, to say what she wanted, to play what she wanted. Not once. I think that's the most important takeaway: you don't have to be afraid. Producers, musicians, trans people, people all over, no matter who you are . . . that's something you could take something from. You don't have to be fearful. I haven't once seen fear on SOPHIE's face, no matter what.'

A posthumous SOPHIE album – developed by her brother over the course of three years – was finally released in September 2024. Before then, only one single song was released in the wake of her passing. In 2015, while they were working on the roll-out for *PRODUCT*, Calum Morton and Jack Nevill suggested to SOPHIE the idea of a remix album. She replied unequivocally – 'no remixes' – until, after a pause, she added a caveat: 'unless it's Autechre.' Morton and Nevill sent the request but didn't hear back for five full years, when they received an email from Sean Booth and Rob Brown with a remix of 'BIPP' attached. 'Sorry this is so late,' they wrote. 'Hope it's still of some use.' On the 14th January 2021, 'BIPP (Autechre Remix)' was released.

Music was part of SOPHIE's life from the day she was born. While her dad rattled the car with the pulse of rave and techno, her mother's disco records brought a soft ecstasy into the hallways of her childhood home. Faris Badwan remembered that, as a teenager, she used to hand out CD rips of David Bowie's BBC sessions and Pixies' *Doolittle* to friends at school. When she was an adult – a DJ of international renown – she kept folders on her laptop labelled '70s', '80s', '90s', ready to match any vibe called for by the moment. Even more than music though, SOPHIE's first love was *sound*. 'We'll be at the beach just chilling out,' Tzef Montana told *Vogue* in 2019. 'She gets a stone and throws it, again and again, just to hear the "plop".'

SOPHIE's music is, above all else, a paean to sound; a devotion to pure sensation which was the driving force of her life, even in small, everyday moments. 'In the morning we would have cookies for breakfast, and she would always buy two,' Hayden Dunham told me. 'She would give me the cookie knowing that I would look up and go "just one?", and then revealing she had another. That says a lot about her. She was into experiencing the world in a very visceral way. Having sushi in her mouth and savouring every flavour; having not just one cookie but two.'

In her music, SOPHIE reimagined the raves of her youth not as a means of escape but as pure utopias, where drugs are welcome but music is the only necessary stimulant. Despite refusing to disguise the artificiality of her songs, and her playfulness about their status as products, it was this love which distinguishes her music from the real art of commerce, because it actually delivers on promises most advertising fails to keep. 'We wanted to change pop culture and make it more real; make it more weird-sounding, make it more authentic,' she told

Office magazine in 2018, 'like Missy Elliot did in the past, like any decent pop star has done.' SOPHIE discovered something euphoric in those Autechre bootlegs, a sensation which she'd never experienced before. From that night onwards, she made it her mission to recreate that feeling for everybody else.

(Outro)

When I spoke to him in spring of 2023, Nicolás Jaar told me about the first time he and FKA twigs met in the studio. It was the very first day of work on the record which would eventually become *MAGDALENE*. 'The most important collaborator on "Thousand Eyes" was twigs' dog,' he told me. He was talking about Solo, the pet Tahliah rescued after finding him hiding behind the bins of an LA nail salon. 'Every time that I listen to that song, I think of the vibe and smell of that dog. Sure, sometimes people might jokingly say "oh let's give a credit to a little dog that was there", but I'm being literal: I don't think we would've made that song without him. Petting him, having him hang out with us, the jokes that we were making . . . That's just one example of something which doesn't get credited, but is part of the history of any creative act.'

Later that year, Spotify announced a new feature for their mobile app called the 'Infinite Scroll'. It was a way of accessing music which allowed users to treat artists like social media influencers: listening to a snippet of a song and then swiping up to the next. In premise, it's a natural extension of features streaming services have offered from the start: the ability to generate whole 'stations' based around one particular song. The novelty of the Infinite Scroll, on the other hand, is that it's bottomless. With 60,000 new songs added to Spotify each day, it grants subscribers the ability to listen to music without interruption, forever. 'There's so much to listen to on Spotify and so little time,' the launch statement read. 'We know you don't want to spend precious hours on titles and tracks you might not enjoy.' This feature was the final destination of the path Peter Goldmark set us down when he invented the micro-groove in 1948. That creation allowed for twenty-two minutes of uninterrupted listening. Seventy-five years later that number has expanded to . . . forever.

Easy and limitless access to recorded music has had many wonderful effects. Ignorance dies in the light, and 2013–23 was a period when many old, suffocating preconceptions about art crumbled in the face of maximum exposure. The streaming age revived forgotten artists and songs in a way that archivists of decades past could only have dreamed of, and the unfairly dismissed music of the past has been given a second life. But features like the Infinite Scroll also do for art what the Silicon Valley technocrats behind Facebook, Google, Amazon and Uber already did to just about everything else: turn the world into a fast, convenient, frictionless mirage. Humans were never actually removed from any of their processes, but they were hidden, so hidden that they're hardly worth a thought, and the same is happening to art. When people once brought LPs off a shelf, hell, even when they were downloading them illegally, it was hard to disguise *who* you were stealing from. No more. Just like Amazon warehouse workers, just like the kids mining lithium for iPhone batteries, degrading the value of humans is exactly the shield which is needed to excuse paying £0.0027 for a piece of art it took years to make. 'The brainwashing worked,' James Blake tweeted in 2024, 'and now people think music is free.'

As the stories of this book show, the ease with which music now comes to us is indeed a complete and utter illusion. 'In order to sustain creative work,' Nicolás Jaar told me, 'a lot of people are involved, because it's not an easy thing to do.

Because of this, for someone's manager to be uncredited on a record is strange, because they might be the main person the artist spoke to during the entire process. What is that if not songwriting? Why wouldn't my partner be credited on an album? How about the *lack* of a certain person? A person's lack might have created a whole slew of music. Someone might have cooked you a delicious meal one night; someone might have brought you a coffee at the right time of day. There's all of this labour which goes into any creative work, yet we have these myths of individuality. When you start peeling back the layers, millions of people made *MAGDALENE*, just like millions of people made every album out there in the world.'

None of the five artists who title the chapters of this book are the biggest musicians on the planet, and yet their ideas – brilliant, original ideas – have drifted out across our culture to touch the lives of millions of listeners across the world. What I hope this book has shown is the labour and lives behind these astounding creative acts. Not a second of their music came easily or simply, their ideas were often utterly confounding in their originality, but in truth only an understanding of their ordinariness – alongside their brilliance – can put humans back into the equation of art. Devonté Hynes is a football fan from Essex. Tahliah Barnett was a girl raised by a single mum in rural Gloucestershire. Thebe Kgositsile was a kid who made music for shits and giggles with friends he met online. Daniel Lopatin released albums to cassette tape from his parents' house in Massachusetts. SOPHIE was, like millions of us, somebody who downloaded a bootleg tape online and fell in love with what she heard. If this is the case – if the next SOPHIE could be just about *anybody*, from the slums of Caracas to the council flats of Essex – then we should ensure that as many people as possible, from as many avenues as possible, have the ability to make it happen. 'The deification works in total opposition to what I'm trying to do, which is to humanise the situation,' Thebe Kgositsile told *Pitchfork* in 2019. 'I want to be normalised. I'm here, n****. Not in a chest-thumping way, but as in: I'm here with y'all on Earth.'

What's even more astounding about the careers of these artists is that, despite the alien-ness of their sound, they did not remain niche musicians, nor did they need to compromise on their art to escape that status. Despite Autechre's incredible talent, they remained decidedly cult concerns throughout their careers. The sheer weirdness of an artist like Alejandra Ghersi Rodríguez, on the other hand, didn't seem to have been much of an impediment to her reaching commercial heights untouched by even the most influential electronic musicians of the '90s, who Arca is an obvious equivalent to. It's hard to conceive of music more alien or abrasive than the likes of *KicK iii*, and yet Ghersi has produced for Frank Ocean, is friend to Cardi B, Beyoncé and Madonna, and features huge, major-label hitmakers like Sia on her songs.

This trajectory is mirrored by the likes of Devonté Hynes: a man who opened for Harry Styles and received a shoutout on a hit Doja Cat album, while touring, predominately, minimalistic classical music. In 2024, when Tyler, the Creator headlined Coachella, one of the biggest festivals in the world, he brought his old friend Earl Sweatshirt out onstage to join him. As Daniel Lopatin said, there has been a great collapsing of everything, and many of the old rules of taste, genre and status are now off the table. It would be easy to point at streaming services or the Internet as the cause of this, but Peter Goldmark didn't guarantee the success of the LP: The Beach Boys did. The same applies to all the brilliant, boundary-less music of the Internet age. 'I'm here through persistence,' SOPHIE told *DJ Mag* in 2019, 'through being really strong in my perspective and letting [the music] make its own point.' Streaming services didn't do it.

The Internet didn't do it. Devonté Hynes, Tahliah Bennet, Daniel Lopatin, Thebe Kgositsile and SOPHIE, and a dozen musicians just like them: they were the ones who made it happen.

During the writing of this book, A.G. Cook announced that, at the end 2023, PC Music would stop releasing original music for good. He closed out the era the following year with *Britpop*, a triple album which interrogated the history of his home country ('a super old place that's trying to be futuristic') and the legacy of PC Music in a new light: as a 'British, eccentric movement'. On the second disc Cook included 'Without', an ode to SOPHIE delivered not as a hyper-pop banger but as a weary, fuzzy rock song. At its end Cook sings an unforgettable refrain over gently strummed guitar: 'I can make you feel better / if you let me . . .' It's an ode to a friend.

As a collective of university students who made pop music on DIY terms, it feels apt to end the story of this book in the year of PC Music's end, exactly a decade after it began. 2013 was, after all, a transformative time for music. *Cupid Deluxe* came out that year. So did *Doris*, *R Plus Seven*, *EP2* and 'BIPP'. It was the year of *Yeezus*, *Sunbather*, *Modern Vampires of the City* and Danny Brown's *Old.* I remember being seventeen, synching that music to my iPod week upon week, and feeling pretty excited for the future of music. Ironically, at that exact moment, others were speculating that the time of newness was over for good.

In 2014's *Ghosts of My Life*, Mark Fisher proposed a metric to measure the stagnation which he claimed had captured culture in the Internet age. 'Imagine any record released in the past couple of years being beamed back in time to, say, 1995 and played on the radio,' he wrote. 'It's hard to think that it will produce any jolt in the listeners . . . [By contrast], play a jungle record from 1993 to someone in 1989 and it would have sounded so new that it would have challenged them to rethink what music was.'

One of the under-appreciated things about *OIL OF EVERY PEARL'S UN-INSIDES*, SOPHIE's only studio album, is the extent to which it is a tribute to the 1990s: to the electronic pioneers Fisher was referring to, and the artists her father played to her in the car. Its title ends with a homage to two classic LPs: Orbital's *In Side* and (of course) Autechre's *Untilted*. SOPHIE quotes Moby's 1995 single 'Into the Blue' in the final seconds of 'Is It Cold in the Water?', and the ninety-five-minute remixes album SOPHIE released the following year (where she remixes every song from her own album herself, in multiple ways), is named after a 1996 album where he'd done the same thing.

Even with all those tips of the hat though, SOPHIE's music doesn't actually *sound* anything like that music. Picture playing a single second of 'Faceshopping' to an audience of jungle fans in 1995. It would have sounded then as it still does now, in 2025: like the future. This isn't only true of outsider music either. Image playing Metro Boomin and Future's 2024 hit 'Cinderella' to a bunch of music fans in the year 2000. Future's flow on that song would have sounded like some extremely experimental art, not a single from a platinum-selling album. It would have blown their little Cool Britannia minds.

This experiment holds true of so much of the music in this book. Play somebody from 1995 a few moments of FKA twigs' 'mary magdalene' or Nicolás Jaar's *Telas* or Danny Brown's *Atrocity Exhibition* or Earl Sweatshirt's *Some Rap Songs* or Sons of Kemet's 'My Queen Is Harriet Tubman' or Playboi Carti's *Whole Lotta Red* or Mabe Fratti's *Se Ve Desde Aquí* or Arca's 'Incendio' or JPEGMAFIA's 'Jesus Forgive Me, I Am a Thot' . . . None of that music has an equivalent in the twentieth century. Some of the most poignant music of the 2010s revealed the fallacy of the logic of perpetual forward motion too. As Proust taught us, memory might just be the most important creative act of all. Devonté Hynes, remembering of the music of Julius Eastman onstage in 2023 is, I would argue, as radical as anything objectively *new*.

In the Earl Sweatshirt chapter of this book, I claimed that his 2021 album *SICK!* wasn't perfect, but that it does contain two perfect tracks. One of those songs was 'Tabula Rasa'. The second is the song '2010'. '2010' holds a special place in my heart. It's probably my favourite song of the entire decade. As should be the case with everybody's favourite music, several of the reasons for this are particular to me and me alone, but I've saved reference to it until the end of the book because it captures the sentiment of what I'm trying to say here more succinctly than I ever could.

The beat, by Michigan producer Black Noi$e, is a thing of majesty. It is, as with many Earl Sweatshirt songs, a loop, formed from of a small section of 1980's 'Saga Unknown', a smooth and chintzy track by Japanese jazz composer Masahiko Satoh. To make it, Noi$e selected one small piano part from a particularly serene moment and pitched one version of it up seven semitones while pitching the other five semitones down, making them an entire octave apart. Noi$e then reversed the second half of that same sample and stitched it to the tail end of the loop, making the keys sound like they're being played in both directions at once. I didn't know any of this when the song was released amid the long COVID winter of 2020, I just knew it sounded like nothing I'd ever heard before: a shimmering, oscillating piece of sound. It's no longer anything like jazz, it doesn't even sound like the piano. It's the new, remade from the old.

Thebe named the song '2010' because that was the year in which he released his debut mixtape with his friend Tyler

Okonma and set this whole thing in motion. For so long Thebe's music had been filled with torment, but this single was different: a moment of pride and celebration after a decade of tribulations. 'Triumph over plight and immense loss,' he raps, 'saw another height, had my ears poppin' / walked outside, it was still gorgeous.' That final lyric is an allusion to the first of a series of antisocial records Thebe had begun making when he was twenty-one years old: *I Don't Like Shit, I Don't Go Outside*. Five years later, after bouts of depression and grief, here was that same kid, coming up for air, ageing into fatherhood, and stepping outside to find that, after all the torment and noise, the sun is still shining.

It's a poignant image, and an apt allegory for what those in love with music can rest assured of too. In the early 2010s, it was claimed that music had lost all originality, that my generation was doomed to regurgitate only shallow imitations of the past. But this wasn't true. The proof is there in the music of this book, in all of these sparkling new songs which have brought more joy than words can express. It's there in the music which has been released since these words were written, and I truly believe that we're only getting started, too. We're all stood in the belly of the Waldorf Astoria now, standing at the precipice of a new and electrifying age. Amazing art is everywhere. Walk outside, put your headphones on: it's still gorgeous.

APPLE MUSIC

SPOTIFY

6. (CODA)

In 2024, science fiction became reality through rap. In the early days of a short but blistering war of rhymes between Drake and Kendrick Lamar, the Canadian pop star, a man who recently equalled Michael Jackson's unbroken hit-singles record, released 'Taylor Made Freestyle', a diss track which doubled as a taunt. Drake was up and hungry, looking to goad his opponent into a response, and to do so Drake taunted Kendrick with two new verses from MCs who are icons in Lamar's home city: Snoop Dogg and Tupac Shakur. Snoop and Drake hadn't actually worked together in nearly a decade. Tupac had been dead since 1996.

The AI verses on 'Taylor Made Freestyle' are immaculate impersonations. The software Drake used didn't simply recreate the voices of Snoop and Shakur; it recreated their cadences and flows too. This had once been the stuff of pure fantasy, the kind written by Mary Shelley. Once-living people, revived, Lazarus-style, from the dead. It was theft, of a kind, a dystopian fiction let loose upon the real world. And what was the reaction to this song? One giant, colossal shrug.

Unlike Drake's first diss track 'Push Ups', 'Taylor Made Freestyle' elicited a sigh from hip hop fandom. Rap fans continued waiting for Lamar's response to the first track, dismissing the second out of hand. More embarrassingly, Shakur's family quickly took Lamar's side and 'Taylor Made Freestyle' vanished, under threat of a lawsuit. Something which the likes of *Blade Runner* had portrayed as revolutionary – magical even – was, when deployed amid a conflict between two real-life artists, completely and utterly boring. People didn't care to hear what a digital, zombified MC had to say about Kendrick Lamar: they wanted to hear what Drake did.

He soon got what he wanted regardless. Kendrick responded with a series of increasingly eviscerating songs, released in quick succession, and Drake simply could not keep up. The death blow came in the form of 'Not Like Us', Lamar's own taunting anthem whose squelching, G-funk beat came direct from the era of Dre and NWA. The battle between the two rappers had become a question of authenticity, and Lamar – a child of embattled Compton, home of some of the most respected names in rap – drew two lines under his. 'Not Like Us' was an enormous hit, registering the highest first-week streaming figures of any rap song in the decade to date, a record once held by Drake.

Since tools like Character.ai and Chat GPT launched in late 2022, much has been said about the grand role artificial intelligence will play in the future of music. That it will play a role is undeniable, but the resounding flop of 'Taylor Made Freestyle' seemed to prove what should have already been obvious: it is very unlikely to take the place of artists themselves. Artificial intelligence does for the act of music creation what streaming services once did for music listening: it reduces the distance between an idea and reality to essentially nothing. There's an important distinction though. Streaming services quicken our access to the fuel of imagination; AI leapfrogs the most valuable thing about it. There is little point to art without people. The only exciting thing about computerised music is the way musicians will go about responding to it.

*

Four months after the story of this book concluded, New York indie band Vampire Weekend released their fifth album, *Only God Was Above Us*. It was an instant classic, and a startlingly apt LP to kick off a new era. Sonically, it traverses genre as effortlessly as artists now tend to: flitting between Californian surf-rock, Q-Tip's stuttering chops, West African hi-life, Gershwin-esque piano and, on the beautiful 'Mary Boone', even some Mancunian baggy, straight out of Factory Records. These disparate elements coalesce like watercolours, serving as a canvas for Ezra Koenig's ruminations on the role of people in the arc of history.

Only God Was Above Us is an electric-sounding record. Violins and piano are shoved up against blown-out bass and careening, screeching guitar. Its songs are as full of life as the in-studio magic of Stevie Wonder's 'I Wish' or D'Angelo's *Voodoo*, but it wasn't played live in a room at all: it was created entirely using software. 'It sounds like a line,' Koenig said about the record's production, '"oh, it's harder to make it sound like that", but in the ProTools era, it literally is . . . in ProTools or GarageBand, the default mode is making music to the grid . . . to not have it be mercilessly gridded takes work.' It was mess by way of meticulousness.

In crafting the album's manic energy, Vampire Weekend were not reacting against AI, but another ubiquity of the Internet age: digital audio workstations. Produced by Ariel Rechtshaid (the man who, alongside Devonté Hynes, helped to forge the indie pop wave in 2013), *Only God Was Above Us* is studiously arranged, pieced together over several years and recorded in several countries; but Rechtshaid and the band chose not to keep that ornateness. Instead the producer used the software to complicate things, smudging and twisting the song's many components until the tracks bristled with life again. As albums go, there is no clearer sign of where the future is headed. Like Caroline Polachek, Vampire Weekend were a once conventional band who saw the writing on the wall. They are now a group in name only, operating essentially as a collaboration between the lead songwriter and producer, and weaving samples and rap production into their songs. Through this adaptation, they have survived where many of their guitar-centric contemporaries faltered.

Around the time of their fifth LP, another indie era anachronism had its day again: an obscure record catching alight after a rave review on a blog. In March 2024, Patrick Flegel released *Diamond Jubilee*, a bumper, two-hour double-album of hypnagogic pop performed under the name of his drag persona, Cindy Lee. *Diamond Jubilee* was an utter anachronism: a borderline unheard-of record which gathered buzz only after *Pitchfork* gave it a score of 9.1. What was most interesting about the album though was the way it was released. *Diamond Jubilee* is not on Apple Music or Spotify. Instead Flagel uploaded it straight to his website and made it available for free, with a link to his PayPal account attached should the listener choose to use it. Like Mach-Hommy, Flegel determined that he could receive more income from a small, dedicated fanbase than he ever would from a streaming service payout. In the wake of several public tirades against streaming platforms, James Blake also began promoting The Vault, an app which offered a subscription-based model for music fandom, where die-hards could subscribe to their favourite artists and be rewarded with deep cuts and unreleased tracks directly. Neither were perfect solutions, but a mood of resistance was rising. Out of all the digital technologies to pick fights against, musicians' warring against the streaming giants have the most daunting challenge of them all.

There is certainly no shortage of brilliant, glistening music to fuel a revolution. Deep into the 2020s, younger artists like Adrianne Lenker are entering purple patches: producing sharp, heart-wrenching songs as easily and prolifically as the greats of generations past. The international scene is bristling with new ideas too. NTS' 2024 compilation *funk.BR – São Paulo* compiled bracing mandelão: jolting, unprecedented party music born in the Brazilian bailes of Helipa, Bega and Casinhas. Belgian band Avalanche Kaito meld the vitriolic griot of their Burkina Faso-born vocalist and animated, punkish drums. Chicago producer Heavee is forging a new iteration of footwork, melding kinetic percussion with buoyant R&B melodies. It's these new ideas, not ones born of software, which will shape the sound of the future.

As a vision for the future, the concept of artificial intelligence is a paradoxical proposition. After all, the software at the forefront of this 'revolution' cannot generate any new ideas of its own; it can only reiterate, remix and rehash ones conceived of by living, breathing humans. It does seem inevitable though, that by the end of the decade, streaming services will be rife with pretty good AI riffs on songs the likes of which we've already heard endless times before. The consequences of this may not be as dire as they sound. After all, 'Taylor Made Freestyle' and the ensuing beef only served to diminish Drake's reputation as an artist. If purely iterative music does one day become the norm, then originality will become an increasingly treasured characteristic, and there are few better things for a culture to hold dear. Basically: don't count the artists out too soon. They haven't failed us yet.

Essential Listening

Ten albums from each of the ten years explored in this book which capture the essence of the era.

2013

Cupid Deluxe – Blood Orange
R Plus Seven – Oneohtrix Point Never
Doris – Earl Sweatshirt
Immunity – Jon Hopkins
Yeezus – Kanye West
Random Access Memories – Daft Punk
Jai Paul [Untitled Leak] – Jai Paul
The Redeemer – Dean Blunt
Nothing Was the Same – Drake
Modern Vampires of the City – Vampire Weekend

2014

LP1 – FKA twigs
Black Messiah – D'Angelo
Soused – Sun O))) & Scott Walker
Piñata – Freddie Gibbs & Madlib

Too Bright – Perfume Genius
You're Dead! – Flying Lotus
Salad Days – Mac DeMarco
Xen – Arca
Cilvia Demo – Isaiah Rashad
Broke with Expensive Taste – Azealia Banks

2015

PRODUCT – SOPHIE
Pomegranates – Nicolás Jaar
To Pimp a Butterfly – Kendrick Lamar
Rodeo – Travis Scott
No Now – Clarence Clarity
E•MO•TION – Carly Rae Jepsen
Garden of Delete – Oneohtrix Point Never
The Epic – Kamasi Washington
At. Long. Last. A$AP – A$AP Rocky
The Powers That B – Death Grips

2016

Freetown Sound – Blood Orange
Atrocity Exhibition – Danny Brown
Black Terry Cat – Xenia Rubinos
The Life of Pablo – Kanye West
Blonde / Endless – Frank Ocean
Fetish Bones – Moor Mother
Blank Face LP – ScHoolboy Q
A Seat at the Table – Solange
Floss – Injury Reserve
HOPELESSNESS – ANOHNI

2017

Culture – Migos
Red Burns – Standing on the Corner
Black Origami – Jlin
Flower Boy – Tyler, the Creator
Crack-Up – Fleet Foxes
Utopia – Björk
Peasant – Richard Dawson
Big Fish Theory – Vince Staples
Ctrl – SZA
Take Me Apart – Kelela

2018

OIL OF EVERY PEARL'S UN-INSIDES – SOPHIE
Some Rap Songs – Earl Sweatshirt
Negro Swan – Blood Orange
Your Queen Is a Reptile – Sons of Kemet
Kids See Ghosts – Kids See Ghosts
AAL 2012-2017 – Against All Logic
Veteran – JPEGMAFIA
El Mal Querer – Rosalía
Die Lit – Playboi Carti
ensley – Pink Siifu

2019

MAGDALENE – FKA twigs
Girl with Basket of Fruit – Xiu Xiu
Pang – Caroline Polachek
SINNER – Moodymann
When Future Unfolds – Damien Locks & Black Monument Ensemble

All My Heroes Are Cornballs – JPEGMAFIA
Hiding Places – Billy Woods & Kenny Segal
GREY Area – Little Simz
Norman Fucking Rockwell! – Lana Del Rey
Titanic Rising – Weyes Blood

2020

Untitled (Rise) / Untitled (Black Is) – Sault
Fetch the Bolt Cutters – Fiona Apple
BRASS – Billy Woods & Moor Mother
Cenizas / Telas – Nicolás Jaar
Source – Nubya Garcia
Sawayama – Rina Sawayama
YHLQMDLG / EL ÚLTIMO TOUR DEL MUNDO – Bad Bunny
Whole Lotta Red – Playboi Carti
After Hours – The Weeknd
RTJ4 – Run the Jewels

2021

Fatigue – L'Rain
KICK ii / KicK iii / kick iiii / kiCK iiiii – Arca
The Turning Wheel – SPELLLING
Call Me If You Get Lost – Tyler, the Creator
SINNER GET READY – Lingua Ignota
LP! – JPEGMAFIA
Sometimes I Might Be Introvert – Little Simz
GLOW ON – Turnstile
Promises – Pharaoh Sanders, Floating Points & The London Symphony Orchestra
Haram – Armand Hammer & The Alchemist

2022

Se Ve Desde Aquí – Mabe Fratti
RENAISSANCE – Beyoncé
Remember Your Northstar – Yaya Bey
Mr. Morale & the Big Steppers – Kendrick Lamar
Aethiopes – Billy Woods
God's Country – Chat Pile
¡Ay! – Lucrecia Dalt
Natural Brown Prom Queen – Sudan Archives
I Love You Jennifer B – Jockstrap
I Don't Give a Fuck About This Rap Shit, Imma Just Drop Until I Don't Feel Like It Anymore – $ilkmoney

2023

Voir Dire – Earl Sweatshirt & The Alchemist
Again – Oneohtrix Point Never
Burning Desire – MIKE
Did You Know That There's a Tunnel Under Ocean Blvd? – Lana Del Rey
Julius Eastman Vol. 3: If You're So Smart, Why Aren't You Rich? – Wild Up, Devonté Hynes & Christopher Rountree
Maps – Billy Woods & Kenny Segal
Scaring the Hoes – JPEGMAFIA & Danny Brown
Fly or Die Fly or Die Fly or Die ((World War)) – jaimie branch
Wallsocket – underscores
Desire, I Want to Turn Into You – Caroline Polachek

Acknowledgements

Firstly, I'd like to thank everybody who I spoke to or interviewed for the book over the course of two years: Daniel Lopatin and Martina Connors, Devonté Hynes and Macolm Hill, Caroline Polachek, Joshua Safdie, Anaïs Ngbanzo, Hayden Dunham, Cecile Believe, Aaron Chan, Ben and Emily Long, Caius Pawson and Nicolás Jaar. I'd like to thank my editor, Lee Brackstone, for his impeccable notes and somewhat baffling faith in me (seemingly based on a shared love for Bruce Springsteen), alongside Ellie Freedman, without whom none of this would have been possible. Much credit is also due to my agent Becky Thomas and the entire White Rabbit/Orion team – Sophie Nevrkla, Clarissa Sutherland, Jamie Groves and Paul Mottram – for their attentiveness and care. I'd also like to thank the various friends who read over various (even less legible) early drafts of the book, including Becky Wyde, Hassan Qadir, Emma Hancox, James Noble, Rob Noble, Maddie Waktare, Rachel Lewis, Rhiannon White, Immy Higgins, Eleanor Gaffney and Kasimiira Kontio. I also want to express my deepest gratitude to Mom and Dad for their wise – and occasionally humbling – advice, and for sparking this journey with their exceptional taste in music. Most importantly, I need to thank my partner Beth for her unwavering support. She patiently endured two years of ramblings on forgotten composers, SoundCloud rappers and the man who invented the LP in 1948. She's the best, and I couldn't have done any of this without her.

Sources for Quotations

Lyrics from 'Chamakay' by Devonté Hynes © 2013 Domino Publishing Co. Ltd.

Details on Kasabian commenting on Test Icicles were from: https://www.nme.com/news/music/kasabian-374-1366927

Lyrics from 'Love Ya' by Eddy Grant and Ta-Nehisi Coates © 2016 Greenheart Music Ltd.

Quote from Simon Reynolds from *Retromania* (Faber & Faber, 2012)

Quote from Lester Bangs from *Psychotic Reactions and Carburetor Dung* (Random House, 1988)

Lyrics from 'Two Weeks' by FKA Twigs and Emily Haynie © 2014 Heavycrate Music and Universal Publishing

Lyrics from 'mirrored heart' by Cy An, Ethan P. Flynn, FKA Twigs and Lewis Roberts © 2019 BMG Rights Management (UK) Limited, Copyright Control & Young Turks Music / Beggars Music

Lyrics from 'mary magdalene' by Benny Blanco (3), FKA Twigs, Magnus Høiberg and Nicolás Jaar © 2019 BMG Rights Management (UK) Limited, Universal / MCA Music Limited, Mattitude Music LLC / Beggars Music & Universal / MCA Music

Lyrics from 'home with you' by Ethan P. Flynn and FKA Twigs © 2019 BMG Rights Management (UK) Limited & Copyright Control

Details on Frank Ocean's childhood were from: https://www.theguardian.com/music/2012/jul/21/frank-ocean-guardian-exclusive-interview and https://www.gq.com/story/frank-ocean-interview-gq-december-2012

Details on Frank Ocean and Def Jam were from: https://www.youtube.com/watch?v=p_ByLe7IPm4 and https://www.theguardian.com/business/2016/aug/23/universal-streaming-exclusives-frank-ocean-release

Credits

White Rabbit would like to thank everyone at Orion who worked on the publication of *Songs in the Key of MP3*.

Agent
Becky Thomas

Editor
Lee Brackstone

Copy-editor
Jamie Groves

Proofreader
Seán Costello

Editorial Management
Clarissa Sutherland
Sophie Nevrkla
Jane Hughes
Charlie Panayiotou
Lucy Bilton
Patrice Nelson

Audio
Paul Stark
Louise Richardson
Georgina Cutler

Contracts
Dan Herron
Ellie Bowker
Oliver Chacón

Design
Nick Shah
Steve Marking
Deborah Francois
Helen Ewing

Photo Shoots & Image Research
Natalie Dawkins

Finance
Nick Gibson
Jasdip Nandra
Sue Baker
Tom Costello

Inventory
Jo Jacobs
Dan Stevens

Production
Sarah Cook
Katie Horrocks

Marketing
Corinne Jean-Jacques

Publicity
Sarah Lundy

Sales
Catherine Worsley
Victoria Laws
Esther Waters
Tolu Ayo-Ajala
Group Sales teams across Digital, Field, International and Non-Trade

Operations
Group Sales Operations team

Rights
Rebecca Folland
Tara Hiatt
Ben Fowler
Alice Cottrell
Ruth Blakemore
Marie Henckel

Index of Artists

50 Cent 217
1975, The 9

A-ha 70
A Tribe Called Quest 19, 20, 209, 224
Aaliyah 114
A$AP Rocky 247
Ab-Soul 204, 245
Action Bronson 240
Actress 289
Adam and the Ants 44, 96
Adele 97, 110, 111
Aesop Rock 205
Aftab, Arooj 13, 149
Aitchison, Charlotte *see* Charli xcx
AKAI SOLO 267
Alchemist, The 202, 224, 240, 270, 274, 275–6, 285
Algiers 55
Analemma 322
Anderson, Laurie 15, 16, 191
André 3000 192, 193, 225
ANOHNI and the Johnsons 153, 192, 316
Aphex Twin 106, 249
Apple, Fiona 13, 32
Arca 105–11, 118, 120–3, 126, 159, 322, 330
Arcade Fire 314
Arce, Jason 63
Arctic Monkeys 24
Armand Hammer 266, 267, 275
Ashley, Robert 171
Autechre 279–81, 285, 289, 296, 325, 327, 330, 332
Avalanche Kaito 340
Avalanches, The 58, 68
Azalea, Iggy 303

B, Lil 27
Bach, Johann Sebastian 20, 21
Backstreet Boys 32
Backxwash 286, 325
Bad Bunny 8
BADBADNOTGOOD 201, 226
Bainbridge, Adam 66
Balls 23
Barnett, Tahliah Debrett *see* FKA twigs
Basinski, William 171–2
Basside 322

BEA1991 57, 66
Beach Boys, The 4
Beastie Boys 32, 60, 247
Beatles, The 69, 162, 247
Bee Gees 5
Beethoven, Ludwig van 20, 72, 191
Behrman, David 171
Believe, Cecile 313–15, 318, 320, 321, 322
Bennett, Syd *see* Syd Tha Kid
Bennett, Taco 206, 225
Beyoncé 34, 37, 50, 92, 125, 215, 221, 330
Bieber, Justin 10–11, 56, 168
Billionaire Boys Club 99
Birdman 233
Björk 108, 121, 149, 158
Black Eyed Peas 202
Blake, James 192, 263, 316, 328, 339
Blondie 61
Blood Orange 15–88, 285
Blur 19
Boards of Canada 34
Bone Thugs-n-Harmony 19
Bonema, Michael *see* MIKE
Booth, Sean 279, 280, 295, 325
Bow Wow 96
Bowie, David 69, 70, 326
Boy George 96
Bra Willie 228–30, 259, 270–1
Brand Nubian 228
Breaux, Lonny *see* Ocean, Frank
Bright Eyes 26
Bromfield, Dionne 100
Brown, Danny 13, 205, 245–7, 248–9, 268, 275, 295, 325
Brown, Rob 279, 280
Burgess, Leroy 294
Bush, Kate 96, 102, 112
Busta Rhymes 262
Butler, Ishmael 192–3
Byrne, David 124, 192

Cage, John 79, 82
Cale, John 58, 87, 205
Cardi B 330
Carey, Mariah 87
Casals, Pablo 20
Cash, Johnny 92
Cave, Nick 70
Chance the Rapper 240, 247
Charli xcx 39, 169, 303–5
Chat Pile 13
Chemical Brothers 28
Chipmunk 252
Cicierega, Neil 69
Clairo 305
Clarity, Clarence 39
Clark Sisters, The 67
Clipse 215
Coldplay 221, 222
Cole, Debbie 44
Coleman, Ornette 15
Coltrane, Alice 88
Coltrane, John 229
Cook, A.G. 300–2, 304, 312, 331
Cooke, Sam 70
Coral, The 23
Corea, Chick 162
Cudi, Kid 111, 202, 247

Da Brat 62
DaBaby 224
Daft Punk 137, 141, 167
Dalt, Lucrecia 77
D'Angelo 59

Danger Mouse 68–9
Dave and Central Cee 252
David, F.R. 31
Dawson, Kimya 205
Death from Above 1979 24
Death Grips 105
Def Jux 261
Def, Mos 225, 242
Del Rey, Lana 12
DeMarco, Mac 8, 105, 313
Depeche Mode 168, 294
Destiny's Child 34
Digable Planets 192, 228
Dion, Celine 167
DMX 19
Doja Cat 87, 330
Dolphin, Jasper 209, 211, 233, 275
Domo Genesis 216, 224
DOOM *see* MF DOOM
Drake 6, 47, 92, 201, 203, 237, 252, 336
Drakeo the Ruler 272
Dua Lipa 70, 196, 201
Dumile, Daniel *see* MF DOOM
Dunham, Hayden 299–300, 301, 302, 306, 326
Dust Brothers 68
Dylan, Bob 4

Eagles, The 221–2
Earl Sweatshirt 200–77, 329, 330, 333–4
Earth, Wind & Fire 207
Eastman, Julius 78–88, 333
Edgar, Jimmy 309, 322
Eilish, Billie 9, 217
El Guincho 101, 156
Elliot, Missy 61, 62, 63, 76, 159, 327
Elsesser, Sage 231, 254
Elucid 266, 273, 275
Eminem 202, 212, 217
Emmanuel, J.D. 176
Eno, Brian 316
Enya 67

Fatboy Slim 141
Feldman, Morton 79
Fennesz 171
Ferreira, Sky 17, 33–4, 37–8
FKA twigs 50, 55, 90–159, 169, 327, 329
Flack, Roberta 144
Flagel, Patrick 339
Flaming Lips, The 248
Fleetwoods, The 30
Flume 202, 307, 314, 322
Forest Swords 289
Forster, Erika 39
Four Tet 290
Franz Ferdinand 22, 24, 31
Fraser, Elizabeth 186
Freddie Gibbs & Madlib 242
Furtado, Nelly 61, 106
Future 151–2

Gaga, Lady 33, 297
GAIKA 307
Gallagher, Liam 155
Gaye, Marvin 29, 95, 227
ghostwriter977 92
Girl Talk 69
Glass, Philip 16, 21, 46, 83
Goddard, Stuart 96, 97
Godspeed You! Black Emperor 171
Good Charlotte 226
Gorillaz 41

Grant, Eddy 64
Green Day 28, 155
Grimes 8, 32–3, 38, 313
Gucci Mane 214

Halpern, Steven 175
Hancock, Herbie 162
Harle, Danny L 196, 306
Harry, Debbie 15, 16, 57, 58
Heavee 340
Heems 55
Hisaishi, Joe 31
Hodgy Beats 209, 210, 225, 232, 233
Hollis, Mark 45, 112
Holy Fuck 101
Hopkins, Jon 290
Hot Chip 24
Hugo, Chad 214, 237
Huxtable, Juliana 322
Hynes, Devonté 15–88, 111, 176, 183, 253, 329, 330, 333

Icona Pop 303
Ikeda, Ryoji 171
Internet, The 224, 237
Iqbal, Nabihah 291
Isaak, Chris 31
Isiah, Ian 67
Isley Brothers 207

Jaar, Nicolás 134–9, 150–1, 159, 193, 198, 327, 328
Jackson, Janet 46, 74
Jackson, Michael 33, 37, 336
Jadakiss 262
Jagger, Mick 70
James, Boldy 274
JAY-Z 6, 32, 37, 69, 202, 214, 221
Jeezy 215, 249
Jepsen, Carly Rae 39, 56, 59, 60
Jessie J 100
Jlin 290, 322
Jockstrap 47
John, Elton 29, 203
Johnston, Daniel 8
Jones, Grace 41, 121
Joy Division 249, 315
JPEGMAFIA 10, 205, 263, 268, 269, 275
Justice 303, 304
Juvenile 268

Ka 243, 263, 272
Kasabian 48
KAYTRANADA 224
K.Dot 151, 309
Kelis 214
Kenny G 177
Kgositsile, Keorapetse *see* Bra Willie
Kgositsile, Thebe Neruda *see* Earl Sweatshirt
Killer Mike 204–5
Kim, Lil' 61
King, B.B. 229
King Krule 97
Knowles, Solange 17, 34–9, 74
Korn 21
Kraftwerk 290
Kuti, Fela 93, 103

Lacy, Steve 224
Lamar, Kendrick 12, 59, 151, 204, 242–3, 245, 308–9, 336–7
Last Poets, The 227–8
Latifah, Queen 98
Latin Rascals, The 60

Le1f 307
Led Zeppelin 249
Lee, Cindy 339
Lee, Tommy 155
Left Brain 209, 214, 232
Lenker, Adrianne 340
Lethal Bizzle 100
Lewis, Jenny 26
Libertines, The 22
Lightspeed Champion 25–31, 53
Little Simz 70, 252
LIZ 322
LL Cool J 31
LMFAO 56, 293, 305
Logg 294
London, Theophilus 32, 35, 55
Longstreth, Dave 43, 45, 48
Lopatin, Daniel *see* Oneohtrix Point Never
Lopes, Lisa 'Left Eye' 62
Louis, Joe Hill 227
Lucki Eck$ 124
Lutz-Kinoy, Matthew 283
Lwin, Annabella 96–7

McCartney, Paul 87
Mach-Hommy 250–1, 272, 339
Machine Gun Kelly 155
Madonna 6, 19, 130, 201, 302, 320–1, 330
Maine, Aaron 58, 66
Manfred Mann 162, 185
Manji, Evita 323
Mansun 41
Marciano, Roc 243
Maria, Tania 93
Maroon 5 151
Martians, Matthew 207–8, 209, 210, 214
Martinez, Angie 62
Masekela, Hugh 260
Massive Attack 41, 113
Meat Loaf 3
MellowHype 209, 224, 231
MF DOOM 202, 241–2, 255, 324
MGMT 222
MIKE 251–4, 257, 266, 272, 275, 277
Mike G 210
Miller, Mac 111, 240, 250
Minaj, Nicki 6, 203, 293
Mingus, Charles 60, 61, 62–3, 76, 78
Minogue, Kylie 56
Mitchell, Joni 315
Mobb Deep 249
Moby 282, 332
Mock, Janet 65
Modest Mouse 69
Monáe, Janelle 222, 263
Monk, Meredith 81
Moon, Keith 155
Moor Mother 262–3, 266, 269
Moroder, Giorgio 317
Motherland 283
Mozart, Wolfgang Amadeus 72
Mozart's Sister 313
Mr. Hudson 222
Muhly, Nico 83
Mystery Jets 23

N-Dubz 252
Nas 200, 233
Native Tongues 224–5, 226
Navy Blue 231, 270
Nelly 214
Neptunes, The 214, 215, 237, 242, 294

New Order 40, 76
New York Dolls 44
Nine Inch Nails 106, 169, 182, 246
Nirvana 19
Noi$e, Black 270, 333
Noise, The 167
Noreaga 214
Notorious B.I.G. 228
NTS 340
Nyman, Michael 315

Ocean, Billy 12
Ocean, Frank 13, 218–24, 226, 242, 276, 330
Odd Future 205, 209–27, 230–6, 241, 242, 276
Okonma, Tyler *see* Tyler, the Creator
Oneohtrix Point Never 129, 131, 132, 161–98, 329, 330
Orbital 282, 332
O'Rourke, Jim 173, 197
OutKast 40, 268

Palmer, Amanda 251
Pat, Project 67, 68
PC Music 196, 300–1, 304–5
Perfume Genius 105
Pet Shop Boys 294
Petras, Kim 322
Pharrell 124, 214, 215, 242, 252, 294
Pink Floyd 247
Pixies 32, 326
Playboi Carti 47, 251, 265
Polachek, Caroline 41–3, 46–7, 48, 67–8, 183–4, 301, 306, 307, 325, 339
Pop, Iggy 71, 225
Poppy 10
Powell, Bud 62
Prince 19, 59, 74, 92, 95, 150
Prodigy, The 296
Public Enemy 224, 228
Puccini, Giacomo 61, 64, 76

Q-Tip 34, 338

Raekwon 202
Raiin, Ava 66
Ranaldo, Lee 173
Rapture, The 31
Rascal, Dizzee 204
Rashad, Isaiah 13
Reed, Lou 15–16, 19, 46, 81
Reznor, Trent 182, 189
Rhianna 107, 110
Rihanna 50
Robeson, Paul 75
Rocky, A$AP 67, 111, 124, 144
Rodrigo, Olivia 196
Rodríguez, Alejandra Ghersi *see* Arca
Rolling Stones 69
Romeo, Lil' 34
Ronstadt, Linda 3
Rosalía 156
Rose, Axl 155
Ross, Rick 32
Rotten, Johnny 155
Rountree, Christopher 84
Rubinos, Xenia 13, 70
Russell, Arthur 81, 88
Russolo, Luigi 186
RXK Nephew 27

Sade 74
Saint Etienne 184

Samiyam 270
Sampha 111, 112
Sanders, Pharaoh 229
Satoh, Masahiko 333
Sawayama, Rina 39
Schaeffer, Pierre 68
Schoenberg, Arnold 91
ScHoolboy Q 277
Scott-Heron, Gil 227
Scott, Travis 43, 247, 297
Sethi, Ali 136
Sex Pistols 44, 70–1
Shabazz Palaces 192
Shakespeares Sister 96, 102
Shakur, Tupac 19, 61, 236, 249, 262, 336–7
Shygirl 322
Sia 330
Simmons, Gene 121
Simon, Paul 15
Simone, Nina 53, 62, 74, 93, 229
Sinatra, Frank 221
Siouxsie and the Banshees 96, 102
Sivan, Troye 305
Skepta 43, 252
Slipknot 21, 86, 226
sLUms 253–4, 257, 266, 268, 275
Sly Tendencies 231
Smalls, Biggie 262
Smash Mouth 69
Smith, Jamie 100
Smith, Jorja 157
Smith, Patti 15
Snoop Dogg 214, 336
SOB X RBE 272
Solange *see* Knowles, Solange
Sons of Kemet 13, 77, 201
SOPHIE 129, 131, 132, 279–334
S.O.S. Band 36, 46, 74
Soulja Boy 214
Soulquarians 209, 226
Soundgarden 182
Spears, Britney 33
Spice Girls 106, 294
Stanley, Bob 184
Staples, Vince 232, 238, 240, 250, 307–8, 309, 313, 314, 325
Stewart, Jamie 173
Stooges, The 71
Stormzy 252
Stott, Andy 289
Stravinsky, Igor 83
Styles, Harry 70, 83, 330
Styrene, Poly 96
Sun Kil Moon 105
Syd Tha Kid 206–7, 209–10, 223, 224, 237, 268, 276

T-Pain 124
Tawiah 43
Tendler, Adam 84, 86
Tesfaye, Abel *see* Weeknd, The
Test Icicles 23–4, 25, 48
The-Dream 222
Timbaland 34, 114, 215
Tinashe 55
Ting Tings, The 157
Topley-Bird, Martina 113
Tricky 113
Turnstile 59
Twigs, The 124
Tyler, the Creator 203, 208–18, 220, 222, 223–6, 231–3, 253, 274–6, 294, 330, 333–4

Uffie 303, 304
Uncommon Nasa 243
Unicorns, The 23

Urbani, Samantha 41, 43, 52
Uzi Vert, Lil 9, 203

Vampire Weekend 338
Veggies, Casey 209, 210
Vernon, Justin 32
Vickers, Diana 28

Wayne, Lil 46, 202, 217, 218, 232–3, 268
Ware, Jessie 55, 70
Weeknd, The 92, 166–8, 183, 194–5
Weezer 86
Welch, Florence 28
West, Kanye 32, 108, 121, 124, 203, 217, 223, 245, 247, 252
White, Betty Ann 44
Wiley 296
Winehouse, Amy 97
Wiz Khalifa 226
Wonder, Stevie 219, 338
Woods, Billy 205, 243, 263–9, 272–4, 275
Woozy, Ben 292
Wright III, Tommy 67
Wu-Tang Clan 202

X-Ray Spex 96, 110
xx, The 100

Yachty, Lil 247
Yellow Magic Orchestra 31
Yo-Yo Ma 20
Young, Neil 21

Zorn, John 15–16
Zutons, The 23